FOREWORD

MOLLY NESBIT
SUSAN DONAHUE KURETSKY
THOMAS E. HILL

One approaches Vassar College on a tree-lined road. After a while a very long neo-Gothic building joins the route, almost like a fellow traveler. Later one learns that this companion is the Library, and that it extends southward into a series of other interconnected buildings. But initially the building is experienced as an ongoing medieval wall. It is interrupted by an archway known as the Main Gate, the formal entrance to Vassar's campus. Underneath the arch, where swallows like to nest, a large wooden door stands in the shadows. The door leads upstairs to the Art Department.

For just over a century, the Art Department has watched over the gateway to the college. The medieval exterior has survived largely unchanged; inside, the department, along with the Art Gallery, grew and evolved to meet the times. This book tells the tale of a decisive turn in that history, the moment in the mid-1930s when the department consciously chose to become modern, but not only modern—it was changing to meet what they all saw to be the future.

It fell to John McAndrew to design a suite of new spaces that would express this new direction. Until now, we have not known much about the steps that led to those decisions, nor have we fully grasped their implications. It was only in 2007, when the restoration of McAndrew's Art Library was undertaken by the firm of Platt Byard Dovell White Architects, that the significance of the Art Library's particular order of modernity became apparent within its broader context. When Nicholas Adams, the architects' on-site liaison and our historian of architecture, began to see more deeply into the building's archaeology, he invited Mardges Bacon, well known for her account of Le Corbusier's first visit to America in 1935, to explore this material further and to share her findings in a public lecture. Her new research opened up a chapter in American architectural history that leads from Poughkeepsie directly to the Museum of Modern Art in New York. Her own further investigation of this episode, combined with the efforts of many librarians and members of the current Art Department, has led to this book.

As it happened, McAndrew's renovation in 1937 formalized the life that would be led in the Art Department to this day. He laid out two long corridors, one atop the other, both marked on one end by the Art Library and on the other by the Vassar College Art Gallery. In between were classrooms and offices (see "The Art Department in New Quarters," plates I, II). The message was clear from the plan: the study

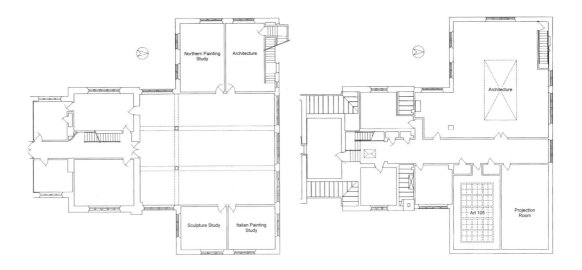

of original works of art and the examination of the written record would be related to one another, and they would be inseparable.

All along, McAndrew had been much aided by his great friend and collaborator, Agnes Rindge (later Claflin), who taught modern art and Northern Old Master painting and at the same time directed the work of the Art Gallery (see plate III). They were both part of a faculty group setting ever-higher standards of inquiry for the study of art at Vassar. The new order of art history, coming from Germany, arrived in the late 1930s with the hiring of the distinguished German émigré scholars Richard Krautheimer and Adolf Katzenellenbogen. The faculty continued to grow. Later, after the Second World War, their student Linda Nochlin would return to teach and, in the late 1960s, would invent feminist art history. As a result, art history at Vassar came to be known as a pursuit at the forefront of the field. At the same time it had become increasingly central to the college's understanding of a liberal arts education.

Generations of students would gather each year to take Art 105, the introductory survey. Like clockwork they streamed into the building, especially at exam times, to ponder the photographic reproductions hung on the walls of the Art Library's four study rooms. The classroom corridors of the entire building had been designed to carry the inevitable overflow and let students study into the night. All this became part of college ritual and lore (see plates IV, V, VI).

Yet McAndrew's plan actually was built upon an existing condition: in 1915 the Main Gate had been expanded laterally on both sides to make an entire freestanding building, Taylor Hall, dedicated both to the teaching of art history and to the collections of the Art Gallery. Taylor Hall restated the seriousness with which the college took the study of art and brought together functions that had been scattered; Avery Hall, for example, had housed the art collection (including scores of full-scale plaster casts). Consequently, on moving

Left:
John McAndrew (with Theodore Muller). Plan of the second floor of the Art Library and Taylor Hall, Vassar College, T19, 1937, redrawn by Antoine Robinson (Courtesy Vassar College Libraries)

Right:
John McAndrew (with Theodore Muller). Plan of the third floor of Taylor Hall, Vassar College, T20, 1937, redrawn by Antoine Robinson (Courtesy Vassar College Libraries)

day in 1915, a startling procession of statuary had wound its way through campus. Vassar's new president, Henry Noble McCracken, later remembered the sight of "tortured Laokoön writhing his way across the snow, the Wingless Victory staggering along behind him," while "Father Tiber took life easy on the skids." Today the casts have largely disappeared, and in 1993 the art collection moved again into the adjacent Frances Lehman Loeb Art Center designed by the New Haven firm of Cesar Pelli, but it is worth remembering just how deep the college's commitment to the study of art has always been. Right from its founding, Vassar had an art gallery, building on the collection of Hudson River School paintings purchased from the Reverend Elias Magoon in 1864. Just as there was an art gallery, there was an art library, also purchased from Magoon, though the books had been folded into the main library. That changed beginning in 1935 with the construction of an extension of the Library building into a new addition that linked the main library, by then called the Frederick Ferris Thompson Memorial Library, to Taylor Hall and the Main Gate. This move created the distinct, and distinctive, Art Library complex for John McAndrew to design.

McAndrew went further to envision a shared corridor south from the Art Library to the Art Gallery, thereby creating and defining the main axis of the Art Department, a route of constant circulation, encounter, and informal conversation among faculty, students, and staff. The original gallery space has since been converted to classrooms, another part of the Pelli design in 1993, but the classrooms continue to be directly attached to the Loeb Art Center so that the same close ties remain, the passage to the art collections having only grown longer.

Since its restoration in 2007, the Art Library spaces have been given digital upgrades. Recently an exhibition case in the center of the reading room was added to accommodate small shows overseen and curated by the art librarian, Thomas Hill. The exhibitions range widely and include objects and/or printed materials relating to art, history, and literature. This open, flexible site extends the integrating logic of McAndrew's basic design and serves as a hub within the Art

Anne Cleveland. "Do You Think We're Supposed to Like This One?" (Anne Cleveland and Jean Anderson, *Vassar*, Poughkeepsie, NY: Vassar Cooperative Bookshop, 1938) (Courtesy Vassar College Libraries)

"DO YOU THINK WE'RE *supposed* TO LIKE THIS ONE?"

Library around which exchanges of all kinds take place. In microcosm it reminds everyone that the direct connections linking the Art Gallery, classrooms, and Art Library are omnipresent, there to be found even in the smallest detail. Seeing actual objects, viewing projected images, and reading texts bring past and present into contact, producing countless combinations, ready to go forward in the mind.

As we move now through these spaces in the course of a normal working day, we still feel the presence of the colleagues who came before us, and sometimes it seems as though we almost hear their echoes. They have left us their momentum to use. Now, thanks to Mardges Bacon's research, it is easier to conjure up a vision of the young John McAndrew and Agnes Rindge trading thoughts, inspired and animated as they plan and present the design, aiming to reflect, as did their courses and exhibitions, the life of the present that meant so much to them both. Agnes Rindge would be the one to formally introduce the Art Library on the pages of the *Vassar Alumnae Magazine* in June 1938. In this case we do not have to imagine her sense of excitement and purpose. Her words speak volumes for their collective vision of what art was and is and could be.

Plate I

VIEW OF TAYLOR HALL GALLERY

The Art Department in New Quarters

The Art Department, like the phoenix of old, has put on new plumage this year and even increased its wing spread. Remodelling, alterations and additions have now given art students the working premises they have so long desired and needed. Perhaps it might interest alumnae readers to have a brief account of this Art Department plant and how it works.

By AGNES RINDGE
Professor of Art

SINCE education in art is perforce visual experience, we have the problem of showing and storing thousands of separate items. They comprise over 20,000 slides for use in lectures and slide reviews, many hundred photographs and large facsimile colour prints, constantly changed on the walls of corridors and study rooms, as well as the permanent collection of original works of art containing prints and drawings, paintings of widely varied epochs, a small amount of sculpture and a large and important collection of Far Eastern pottery and jade. In addition two galleries are devoted to loan exhibitions where new material goes and comes about once a month in the academic year. These exhibitions are intended to supplement the permanent collection and wherever possible are planned to coincide with current material in the courses in college.

This unwieldy and semi-fluid mass of material is for the first time now really manageable. We have a room for the storage of slides where members of the department can prepare their lectures. The same room accommodates the large mounted colour prints. Another room adjacent to the secretary's office houses the photograph collection. These rooms and the large study room for the Introductory course (Art 105) are in the remodelled part of Taylor Hall which adjoins the new Van Ingen Library, the top two floors of which serve the Art Department.

The Vassar Art Department has devised its own peculiar method of instruction in art, differing from other colleges and universities in the greater stress placed upon visual learning. Because we believe art courses consist in knowing and understanding works of art, we require an extensive mastery of these several objects themselves. For this reason every possible wall surface in Van Ingen is equipped with strips to hold photographs or to hang prints upon, so that the student reading the current assignment will have constantly available before her eyes the material referred to in the books and a good deal more besides. She is required to give evidence of such familiarity in slide quizzes, either in the lecture rooms or in the special slide review room on the top floor. This room is also accessible to other departments wishing to supplement their courses with illustration in slides. For example, the English Department this year used it to show aspects of English XVIIIth century life, and the History Department to show manuscripts of the Carolingian and Ottonian periods, and Renaissance paintings.

Separate study rooms adjoining the main reading room of Van Ingen (Pl. V) are provided for the introductory and intermediate courses, since they employ the largest volume of illustrative material. There is one for Sculpture, one for Architecture, one for Italian and one for Northern Painting. The Art 105 room in the remodelled part displays Dutch, Flemish and Spanish XVIIth century painting one week, while the student is reading that assignment. The next week the material is transferred to the Art 105 Conference room (Pl. VI) on the floor above, a room with a skylight to insure maximum wall space. The student is thus exposed to many more examples than she is required to remember and has the opportunity of increasing her visual capacity and her sense of style as far as she is able.

The top floor of Van Ingen also contains a large draughting room (Pl. VII) where the students in landscape and domestic architecture do their work, as well as three departmental offices. Seminars for the advanced students in history of art are in the central part of Taylor Hall, on the floor above the galleries.

This then is the functional premise for the recent reconstruction and addition for the Art Department. There are nineteen courses given, exclusive of practise in art, and something over 450 students enrolled. For the first time the present library facilities are adequate for the traffic. Perhaps now it would not be amiss to explain the character of the execution of the addition. This we felt must be designed in accordance with contemporary functional thinking in architecture; it must give us the best possible exploitation of the limited sum at our disposal, and it must be beautiful. Since we are engaged in the study of art, mere function is not enough. In other words, our aim was as far as possible to practise what we preach. And what works best can generally be made to look best. Although the exterior design was determined by the existing buildings, we did not feel that interior design needed to conform to the Tudor Gothic of the 1914 Taylor Hall in the Van Ingen of 1937. The problem was to make the new and remodelled premises look so well and work so well that they could be accepted in their own right, irrespective of earlier stylization. We also believed that there is real beauty to be had from the modern architectural vocabulary and that judicious use of its principles need not be inharmonious in effect. The reception accorded to Van Ingen by our very numerous visitors this year seems to be a real justification. Already other colleges are taking heart from it. Lighting, colour areas, textures and spaces have proved enjoyable to all kinds of persons. Our only difficulty has been to persuade the seniors to use the old seminar rooms at all.

Most visitors from other colleges cannot believe the job was done so economically. The money was spent where it would serve best—for the bright deep blue metal bookcases, making the books look inviting and handsome, for the specially designed lighting fixtures, which were to give not only the proper power and distribution of light but real beauty of illumination as well, for the dark cork floor and bulletin board and for the large specially built tables. The entire scheme of Van Ingen was limited to nine colours of paint used in various combinations according to the character of the rooms themselves and according to the relations of the rooms to each other so that variety is given to the general aspect of the whole building. Strong colour contrasts appear, for example, in the Sculpture Study room (Pl. V.) where the illustrative material is necessarily black and white; soft blue and dull terra cotta with white serves to enhance the character of Italian painting, and so forth. The walls of the study room are different colours, first to insure maximum illumination from white reflecting walls, and second to subdivide the material displayed, giving the eye one wall at a time to consume, thus reducing the inevitable fatigue of the very powers of attention we try to evoke. The treatment of the walls as plane surfaces of course increases the appreciation of the room as a volume of light and air and this is aided, too, by the Venetian blinds which minimize the leaded panes of the windows determined by the exterior design. The chairs are comfortable, easily moved and cleaned, and finished in natural wood stain. The tables are mounted on chromium legs, finished with natural wood, and covered with linoleum of putty grey, soft blue, or deep rust. All the tables from the old Taylor Hall library were remodelled to fit the new scheme.

One of the most satisfactory features of the lighting design is the use of that new architectural material, glass brick—in this case the square, solid blocks of clear glass, made familiar to many by the Cooperative Bookshop, where they are sold as bookends. Crowning the metal bookcases, these translucent walls admit light from the study rooms into the main reading room (Pl. II) and an entire wall of them between two of the study rooms transmits added light from the Northern painting room (Pl. IV) where there are two windows, to the Architecture room where there is but one. The texture and semi-transparency of this brick gives very much the effect of a wall of large uncut moonstones, so that seen from the outside of the building at night one might almost expect Arabian Nights within!

In general the walls are painted plaster with wood strips except for the absorbex blocks on the Art 105 Conference room (Pl. VI), which give a beautiful texture while improving the acoustics for recitations. The design of the building consists primarily, then, in the distribution of areas of colour and texture—the most difficult and interesting form of abstract composition in architecture. The stairway, as the circulatory center of the unit, is a rounded wall mass in the midst of curved walls, which appear to make more room for it and to ease the flow of traffic. At the head of the stair on the top floor a stone sculpture by Flannagan, a recent gift to us, serves to emphasize the termination of the stairway and to dominate the long corridor ending in a large window. An actual inch-foot scale and casts of capitals and orders serve as decoration in the draughting room (Pl. VII), supplementing the functional character of the freely exposed steel girders. So much for Van Ingen.

The department has again the grateful task of recording the lavish generosity of the Pratt family on our behalf, not only of Mr. and Mrs. Charles M. Pratt but of our present trustee, Mr. Richardson Pratt. Not content with the erection of Taylor Hall itself in 1914 and the munificence of their gift of Italian paintings assembled at that time, they have added to their earlier gift of a jade collection many additional items including an important collection of Chinese and Japanese pottery, representing many periods and types. Dr. Salmony, the distinguished oriental scholar we have asked to catalogue and install the collection, considers it to be next in importance after the collections in the Metropolitan Museum and the Chicago Art Institute in the Japanese field.

The gift deserved some special accommodation to do it justice and the donors once more made the present installation possible by granting us the necessary funds for remodelling the South gallery. The original gallery was one enormous room with a very high ceiling and no reflecting walls, making it very difficult to show to good advantage the paintings we possessed of different schools and very different sizes. The present new investiture has been designed to be as becoming as possible to all the objects in our permanent collection. The muted colours of the walls, the greatly improved diffusion of light, the proportions of all the parts were determined with this in mind. At one end the Far Eastern pottery is installed in specially lighted cases, subdivided so that not too many are seen at one

Plate II   GENERAL VIEW OF VAN INGEN MAIN READING ROOM

Plate III   VAN INGEN LIBRARY DETAIL

Plate IV   NORTHERN PAINTING STUDY ROOM   *Wurtz Bros., N.Y.*

Plate V   SCULPTURE STUDY ROOM   *Wurtz Bros., N.Y.*

Wurtz Bros., N.Y.

Plate VI   ART 105 CONFERENCE ROOM

Wurtz Bros., N.Y.

Plate VII   DRAUGHTING ROOM FOR ARCHITECTURE

Plate VIII   VIEW OF TAYLOR GALLERY   *Wurtz Bros., N.Y.*

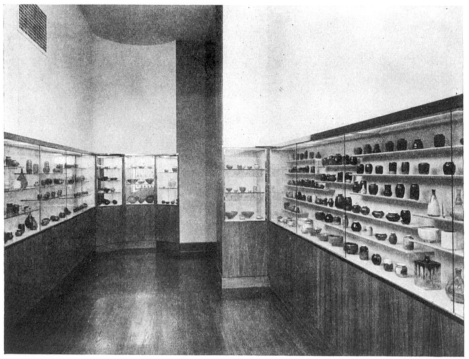

Plate IX   ORIENTAL POTTERY COLLECTION   *Wurtz Bros., N.Y.*

time, and varied with different kinds of shelving. The figured walnut veneer and the white walls give the deep glazes of the pottery every opportunity to focus the visitor's attention after catching a glimpse of them from the main room (Pl. IX). The remaining space at this end of the gallery, almost a square, contains the prints and original drawings of old masters in such a fashion that they can be examined at close range as they should be.

At the other end of the main room (Pl. I), with a wide opening, there is a smaller supplementary gallery so that works of greatly different character may look well apart from the dominant character of the main gallery. For example, modern paintings can be shown here, or Flemish and Dutch paintings that are not happy amongst the Italian pictures. These various subdivisions not only increase the actual wall hanging space, but make rearrangement and additions possible. After a time people get used to the position of a picture and no longer notice it. When we finally restored the paintings to our Vassar public several people thought we had brand new ones and nearly everyone thought they had all been newly cleaned and varnished because the lighting of the picture surface was so much improved. The walls of the center gallery are covered with material of an unobtrusive diagonal weave, the long side walls are a rather pinkish beige, the two screen walls at one end a warm grey, the single screen wall at the other end more terra cotta, but neutralized (Pl. VIII). The floor is a warm deep brown—our old hard wood floor refinished—the ceiling white with really beautiful glass, sometimes faintly green or lavender. One whole wall is devoted to the magnificent Taddeo Gaddi, the two important XVth century Piero di Cosimo school pieces have each a separate wall, and the later works, both French and Italian, are easily disposed on the long wall opposite the entrance. We hope that in such a satisfactory setting people will pay more attention to our very respectable collection. Actually it is well enough known so that the Hubert Robert traveled to Texas, the Tiepolo drawing to Chicago, the Marieschi and the Wilson are now at Oberlin for a festival there, and the Bartolommeo Vivarini has just returned from the Venetian show at Knoedlers' in 57th Street, while the Courbet goes out to an important exhibition of that master in Baltimore in May. Out of our storage of watercolours we are putting a good number on view in various offices and study rooms about the campus, since pictures are meant to be looked at as much as possible. The corridor by the offices, and the former jade room, contain examples of English and American painting, chiefly from the earlier collection given by Matthew Vassar himself. We still have to publish our catalogue, now underway; we still have some remodelling and improvements to make in the main hall and the large lecture room, but we are ready to welcome visitors with some pride this Commencement.

During the current academic year the department has acquired, in part through the generosity of the Friends of Taylor Hall, a fine XVIth century Italian drawing by Raphael's contemporary, the painter-architect, Baldassare Peruzzi, a small oil sketch of the Finding of Moses attributed to the Florentine XVIIth century artist, Lorenzo Lippi, and the large signed oil painting of Saint Rosa of Lima by the Late Neapolitan, Luca Giordano. All of these items are used in courses during the year as part of the regular study material.

During the year we have exhibited the enormous print rental collection operated by the Cooperative Bookshop; facsimiles of William Blake's Book of Job watercolours for the English Department; the Piranesi prints in our collection for the benefit of Roman architecture; facsimiles of the XVth century engraver, Master E.S., which the German Club took advantage of as a background for a tea; photographic enlargements of mediaeval minor arts made by the Walter's Gallery of Baltimore; Wesleyan University's circulating collection of photographs of Baroque Church façades; collage-fantasies by Halicka; Spanish War posters for the A.S.U.; paintings and costume designs by the artists of the American Ballet Caravan; the paintings of Pavel Tchelitchew (with the artist present), which were only shown in New York, Hartford and Chicago; a show of oil paintings by six young American painters from the East River Gallery; a large retrospective show of watercolours; and in April when two of the courses were working in the field, an exhibition of old masters of the XVIIth and XVIIIth centuries, Dutch, Flemish, Italian and Spanish schools. We plan to round out the year with Abstract Art, including the Constructions of Naum Gabo, who will lecture, exhibiting in America for the first time this year, and abstract paintings lent by the Museum of Modern Art. This is intended to electrify the students and startle the alumnae as far as possible, and perhaps provide common ground for conversation by Commencement parents. The whole operation of Taylor Hall and the Art Department is designed to belong in the present day. Without condoning any of the foibles of the XXth century, we believe that the history of art has continuity right up to 1938, in spite of the fact that the department obliges students to begin acquaintance with the subject nearly four thousand years ago.

Commencement Exhibitions in the Library

Exhibitions of special interest to reunion classes will be arranged in the library. For the class exhibitions publications of members of the class, photograph albums and memorabilia, Vassarions and class photographs will be shown. Selections of books purchased from class gifts and of books given by individual members of the class, and groups of books purchased from library book funds in which reunion classes have special interest will also be displayed.

THE ART LIBRARY IN NEW PHOTOGRAPHS

PHOTOGRAPHS BY ANDREW TALLON
CAPTIONS BY TOBIAS ARMBORST

The Northern Painting Study room

Left: View toward the southwest corner of the study room (the former Northern Painting Study room), showing the linoleum-topped reading tables, tubular steel chairs, blue bookcases, and polychromatic walls.

Right: View of the glass-brick partition between the former Northern Painting Study room and the Architecture room on the west side of the library; horizontal steel rails between alternating rows of glass bricks allow photographs and prints to be mounted along the translucent wall.

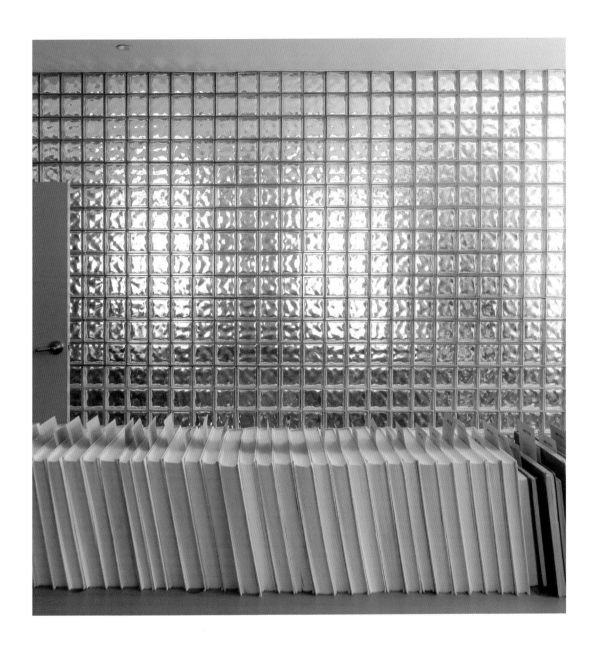

The Architecture room

The translucent glass-brick wall between the
two study rooms on the west side of the library,
seen from the Architecture room.

The large study room

Views of the large study room on the east side of the library that resulted from the combination of two original study rooms: the Italian Painting Study room and the Sculpture Study room. The images show the glass-brick clerestory that admits light from the study room to the reading room.

The staircase on the entry level of the
Art Library

Views of the staircase adjacent to the Art
Library entrance, looking from the third
floor of Taylor Hall toward the Art Library
entrance (left), and from the second floor
of Taylor Hall (right).

The window of the seminar room

The resolution of window and ceiling shows the negotiation between the modern interior and the Tudor Gothic exterior of the Art Library.

A table and chairs in the stacks below the
library's main reading room

Views from the main reading room to the study rooms (previous page) and out to the Frederick Ferris Thompson Memorial Library (this page).

The view on the previous page highlights the complex relationship between the Art Library's Gothic exterior and its modern interior, with the juxtaposition of sash-bar window and glass-brick clerestory with stone window mullions and flat, white ceiling.

JOHN MCANDREW'S MODERNIST VISION

FROM THE VASSAR COLLEGE ART LIBRARY TO THE MUSEUM OF MODERN ART IN NEW YORK

MARDGES BACON

PREFACE: MCANDREW AND THE GEOGRAPHIES OF MODERNISM

During the 1930s, John Thomas McAndrew (1904–1978) stood at the crossroads of modernism in American architecture as its many transatlantic elements converged. Trained as an architect, he designed the Vassar College Art Library (1935–37), which was enclosed within a Tudor Gothic shell by the firm of Allen & Collens (later Allen, Collens & Willis, 1935–37) (see pages 34 and 35). McAndrew also designed (with Alfred Barr) the first sculpture garden for the Museum of Modern Art (MoMA) in New York (see fig. 3.3). He was a professor at Vassar College from 1932 to 1937 and then served as curator at MoMA's Department of Architecture until mid-1941. After World War II, he returned to academia as a professor at Wellesley College, where he also served as director of its art museum. Little has been written about McAndrew and his design work; his writings have also remained largely unexamined.[1] This book constructs McAndrew's modernist vision as it emerged during his undergraduate years at Harvard College and his time in architecture school at Harvard; it is then explored through the prism of his Vassar College Art Library and his curatorial and design work at MoMA. This study also examines McAndrew's writings for their astute insights and their capacity to contextualize both his design for the Art Library and the MoMA exhibitions he curated. Throughout his early years, from Cambridge to New York City to Poughkeepsie and back to New York City, McAndrew kept the company of friends and colleagues who would help to shape the modern movement. They, in turn, admired the brilliance of his intellect and his role in the formation of modernism. As McAndrew's career shifted from the practice of architecture to its history, criticism, and connoisseurship, he continued to acquire firsthand knowledge through his regular trips to Europe and the Americas.

John McAndrew (with
Theodore Muller).
Art Library (originally
Van Ingen Library),
Vassar College,
1935–37, Platt
Byard Dovell White
Architects (Photo
© Jonathan Wallen)

My aim in this book has been to situate McAndrew's design and curatorial work within the currents of modernist thought in both the United States and Europe. In its narrowest terms, modernism represented a practice of design from 1914 to 1939—from the beginning of World War I to the start of World War II. As a manifestation of art, culture, and intellectual exploration, modernism carried multiple meanings. In contradistinction to an aesthetic based on tradition, modernism was associated with a consciousness of the present, of "self" and a state of self-awareness.[2] It embodied a shift toward the transitory and ephemeral. Expressions of the modern and modernism were intrinsically authentic. As the architectural and social critic Lewis Mumford declared in 1934, "'Modern' is something that you are, not a theatrical effect you try to achieve."[3] While the arrival of modern painting and music was often greeted with outrage and scandal, the emergence of modern architecture met with more measured controversy among practitioners cleaving to tradition.[4] However, modern architecture frequently forged paradoxical relationships. On the one hand, most proponents eschewed historical representation and academicism. On the other hand, many modernists still held to classical principles, e.g., Le Corbusier's use of "regulating lines."[5] In contrast to the term "modern architecture," which was used by polemicists from Antonio Sant'Elia to Le Corbusier to Bruno Taut (Frank Lloyd Wright preferring the term "organic architecture"), "modernism" has been generally regarded as a later designation.[6] But in reference to art, as discussed in Chapter Two, Vassar professor Oliver Tonks did use the term "modernism" in 1923 to describe a new development in painting.

In this book I have referred to two geographies of modernism, which were informed and enriched by transatlantic exchange: American and European. Since the early twentieth century Wright's work and ideas had influenced architects associated with the German Werkbund.[7] Moreover, American grain elevators, daylight factories, and skeletal steel skyscrapers not only provided evidence of native technological advancement but also served as models to such European modernists as Walter Gropius and Le Corbusier.[8] The historian Henry-Russell Hitchcock recognized that the roots of American modernism were as deep as those of European modernism. They existed in the United States, he claimed, "at least as effectively as in Europe before 1922."[9] Identifying the sources of modern architecture, he assigned Wright (and Louis Sullivan and H. H. Richardson before him) and Barry Byrne in America to an older generation of architects within what he called the "New Tradition," while Peter Behrens and Otto Wagner remained key figures within that tradition in Europe. But to Hitchcock, Europe still held the lead in establishing a cadre of "New Pioneers," notably Gropius and Le Corbusier. In the United States such modernists as A. Lawrence Kocher were simply outnumbered by the European émigrés of the 1920s, including Rudolph Schindler, Richard Neutra, and William Lescaze. A second wave of European émigrés followed in the 1930s, including Gropius, Marcel Breuer, and Ludwig Mies van der Rohe.

McAndrew's modernist vision, which suffused his teaching, design and curatorial work, as well as his writings, is the primary theme of this book, which is organized into three chapters and an epilogue. Chapter One examines McAndrew's years at Harvard College and his subsequent education as an architect, along with those key early experiences that shaped his understanding of modernism. In Chapter Two, the Vassar College Art Library (originally the Van Ingen Library), in conjunction with the Taylor Art Gallery, for which McAndrew produced tandem designs, provides a case study of American modernism. During McAndrew's Vassar years, his design work, rather than his writings, embodied his thinking on modernism. Redolent with the transnational ideas of its times, the Art Library lays claim to be the first modern interior of an academic building on an American campus.[10] This raises the question: What were the artistic and cultural conditions that made Vassar College receptive to modernism in general and modern architecture in particular? McAndrew's Art Library underscores the point that even though in the United States modernism was well established, especially in houses and skyscrapers, its appearance on the American campus was relatively late at a time when most academic buildings were still governed by Beaux-Arts design and planning with neo-Gothic or colonial revival representation. Even leading American architecture schools—in the throes of a curricular reform during the mid-1930s that transformed their teaching from Beaux-Arts to modern design principles—were slow to embrace modernism in the designs of their respective buildings.[11] In fact Vassar's new library was completed just prior to the landmark competition of 1938, sponsored by the Museum of Modern Art, for an art center on the campus of Wheaton College in Norton, Massachusetts, which formally launched modern design for collegiate buildings (see Chapter Three).[12]

Although at the time of its dedication the Art Library was the subject of positive commentary in both the *New York Times* and the campus press, it was not reviewed in the professional press. Since the library's completion, its groundbreaking interior has been virtually unknown outside the Vassar campus, where McAndrew's design has been greatly admired and appreciated. In 2007–09 the Art Library was restored by the late Paul Spencer Byard and his partner Charles A. Platt, of the firm of Platt Byard Dovell White Architects, who understood the difficult task of walking in McAndrew's steps to produce a lucid, thoughtful, and authentic execution. Among their greatest challenges (and successes) was to re-create the vibrant polychromy of the library's original color scheme. This has led to an important question: If International Style principles eschewed ornament, and its palette was viewed as a neutral one that largely occluded color, what other theoretical precedents might account for the Art Library's complement of vivid colors, and how did it challenge prevailing American assumptions about modernism?

In Chapter Three I examine McAndrew's contributions to modernism as both maker and curator at the Museum of Modern Art. I analyze his design (with Alfred Barr) for the Museum's first sculpture garden, one specifically conceived to provide a flexible urban space for changing outdoor sculpture exhibitions. By

investigating McAndrew's most important exhibitions and his con-
current writings on architecture and utilitarian design, I consider
the curator's critical position and its relationship to the formalism of
Barr, Hitchcock, and Philip Johnson and to the sociocultural assumptions of Mumford. I situate McAndrew's modernist vision within
the currents of transatlantic exchange at the moment in which the
Museum of Modern Art was experiencing its own reappraisal. In
effect I frame McAndrew's view of modernism as a cross-cultural
project. If he understood that Le Corbusier and Breuer had transformed their work in the 1930s through regional, vernacular, and
human-centered concerns as well as organic processes, he viewed a
similar progression among the work of their American counterparts.
McAndrew's design work and his seminal MoMA exhibitions were
instrumental in helping to craft a more pluralistic American modernism before World War II, which would lead to its postwar acceptance
by both practitioners and the public.

The Epilogue considers briefly McAndrew's academic career
after World War II, first as a professor at Wellesley College and
director of its art museum, and then as a cofounder of Save Venice
Inc. Notwithstanding their importance, these professional pursuits
lie largely beyond the scope of this study to situate the Vassar College
Art Library within international modernism, to parse the core principles of McAndrew's modernist vision, and to define his contributions
as both architect and curator to prewar architectural discourse.

1   My article "Modernism and the Vernacular at the Museum of Modern Art, New York," based on a paper presented at the Deerfield/Wellesley College Symposium on American Culture in 2002, was a first attempt to examine McAndrew's concept of "naturalization" in conjunction with his contributions to transatlantic exchange in American architecture during the 1930s and to the discourse on modernism and the vernacular at the Museum of Modern Art. It appeared in Maiken Umbach and Bernd Hüppauf, eds., *Vernacular Modernism: Heimat, Globalization, and the Built Environment* (Stanford, CA: Stanford University Press, 2005), 25–52, 205–15. Keith L. Eggener subsequently published "Nationalism, Internationalism and the 'Naturalisation' of Modern Architecture in the United States, 1925–1940," *National Identities* 8, no. 3 (September 2006): 243–58, and "John McAndrew, the Museum of Modern Art, and the 'Naturalization' of Modern Architecture in America, ca. 1940," in *Architecture and Identity*, ed. Peter Herrle and Erik Wegerhoff (Berlin: LIT Verlag, 2008), 235–42.

2   On the concept of the "present" within the construction of modernity, see William H. Jordy, "The Symbolic Essence of Modern European Architecture of the Twenties and Its Continuing Influence," *Journal of the Society of Architectural Historians* 22, no. 3 (October 1963): 177–87, reprinted in William H. Jordy, *"Symbolic Essence" and Other Writings on Modern Architecture and American Culture*, ed. Mardges Bacon in association with the Temple Hoyne Buell Center for the Study of American Architecture, Columbia University, New York (New Haven, CT: Yale University Press, 2005), 135–50. See also Jürgen Habermas, "Modernity—An Incomplete Project," in *The Anti-Aesthetic: Essays on Postmodern Culture*, ed. Hal Foster (Port Townsend, WA: Bay Press, 1983), 3–15; Matei Calinescu, *Five Faces of Modernity: Modernism, Avant-Garde, Decadence, Kitsch, Postmodernism* (Durham, NC: Duke University Press, 1987), 8.

3   Lewis Mumford, "The Art Galleries: Memorials and Moderns," *New Yorker*, April 14, 1934, 64, reprinted in Lewis Mumford, *Mumford on Modern Art in the 1930s*, ed. Robert Wojtowicz (Berkeley: University of California Press, 2007), 120.

4   On the debate between modern and tradition from 1934 to 1936, in which the architect and designer George Nelson offered a "new voice" in opposition to the position that architect H. Van Buren Magonigle had taken in a series of articles, "A Half Century of Architecture," in the journal *Pencil Points*, see Tom Fisher and Philip Langdon, "The Debate Goes On," *Progressive Architecture* 76, no. 4 (April 1995): 66–69.

5   Le Corbusier-Saugnier, *Vers une architecture* (Paris: G. Crès [1923]), 53–63.

6   Christopher Wilk makes this point in his introduction to *Modernism: Designing a New World, 1914–1939* (London: V&A Publications, 2006), 14. For uses of the term "modern architecture," see Antonio Sant'Elia, "The New City," in *Nuove Tendenze* (Milan: Famiglia Artistica, May–June 1914), reprinted in *Architecture and Design, 1890–1939: An International Anthology of Original Articles*, ed. Tim Benton and Charlotte Benton with Dennis Sharp (New York: Whitney Library of Design, 1975), 71–72; Le Corbusier-Saugnier, *Vers une architecture*, 199; Bruno Taut, *Modern Architecture* (London: Studio [1929]). For an earlier use, see Otto Wagner, *Moderne Architektur: seinen Schülern ein Führer auf diesem Kunstgebiete* (Vienna: Anton Schroll, 1902).

7   Henry-Russell Hitchcock Jr., "Wright's Influence Abroad," *Parnassus* 12, no. 8 (December 1940): 11–15; Anthony Alofsin, *Frank Lloyd Wright—The Lost Years, 1910–1922: A Study of Influence* (Chicago: University of Chicago Press, 1993), 1–4.

8   Walter Gropius, "Die Entwicklung moderner Industriebaukunst," in *Die Kunst in Industrie und Handel. Jahrbuch des Deutschen* Werkbundes, *1913* (Jena, Germany: Eugen Diederichs, 1913), 17–22; Le Corbusier-Saugnier, *Vers une architecture*, 25–27. In his book *Urbansime*, Le Corbusier applauded the skeletal frame of the American skyscraper for its clarity of functional expression and as a means to achieve spatial volumes. Le Corbusier, *Urbanisme* (Paris: Éditions Crès, 1925), 185.

9   Henry-Russell Hitchcock Jr., *Modern Architecture: Romanticism and Reintegration* (New York: Payson & Clarke, 1929), 206.

10   An argument could be made that Joseph Urban's New School for Social Research, New York (1930–31), is the first academic building of modern design, although it is not located on a college or university campus. There is also the establishment in 1932 of Taliesin, Wright's home studio in Spring Green, Wisconsin. Karcher and Smith's Field House at Swarthmore College in Pennsylvania (1935–36) predates Vassar's Art Library, but it is a utilitarian rather than academic building. Modernism found its way into elementary school design in 1929 with Lescaze's Oak Lane Country Day School, Oak Lane, Pennsylvania. Following the appointment in 1938 of Mies van der Rohe to head the Architecture Department at Chicago's Armour Institute of Technology (later Illinois Institute of Technology), the architect then designed its new campus (1939–58). Many historians have considered Anderson & Beckwith's Alumni Swimming Pool at Massachusetts Institute of Technology, in Cambridge (1939–40), to be the first modern building on an American campus, although it is not an academic building. It was featured in Elizabeth Mock, ed., *Built in USA: 1932–1944* (New York: Museum of Modern Art, 1944), 82–83.

11 Joseph Hudnut is credited with the transformation of the architecture curriculum at Columbia University (1934–35) and then at Harvard University, where he was named dean of the Faculty of Architecture and began to implement his modernist agenda in the summer of 1935. By the spring of 1937 Gropius had joined the faculty. Anthony Alofsin, *The Struggle for Modernism: Architecture, Landscape Architecture, and City Planning at Harvard* (New York: W. W. Norton, 2002), 119, 134, 138; Jill Pearlman, *Inventing American Modernism: Joseph Hudnut, Walter Gropius, and the Bauhaus Legacy at Harvard* (Charlottesville: University of Virginia Press, 2007).

12 McAndrew served as chairman of the jury for the Wheaton College Art Center competition. Four firms accepted MoMA's invitation to compete: William Lescaze, Lyndon and Smith, Walter Gropius and Marcel Breuer, and Richard Neutra. "Report of the Jury for the Competition for an Art Center for Wheaton College," *Architectural Forum* 69, no. 2 (August 1938): 143–58; "Faculty Notes," *Vassar Miscellany News*, June 17, 1938, 5; "An Architectural Competition," *Bulletin of the Museum of Modern Art* 5, no. 2 (February 1938): 2–3.

I. JOHN MCANDREW'S INTRODUCTION TO MODERNISM

John McAndrew shared with others of his generation a wide-eyed curiosity about the modern world, especially its art and culture. Although his background was modest, he was given exceptional opportunities to develop his intellectual interests and indulge his free-spirited love of travel. His education and his explorations would be decisive factors in shaping his modernist vision.

John McAndrew was born in Brooklyn in 1904. His father, William McAndrew, was then the principal of Washington Irving High School in Manhattan.[1] His mother, Susan Irvine (Gurney) McAndrew, was a housewife. Raised in Kingsbridge, New York, John was schooled at home until the age of eight, when he attended the nearby Riverdale Country School, where he was described at ten as a boy of "superior intelligence and power" and "full of fun, but extremely conscientious."[2] By this time his father had become associate superintendent of schools in New York.[3] William McAndrew subsequently served as superintendent of Chicago public schools from 1924 to 1927, when he was ousted by Mayor William Hale Thompson on a charge of "insubordination," though later vindicated. John's father was known as a highly principled, if overbearing, educator. Strong willed and not always popular, William McAndrew was nonetheless admired by colleagues for supporting educational policy in the face of political influence.[4] William may have acquired his unbending ethical positions from his Scottish-born mother, who was the first woman physician in Michigan, and Scottish-born father, a cabinetmaker in Ypsilanti. In addition to their vocations, William's parents were committed to late nineteenth-century liberal causes, notably temperance and the abolition of slavery. William and Susan McAndrew also championed such causes as juvenile temperance and women's suffrage.[5] The high principles embedded in William's character and the vicissitudes of his career would lead to shifts of employment, resulting in traits that his son inherited and patterns that he acquired. However, while at the Riverdale School, John excelled by virtue of his intellect and tenacity. He graduated at sixteen and soon enrolled in the class of 1924 at Harvard College.

John McAndrew was introduced to modern art and culture at a time when Harvard students were increasingly attracted to their allure (fig. 1.1). Like his classmate Henry-Russell Hitchcock Jr., whom he met freshman year, McAndrew was an undergraduate major in the fine arts. Hitchcock and Julien Levy, another Harvard classmate, remained his lifelong friends (figs. 1.2, 1.3). McAndrew's avocation at college was

Left: Figure 1.1
John McAndrew, freshman class photograph, 1920 (Courtesy Peter J. Fergusson)

Left: Figure 1.2
George Platt Lynes.
Photograph of Henry-
Russell Hitchcock,
1935. Gelatin silver
print (Frances Lehman
Loeb Art Center,
Vassar College)

Center: Figure 1.3
Jay Leyda. Photograph
of Julien Levy, ca.
1932. Gelatin silver
print (Philadelphia
Museum of Art, 125th
Anniversary
Acquisition. The Lynne
and Harold Honickman
Gift of the Julien Levy
Collection)

Right: Figure 1.4
A. Everett Austin, 1927
(The Virgil Thomson
Papers, Gilmore
Music Library, Yale
University)

designing scenery and costumes for school productions. In their sophomore year he and Hitchcock were elected to the Dramatic Club in the category of Art at the same time as Walter Hamor Piston (class of 1924) was elected in the category of Music. This affiliation bound McAndrew artistically not only to a group of drama students but also to a circle of gay men, which included Virgil Thomson (class of 1923).[6] In his senior year he designed the sets for the Dramatic Club's production of Carlo Goldoni's comedy *Liar*.[7] His design of a Venetian carnival street scene turned out to be a prophetic experience, which would later prepare him to mount the Venetian balls that crowned many early fund-raising efforts of Save Venice Inc., the organization he would cofound in 1971 to restore Venetian works of art and architecture (see Epilogue). His college experience in scenic design also helped him to develop his gift for staging, one on which he would later draw for gallery and museum installations.

In the spring of his senior year McAndrew met A. Everett Austin, known as "Chick," in Edward Waldo Forbes's course Methods and Processes of Italian Painting (fig. 1.4).[8] Forbes, the director of Harvard's Fogg Art Museum (now Fogg Museum), loaned many works from his own collection of classical sculpture and Italian Renaissance painting to the museum. An exposure to original works rather than reproductions was central to the Fogg experience; it was a hallmark of Forbes's teaching method and a touchstone for McAndrew's training in fine arts at Harvard. "When a student sees the actual work of art itself, if that work of art is explained in a stimulating way and is studied as a vital object in the chain of real experiences of real people," Forbes believed, "then art becomes living and the student can understand it as one of the great forms of the expression of human emotions."[9] Forbes was also a practicing artist, and his methods course placed great emphasis on understanding the techniques and processes that informed painting and sculpture. According to Sybil Gordon Kantor, Alfred Barr's biographer, "Students were required not only to replicate oil paintings, frescoes, and tempera panels in the Renaissance manner but also to prepare their own plaster and gesso and lay on their own gold leaf."[10] As Lincoln Kirstein (Harvard class of 1929) recalled, the laboratory for conservation and restoration that Forbes founded "did much to temper the museum's former compulsory aesthetic of Ruskinian and Paterian 'appreciation.'"[11] The students' immersion in a balance of technique and connoisseurship, which reflected the close relationship between the Fogg Art Museum and the Department of Fine Arts, was then called the "Fogg method."[12] To Forbes, such courses were not intended to create artists but to instill in Harvard men "the art heritage of our civilization…[a] love of the arts," making it "an integral, vital part of their lives," and to provide a few with "the training and experience necessary to enable them to serve as curators and directors of museums, or connoisseurs, critics, and teachers of the arts."[13] McAndrew appreciated how Forbes taught "what you could do and what you couldn't do and what went wrong and what changed color over time."[14] That experience helped to nurture McAndrew's sensitivity to color, enabling him later to grasp the nuances of modernist color theory advanced by De Stijl artists in Holland, Bauhaus artists and designers in Germany, and Le Corbusier in France. In short, as McAndrew later recalled, "such work made me SEE more [McAndrew's emphasis]."[15]

In the spring of 1924 McAndrew graduated magna cum laude in fine arts with a bachelor of science degree.[16] He was only twenty years old.[17] While he would position the fine arts at the center of his professional life, he did not initially seek a career as either an educator or a museum curator. Instead, that fall he enrolled in a four-year program of study at the Harvard School of Architecture.[18] These were heady years of avant-garde exploration in European art and architecture that included De Stijl developments, most notably Gerrit Rietveld's Schröder House in Utrecht, Netherlands (1924–25); the founding of the Bauhaus in the German cities of Weimar, in 1919, and Dessau, in 1925; Walter Gropius's Bauhaus building in Dessau (1925–26) (fig. 1.12); and Le Corbusier's early villas in the suburbs of Paris. Moreover, the new pedagogy of the Bauhaus, under the direction of Gropius and his successors Hannes Meyer and Ludwig Mies van der Rohe, had transformed the teaching of design in Central Europe. But American architecture schools during the 1920s were still governed by the Beaux-Arts system and its curriculum. When McAndrew entered Harvard's School of Architecture, George Harold Edgell, an art historian, was dean. The principal design teacher was Jean-Jacques Haffner, a French graduate of the École des Beaux-Arts in Paris, student of Victor Laloux, and winner of the Grand Prix de Rome in 1919. Haffner instructed students in Beaux-Arts theory and design.[19] As Louis Kahn recalled of his Beaux-Arts training under Paul Cret at the University of Pennsylvania (1920–24), the system called for skilled drawing and rendering with emphasis on *analytiques* and *projets*, as well as the *esquisse* (sketch) guided by, among other things, the concept of *poché* (or a "pocketed" plan), in which structural elements were revealed by the voids between them.[20] During

McAndrew's years at Harvard, the school shared with Massachusetts Institute of Technology (MIT) and the Boston Architectural Club (now the Boston Architectural College, or BAC) what were known as "conjunctive problems" or "sketch problems." Skilled at rendering, McAndrew won a Second Medal for his project for "A Summer School of Fine Arts" (fig. 1.5).[21] The Beaux-Arts system had limitations, however; with a residual emphasis on historical styles, its pedagogy paid little attention to such pragmatic issues as site conditions, contemporary social or cultural concerns, and economic developments, notwithstanding the increasing weight given to computation and engineering in the schools.[22] According to Lawrence Anderson, later dean of MIT's School of Architecture, the architecture programs at Harvard, the BAC, and MIT were linked to the conservative culture of Boston, which at the time reflected the ambience of such institutions as the Isabella Stewart Gardner Museum.[23] This meant that most Harvard design teachers were unwilling to introduce students to the new architecture from Europe.

Yet McAndrew's fellow design students were alive to American and European modernism, although it was largely as an underground movement. They did know about Frank Lloyd Wright from Edgell's lectures in 1926.[24] That year Edgell wrote to Wright to request photographs of his Imperial Hotel in Tokyo (1913–23) and also of one of his houses to use in a lecture and then publish in his forthcoming book, *The American Architecture of To-day* (1928).[25] Harvard students of McAndrew's generation were excited about the buildings of the 1925 Exposition internationale des arts décoratifs et industriels moderns (International Exposition of Modern Decorative and Industrial Arts) in Paris as well as European manifestos and ground-breaking studies of American modernism. But their investigations were still largely covert. Writing to Lewis Mumford in the late 1930s, McAndrew recalled his earlier debt to him. Students were "floundering in architectural school," he told Mumford, but "beginning to take architecture seriously when *Sticks and Stones* appeared."[26] He called it the "book that changed our minds," recounting how "we used to circulate it secretly under the draughting tables, sometimes with *Vers une architecture* or [Geoffrey Scott's] *The Architecture of Humanism*."[27] Walter Kilham Jr., a fellow Harvard student (1925–28), later remembered carrying around copies of both Le Corbusier's *Vers une architecture* (1923) (fig. 1.6) and *Urbanisme* (1925).[28] Thus McAndrew was drawn to Wright's organic tradition at the same time as he was absorbing Le Corbusier's symbolic thinking, which was embedded in modern experience, as well as his preoccupation with industrial buildings, which would later resonate with McAndrew as a form of technological vernacular (see Chapter Three). The impact of these books, along with Edgell's lectures, on fellow architecture students such as George Thomas Daub, Howard Fisher, Henry Hoover, Carl Theodore Larson, George Lyman Paine, G. Holmes Perkins, Peter van den Meulen Smith, and Edward Durell Stone would be measured by the increasing tilt toward modern design in their work.[29] In large measure, the early exposure to Wright and Le Corbusier predisposed McAndrew and others to renounce conventional historicism and to accept a pluralistic and cross-cultural view of modernism.

Figure 1.6
Cover, Le Corbusier-Saugnier, *Vers une architecture*, Paris: G. Crès [1923] (Private collection © FLC-ADAGP, Paris / Artists Rights Society [ARS], New York 2017)

McAndrew acquired an exceptional knowledge of European avant-garde movements, nurtured by his enduring friendships with the well-traveled Hitchcock and Austin, who were also enrolled in the Harvard School of Architecture (in 1923–24 and 1925–26, respectively) and kept him informed about new design developments.[30] Hitchcock continued his studies at Harvard as a graduate student in fine arts from 1925 to 1927, during which time he also found inspiration in *Vers une architecture*. He later recalled that "we had our own copies of one of the Paris issues, soon worn out by repeated reading."[31] And when Hitchcock gave his first lectures at Wellesley College in the spring of 1927, as Barr remembered, he "emphasized Corbu."[32] By the early 1930s he would become Le Corbusier's chief American supporter. Along with Philip Johnson and Alfred Barr, Hitchcock would also be responsible for constructing the dominant formalist canon of European modernism, as it was understood in the United States. Through his friendship with Hitchcock and Austin, McAndrew was also in touch with the Harvard circle associated with Paul Sachs's graduate course Museum Work and Museum Methods, or simply Museum Course, which was held in Sachs's house, Shady Hill.[33] In January 1927 McAndrew attended a lecture by Barr at the Fogg Art Museum and afterward met him at a party (fig. 1.7).[34] That encounter sparked a friendship that would lead Barr to serve as McAndrew's unfaltering mentor. Attending a farewell dinner at Shady Hill toward

the end of the academic year 1926–27 were not only Hitchcock
and Austin but also Barr (who had pursued his doctoral studies at
Harvard in 1924–25 and was then teaching at Wellesley College),
Agnes Rindge (who had left an appointment at Vassar College, where
she had taught from 1923 to 1926, to undertake a doctoral program
at Radcliffe College), Kirk Askew, and Jere Abbott (Barr's Harvard
roommate with whom he would travel to Europe and Russia in
1927–28). These students formed part of a core group now known
collectively as "Harvard modernists."[35]

In September 1927 the first issue of the avant-garde student
review *Hound & Horn: A Harvard Miscellany* was published (fig. 1.8).[36]
Founded by Kirstein and his Harvard classmate Varian Fry, this arts
and letters journal published three volumes during its first academic
year (1927–28). Hitchcock, having left graduate school, and Austin,
having subsequently dropped out of architecture school, were both
involved. Hitchcock published his essay "The Decline of Architecture"
in its first issue. With references to Le Corbusier, the architect Erich
Mendelsohn, and the French painter Fernand Léger, Hitchcock

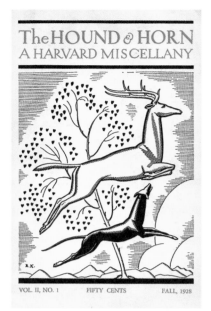

sought to decode the meaning of European modernism, especially its relation to contemporary life, for American readers. He was particularly interested in pointing out the current tension in the new architecture between technical precision and artistic expression.[37] The debut issue also contained four abstract photographs by Jere Abbott of the Necco candy factory in Cambridge, Massachusetts (1927), which Hitchcock considered "the finest fragments of contemporary building" (fig. 1.9).[38] Such factories spoke to the vitality of American modernism invested in its vernacular buildings, which served as a source of inspiration for contemporary designers. In the March 1928 issue, Kirstein published two watercolors by Chick Austin, one of Carcassonne, France, and the other of Venice.[39] During the fall of 1927, McAndrew followed Hitchcock and Austin by withdrawing from the School of Architecture. Although he left for New York, he maintained his contacts with many of the Harvard modernists.

Left: Figure 1.8
Cover, *Hound & Horn:
A Harvard Miscellany*
2, no. 1, Fall 1928
(Private collection)

Right: Figure 1.9
Jere Abbott.
Photograph of the
Necco candy fac-
tory, Cambridge,
Massachusetts,
1927 (Jere Abbott,
"Four Photographs,"
Hound & Horn 1,
no. 1, September 1927,
opp. p. 36; Private
collection)

JOHN MCANDREW AND PHILIP JOHNSON IN EUROPE

Notwithstanding his success at the Harvard School of Architecture during three years of study (1924–27), McAndrew left without submitting a thesis or completing his degree. At architecture school, he later disparaged, "I learned little."[40] His predilection for modernism, cultivated by Hitchcock, Austin, and Levy and stimulated by Wright's work and the writings of Mumford and Le Corbusier, was decidedly at odds with the school's Beaux-Arts curriculum. By late 1927 McAndrew was employed as a draftsman in the New York office of Aymar Embury, a well-established and fashionable academic architect. Embury specialized in residential architecture and schools.[41]

In 1929 McAndrew took a long break from Embury's office to travel in Europe. Visiting a museum gallery in Mannheim, Germany, that summer, he caught the eye of Philip Johnson, who stood in front of a "most disappointing Van Gogh." Johnson observed that the young man "looked much better than his clothes.... His face was American."[42] Although their student years at Harvard had overlapped—Johnson entered the college in the fall of 1923—they had not encountered each other on campus. Paralleling McAndrew's departure from graduate school, Johnson had recently left Harvard without completing his undergraduate degree. With McAndrew in tow, Johnson returned to his base in Heidelberg, Germany. Together they toured the country, visiting the cities of Worms, Mainz, Darmstadt, and Lorsch in Johnson's ostentatious Packard convertible. They agreed to meet up in another month for a more extensive tour in order to gather material for a collaborative project that Johnson described as "popular articles on modern architecture." [43] Their overall plan encompassed a two-month architectural excursion, studying sites that Barr, an early mentor to Johnson, had suggested.

Johnson was wild about McAndrew. He told his family that McAndrew "knows everyone in Cambridge that I do, and the two days he was with me, we talked ourselves so excited that neither of us could sleep."[44] Glad that he was traveling alone, which allowed him to meet someone like McAndrew, Johnson reported that his new companion was "charming, and 'hates the people I hate' etc." Moreover, "he is...crazy about modern architecture as am I."[45] By mid-September he and McAndrew had launched their grand tour, visiting the Kiefhoek housing estate in Rotterdam, Netherlands (1925), by J. J. P. Oud; they were "quite fanatic" about him and "under his spell."[46] However, in comparison to the formal élan of Oud's Hook of Holland housing development (1924–27), which Johnson considered the "Parthenon of modern Europe," the Rotterdam housing lacked "genius" and "charm" (fig. 1.10).[47] In Rotterdam they also visited Brinkman & Van der Vlugt's Van Nelle Factory (1926–29).[48] Johnson wrote home that they planned to make a "fact-picture book, with a minimum of metaphysics and aesthetics in it," focusing on leading architects and "the styles" in each country accompanied by a brief article. Nonetheless, aesthetics still seems to have governed the enterprise, with Johnson conceding that he would "sacrifice the best buildings if they don't photograph well."[49] Johnson described McAndrew as the "perfect traveling companion" because he "knows much more than I, but is very modest, just as enthusiastic as I but less prejudiced, less apt to be a fanatic. I am learning a lot from him....Quicker than I, we make a good team."[50] From the Hague they traveled to Berlin by way of Cologne, Dusseldorf, and Essen, whose "best...advanced ideas of regional planning of the Ruhr" impressed them as "progressive." When they reached Frankfurt they visited what Johnson described as its "great Modern suburbs," notably the Römerstadt Siedlung by Ernst May, C. H. Rudloff, and others (1927–28).[51]

Figure 1.10
J. J. P. Oud. Housing
Development, Hook
of Holland, 1924–27
(Marcel Chappey,
*Architecture
Internationale*, Paris:
Vincent, Fréal [1929],
plate 79; Private
collection)

In early October, when the two travelers settled in Berlin, Johnson enlisted McAndrew's help in designing a renovation for his family's Barrett House, at Townsend Farm, near New London, Ohio. Johnson assured his mother that "as far as an architect goes, John is quite a capable one himself, so we ought to have lots of fun."[52] Attempting to match the astonishing architecture they had just encountered and to draw on De Stijl color concepts, they planned to deploy a white palette with "the purest possible primary colors… much more yellow than blue, and much more blue than red."[53] The window sills and jambs would be yellow (recalling Kiefhoek) and the front door painted red. Johnson added that "the walls would be a shiny white Duco, the carpet and stuffed chairs, gray or a mixture of gray and black…rather a silvery. The lighting fixtures and door knobs and things of chromium plate and ground glass.…My color scheme is exactly that used by Oud in those famous buildings at the Hook."[54] Even though the Barrett House renovation was never executed, the two Americans hoped to realize on their shores design ideas that they had discovered in Europe, which McAndrew would further explore in Le Corbusier's color palette and later adapt to the Vassar College Art Library interior.

When not attending the opera, theater, concerts, and films or enjoying the city's crowded cafés, they continued their "search for the modern," a search that had become their obsession.[55] While in Berlin, Johnson commissioned the photographer Helmar Lerski to take his portrait, a tightly framed close-up (fig. 1.11). Together McAndrew and Johnson visited a house in the suburbs of Berlin by Mendelsohn, most likely the architect's own Am Rupenhorn (1929–30). Johnson

Figure 1.11
Helmar Lerski.
Photograph of Philip
Johnson, Berlin,
1929 (Helmar Lerski/
Getty Research
Institute, Research
Library Los Angeles
© Estate Helmar
Lerski, Fotografische
Sammlung, Museum
Folkwang, Essen/Philip
Johnson Tapes, 34,
208)

described its "plain white plaster" with "no ornament on the house whatsoever" and wrote that its "whole lower floor is glass, plate glass which lowers into the floor and makes practically a porch of the living room and dining room in hot weather."[56] Exhilarated by the experience, Johnson told his mother that "John and I have been going around singing the rest of the day."[57]

The two former Harvard students were kindred aesthetes. Johnson confided to his mother that "having John with me has been gorgeous, because it keeps the focus on art all the time."[58] With a letter of introduction from the architect Jan Ruhtenberg, the two Americans visited the Bauhaus at Dessau (and met with Gropius on a second visit), which McAndrew remembered as the "climax of our trip" and Johnson simply called "our Mecca" (fig. 1.12).[59] They were impressed by what they learned there from an American Bauhaus student, most likely either Howard Dearstyne or Edward Fischer.[60] The school was then under the leadership of the Swiss architect Hannes Meyer after Gropius had officially left in 1928, ostensibly to return to his architectural practice in Berlin, but remained a visitor. McAndrew concluded that the American student was getting a better education at the Bauhaus than at any American architecture school.[61] For his part, Johnson responded to the Bauhaus's "beauty of plan," saying, "The very idea of working in such a magnificent building thrills me."[62] There he purchased a number of lighting fixtures, which he planned to use in a future exhibition back home to show what "the modern work is like here."[63] Many of the new buildings they discovered on their travels belied the clichés that later framed Johnson and Hitchcock's concept of an International Style. For example, what Johnson and McAndrew admired in Oud's treatment of color—the counterpoint between white surfaces and judicious color accents—was what fascinated Johnson in a school designed by Otto Haesler, which they also visited. At the Alstädter School in Celle, Germany, near Hanover (1927–28), Johnson told Barr, Haesler "uses color better than anyone but Oud," with a similar play of white surfaces and intelligently executed primary colors.[64]

But their "search for the modern" was not the only object of their travels. Seeking aesthetic diversion in the baroque and rococo, they traveled to other sites in Central Europe, including the German cities of Leipzig and Dresden. In Dresden they were particularly impressed with Matthäus Daniel Pöppelmann's Zwinger Pavilion (1710–19), Johnson comparing it to a Bach fugue because each part was an "elaboration on a very simple theme."[65] They also spent time in Prague, which Johnson considered a baroque city. The two travelers continued to enjoy each other's company. Johnson confided to Barr that he found McAndrew "a charming talker, and while not profound, has a good eye. I have learned a lot from him, especially about Barock [using the German spelling]."[66]

Johnson and McAndrew's absorption in aestheticism and adventure was energized by the zeitgeist in Berlin. There, Johnson later reflected, "it was sin, mainly, as it was for [W. H.] Auden and

Figure 1.12
Walter Gropius.
Bauhaus building,
Dessau, Germany,
aerial view, 1925–26
(Foto Marburg / Art
Resource, NY © 2017
Artists Rights Society
[ARS], New York / VG
Bild-Kunst, Bonn)

[Christopher] Isherwood, that attracted us there. And the life that went with the sin. The incredible music and dance, the plays…art exhibitions."[67] Those months in Berlin had been free and unfettered by contemporary conventions, an opportunity to immerse themselves in the local gay culture. Of his time in Berlin with McAndrew, Johnson recalled, "I guess it was mostly sex. Isherwood period."[68] But their relationship would not last. By mid-November 1929 McAndrew had left Berlin. When Johnson told his family about "John's going away," he consoled himself with a twinge of melancholy: "Well, that is almost forgotten now in the dim and distant past."[69] As a result of the split, they abandoned their proposed book about European modernism. In the summer of 1930 Johnson would resume his research and travel, not with McAndrew but with Hitchcock, for what would become the *International Style* book of 1932.[70] However, the Johnson-McAndrew interlude was a formative experience for both men. Their breakup led to lifelong periods of ambivalence and discord between them, although they maintained a professional relationship until Johnson entered into right-wing and fascist politics in late 1934.[71]

NEW YORK'S ART SCENE: THE JULIEN LEVY GALLERY AND THE ASKEW SALON

McAndrew returned to New York at the end of 1929 to resume his drafting job with Aymar Embury, while Johnson returned to Harvard in January 1930 to finish his undergraduate degree. By late 1930 McAndrew was assisting his former classmate Julien Levy in establishing his gallery specializing in surrealist art (fig. 1.3). Levy felt that it was a good opportunity for McAndrew during a period in which he was "marking time between a dreary job in an architect's office"

and "a hoped-for career teaching architectural history."[72] As the Julien Levy Gallery's first secretary, McAndrew helped to design its interior, remodeling rooms in a brownstone at 602 Madison Avenue, using his "celluloid French curve" to transform "an awkward corner" into a serpentine wall. Although it was Levy's initial idea, the curved wall was executed by McAndrew. For a subsequent gallery on East Fifty-Seventh Street, Levy would also use a curved wall, one that would become not only its signature design element but also one of McAndrew's (fig. 1.13).[73] For a year McAndrew worked in both the Levy Gallery and the Embury office. But in October 1931 Embury would have less work on the boards due to the effects of the Great Depression that followed the business boom of the 1920s and the stock market crash in 1929, which obliged him to sever his relationship with his draftsman.[74] As McAndrew later remembered, "I was overtaken by the Depression, and discouraged from trying to survive as an architect."[75]

In spite of the challenging economic conditions of the early 1930s, Levy's new gallery experienced a surge of success. Given greater responsibilities with exhibitions, McAndrew thrived. He arranged for the loan of paintings by Salvador Dalí and Max Ernst to the Wadsworth Atheneum, in Hartford, Connecticut, whose director, Chick Austin, staged the first surrealist show in America (fall 1931). McAndrew helped to organize the Levy Gallery's first group exhibition of surrealist works in a show called *Surréalisme* (January 1932), despite Levy's apprehension about debuting Salvador Dalí's explicit imagery to an unaccustomed public.[76] The announcement was designed by Joseph Cornell (fig. 1.14). McAndrew was instrumental in advancing the careers of photographers George

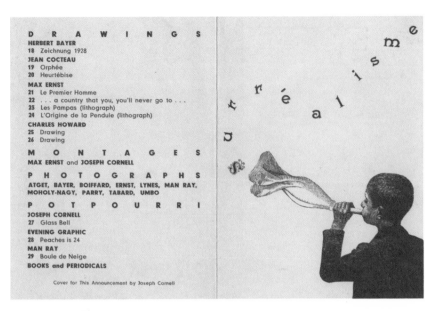

Platt Lynes and Walker Evans. He introduced Levy to Lynes, which resulted in several exhibitions featuring Lynes's photographs.[77] He also introduced Levy to Evans, whose work was subsequently shown in several Levy Gallery exhibitions.[78] Lynes, in particular, was developing a close friendship with McAndrew, whose intelligence and opinion he valued.[79] In 1931 the two shared an apartment with Lloyd Wescott (brother of the writer Glenway Wescott) at 425 East Fifty-First Street, where McAndrew was remembered for having painted the smaller of its two rooms "cinnamon," a color used by Le Corbusier and other avant-garde artists in the 1930s, which called to mind organic materials.[80] During the years from 1931 to 1935, McAndrew's small circle of friends included not only Lloyd Wescott but also Lloyd's brother Glenway, who had long formed a ménage à trois with Monroe Wheeler and George Platt Lynes, as well as Lynes's brother J. Russell Lynes. Together they met at the Lynes family homes in Englewood, New Jersey, and North Egremont, Massachusetts, in the Berkshires. In April 1934 in North Egremont, George Platt Lynes captured one facet of McAndrew's persona in a homoerotic photograph with his boyish head encircled in a wreath of white fern fronds (fig. 1.15).[81]

McAndrew's association with Levy renewed his friendships with the Harvard modernists. During their student years some had been associated with *Hound & Horn*. Others had been members of an affiliated group called the Harvard Society for Contemporary Art, founded in December 1928.[82] Initiated by Lincoln Kirstein with John Walker III and Edward M. M. Warburg, who formed an executive committee, the Harvard Society relied on the support of Paul Sachs, with Alfred Barr as its intellectual fountainhead.[83] Decidedly a men's club, it nonetheless embraced two women: Agnes Mongan, a Sachs protégé who would later become director of the Fogg Art Museum, and Agnes Rindge, who rejoined the Vassar College Art Department faculty in

1928 after completing her PhD at Radcliffe College.[84] This precocious group organized a run of astonishingly creative exhibitions (in two second-floor rooms of the Harvard Cooperative Building), which were then (as now) recognized as precursors to those at the Museum of Modern Art. Barr defined its gallery space as "elegantly refitted with a silvered ceiling, steel café chairs and severe, highly polished metal-topped tables."[85] The Harvard Society's first academic year included exhibitions devoted to American art (February 1929), the School of Paris (March 1929), Maurice Prendergast (April 1929), and Buckminster Fuller's Dymaxion House (May 1929).[86]

As part of her efforts to help found the Museum of Modern Art in November 1929, Abby Aldrich Rockefeller visited the Harvard Society and determined that New York should copy "*en gros* what they were doing."[87] Rockefeller and founding president A. Conger Goodyear were instrumental in appointing Barr as the museum's first director.[88] At this exciting moment in the maturation of American modernism an axis was drawn between Cambridge and New York. Following the establishment of MoMA, a proliferation of New York galleries devoted to modernism emerged, most notably the Marie Harriman Gallery (1930), the John Becker Gallery (1930), and the Pierre Matisse Gallery (1931), in addition to the Julien Levy Gallery (1931). These joined with the established galleries New Art Circle, Valentine Gallery, and Brummer Gallery, which now embraced modernism.[89]

During the early 1930s, the anchor of New York's avant-garde art was formally the Museum of Modern Art, which, beginning in 1933, was headquartered at the Rockefeller house at 11 West Fifty-Third Street.[90] But informally it was a brownstone at 166 East Sixty-First Street, where Kirk and Constance Askew hosted Sunday parties and served bootlegged homemade liquor. As actor John Houseman described the scene, as many as five dozen guests would arrive shortly after five in the afternoon during the *R* months (September through April). The core of this weekly reunion was a group of former Harvard students, principally those who had trained in the fine arts under Sachs, as had Kirk Askew, a representative of the London art dealers Durlacher Brothers; the group included Alfred Barr and Jere Abbott (then associate director of MoMA), Chick Austin, Henry-Russell Hitchcock (professor at Wesleyan University from 1929 to 1948), Philip Johnson, Julien Levy, and Agnes Rindge. They were often joined by artists who had either gravitated to New York or were passing through, including Salvador Dalí, Pavel Tchelitchew, Eugene and Leonid Berman, Juan Gris, Wassily Kandinsky, and René Magritte. But it was more than that: also a magnet for music, arts and letters, theater, and dance, the Askew salon was frequently attended by composers Aaron Copland, Virgil Thomson, and Roger Sessions; Lincoln Kirstein; the curator Hyatt Mayor; photographers George Platt Lynes and Lee Miller; various *New Yorker* writers; poets Elizabeth Bowen and e. e. cummings; a few select critics, including Gilbert Seldes and Henry McBride; dance choreographers Agnes de Mille and George Balanchine; art dealers Marie Harriman and Pierre Matisse; and the Museum of Modern Art's founding film librarian, Iris Barry, among others.

Houseman recalled that the group was evenly divided between the sexes, with many spouses present.[91] "Flirtation (homo- and hetero-sexual) was tolerated," Houseman recalled, "but not encouraged. If it threatened to hold up traffic or disrupt the interchange of ideas it was soon ferreted out and broken up" by the hosts.[92] At a time when the culture of art, and certainly modern art, was fresh and not yet fully professionalized, these informal gatherings were stimulating opportunities to absorb and exchange ideas. McAndrew remembered

the Askew salon as an intimate circle: "There weren't so many people who were interested in these things so everybody knew each other."[93] Virgil Thomson viewed the salons as a form of networking enterprise. "The mechanism of taste forming is complex," he recalled, "the people at the Askews were not so much picture buyers, but talkers."[94] Taken as a whole, this group exerted an enormous influence on the contemporary art scene. McAndrew and Agnes Rindge were regulars. Lynes's 1935 portrait of Rindge shows the Vassar professor with the allure of glamour that embodied this circle (fig. 1.16). It was a persona to which McAndrew aspired.

During the late 1920s and early 1930s, McAndrew's prospects both narrowed and expanded. He had left the formal discipline and practice of architecture for an exploration of modernism through European travel and immersion in the New York art scene.

Figure 1.17
Audience for first
performance, *Four
Saints in Three Acts*,
Wadsworth Atheneum,
February 7, 1934. Fifth
row, from the left: A.
Everett "Chick" and
Helen Austin, Kirk
and Constance Askew,
John McAndrew,
Agnes Rindge, Julien
and Joella Levy
(*Hartford Courant*,
February 8, 1934,
Wadsworth Atheneum
Archives, Hartford,
Connecticut)

He retained his close personal friendships with Hitchcock, Levy, Austin, Barr, Askew, Rindge, and other Harvard modernists, but with Johnson he kept his distance. He and Rindge continued to socialize together and were among a group of New Yorkers from the Askew salon who attended the first performance at the Wadsworth Atheneum of the opera *Four Saints in Three Acts*, composed by McAndrew's Harvard classmate Virgil Thomson and with a libretto by Gertrude Stein (fig. 1.17). McAndrew would soon draw on his abiding friendship with Rindge as he sought to enter the academy and begin a teaching career.

1   Clyde R. Jeffords and Claude F. Walker, *The High Schools of New York City: A Hand-book of Procedure and Personnel* (New York: High School Teachers' Association of New York City, 1921), 10.

2   "Progress Reports" [Riverdale Country School, 1914] (John McAndrew Papers, Courtesy of Wellesley College Archives; hereafter cited as John McAndrew Papers, WCA).

3   *NEA* [National Education Association] *Bulletin* 5 (September 1916): 230.

4   "Wm. M'Andrew, 73, Educator, Is Dead," *New York Times*, June 29, 1937, 21; "McAndrews Dies, Famed Schoolman," *The Daily News—Ludington, Michigan*, June 29, 1937, 4.

5   Caryn Hannan and Jennifer L. Herman, et al., *Michigan Biographical Dictionary* (Hamburg, MI: State History Publications, 2008), 115; William McAndrew, *Helen Walker McAndrew, 1826–1906*, 1931, https://babel.hathitrust.org/cgi/pt?id=mdp.39015071151198.

6   "Results of Dramatic Club Competitions are Announced," *Harvard Crimson*, May 16, 1922, accessed December 18, 2012, http://www.thecrimson.com/article/1922/5/16/results-of-dramatic-club-competitions-are/. In his sophomore year McAndrew was given an honorable mention for set designs to a 47 Workshop Company production of the play *Pastora Impera*. "Announce Results of Workshop Competition," *Harvard Crimson*, December 13, 1921, accessed December 18, 2012, http://www.thecrimson.com/article/1921/12/13/announce-results-of-workshop-competition/. In his junior year he designed costumes and "scenic effects" for the Dramatic Club's production of two miracle plays and also scenery for an Agassiz House production of Thomas Wolfe's *Welcome to Our City*. "To Present Miracle Plays This Evening," *Harvard Crimson*, December 20, 1922, accessed December 18, 2012, http://www.the crimson.com/article/1922/12/20/to-present-miracle-plays-this-evening/; "Workshop to Present 'Welcome to Our City,'" *Harvard Crimson*, May 11, 1923, accessed December 18, 2012, http://www.thecrimson.com/article/1923/5/11/workshop-to-present-welcome-to-our/.

7   "Dramatic Club Choses [*sic*] Settings for 'Liar,'" *Harvard Crimson*, November 20, 1923, accessed December 18, 2012, http://www.thecrimson.com/article/1923/11/20/dramatic-club-choses-settings-for-liar/.

8   McAndrew met Austin when the latter returned to Harvard from an archaeological expedition to the Sudan in February 1924. John McAndrew, interview by Jill Silverman, November 4, 1974 (Wadsworth Atheneum Archives, Hartford, CT; hereafter cited as WAAHC); Eugene R. Gaddis, *Magician of the Modern: Chick Austin and the Transformation of the Arts in America* (New York: Alfred A. Knopf, 2000), 40, 57.

9   Edward W. Forbes, "The Campaign for a New Museum," *Fogg Art Museum, Harvard University, Notes* 2 (April 1925): 23.

10   Sybil Gordon Kantor, *Alfred H. Barr, Jr. and the Intellectual Origins of the Museum of Modern Art* (Cambridge, MA.: MIT Press, 2002), 50. Kantor's analysis is based in part on her interview with the art historian, curator, and former director of the Fogg Art Museum Agnes Mongan, October 1983.

11   Lincoln Kirstein, *Mosaic: Memoirs* (New York: Farrar, Straus & Giroux, 1994), 163.

12   Kantor, *Alfred H. Barr, Jr.*, 49.

13   Forbes, "Campaign for a New Museum," 21.

14   McAndrew, interview by Silverman, November 4, 1974 (WAAHC).

15   John McAndrew to Oleg Grabar, December 10, 1977 (John McAndrew Papers, WCA).

16   [John McAndrew transcript, 1924] Graduate School of Design. Student folders (graduate), 1893–1986 (inclusive). UAV322.282 Box 25, Folder: McAndrew, John (Harvard University Archives). Russell Lynes explained that the "Bachelor of Arts at Harvard was awarded only to students who qualified in Latin or Greek. McAndrew's father [William], who had been Superintendent of Schools in Chicago, did not believe in the teaching of Latin in his school system or in having his children study it." Russell Lynes, *Good Old Modern: An Intimate Portrait of the Museum of Modern Art* (New York: Atheneum, 1973), 177.

17   Although biographical sketches claim that McAndrew graduated from Harvard College at nineteen, his commencement was on June 19, 1924, following his twentieth birthday on May 4.

18   *First Report of the Alumni in Architecture of Harvard University* (Cambridge, MA: Harvard University Press, 1932), 92.

19   Anthony Alofsin, *The Struggle for Modernism: Architecture, Landscape Architecture, and City Planning at Harvard* (New York: W. W. Norton, 2002), 55.

20   William H. Jordy, "The Span of Kahn—Kimbell Art Museum, Fort Worth, Texas; Library, Phillips Exeter Academy, Exeter, New Hampshire," *Architectural Review* 155 (June 1974): 332.

21   William Wirt Turner, *Fundamentals of Architectural Design* (New York: McGraw-Hill, 1930), 155, plate 16.

22   Alofsin, *Struggle for Modernism*, 58–59.

23   Lawrence B. Anderson, interview by the author, Lincoln, Massachusetts, January 5, 1988.

24   Alofsin, *Struggle for Modernism*, 83.

25 Alofsin, *Struggle for Modernism*, 279n103. Calling Wright the "greatest living protagonist" of the modern rural and suburban dwelling, Edgell published photographs of the Imperial Hotel, the Coonley House in Riverside, Illinois, and Taliesin in Spring Green, Wisconsin. George Harold Edgell, *The American Architecture of To-day* (New York: Charles Scribner's Sons, 1928), 122–23, 342, 345; figs., 71, 72, 108, 335–37.

26 Lewis Mumford, *Sticks and Stones: A Study of American Architecture and Civilization* (New York: Boni & Liveright, 1924); John McAndrew to Lewis Mumford, March 9, 1939 (Lewis Mumford Papers, folder 3642, Kislak Center for Special Collections, Rare Books and Manuscripts, University of Pennsylvania; Courtesy of the Estate of Lewis and Sophia Mumford; hereafter cited as Mumford Papers, KCSC, RBM, UP).

27 McAndrew to Mumford, March 9, 1939 (Mumford Papers, folder 3642, KCSC, RBM, UP). See Le Corbusier-Saugnier, *Vers une architecture* (Paris: G. Crès [1923]); Geoffrey Scott, *The Architecture of Humanism: A Study in the History of Taste*, rev. ed. (1914; repr., London: Constable, 1924).

28 Walter H. Kilham Jr., *Raymond Hood, Architect: Form through Function in the American Skyscraper* (New York: Architectural Book Publishing, 1973), 14.

29 *First Report of the Alumni in Architecture of Harvard University 1932* (Cambridge, MA: Harvard University Press, 1932), 54, 60, 74, 81, 85, 101, 103, 121, 157.

30 During his senior year Hitchcock was a Harvard architecture student. In 1923–24 Austin traveled to North Africa and Europe; by 1925 Hitchcock had traveled to Europe twice, his second trip in 1924–25. Helen Searing, "Henry-Russell Hitchcock: Architectura et Amicitia," in *In Search of Modern Architecture: A Tribute to Henry-Russell Hitchcock*, ed. Helen Searing (Cambridge, MA: MIT Press in association with Architectural History Foundation, New York, 1982), 4.

31 Henry-Russell Hitchcock, "Modern Architecture—A Memoir," *Journal of the Society of Architectural Historians* 27 (December 1968): 229.

32 Hitchcock, "Modern Architecture—A Memoir," 229.

33 Sybil Gordon Kantor, "The Beginnings of Art History at Harvard and the 'Fogg Method,'" in *The Early Years of Art History in the United States*, ed. Craig Hugh Smyth and Peter M. Lukehart (Princeton, NJ: Department of Art and Archaeology, Princeton University, 1993), 170–72.

34 Barr, then an assistant professor at Wellesley College, gave his lecture on "French Painting of the Twentieth Century." See "Barr to Lecture," *Harvard Crimson*, January 19, 1927, accessed January 10, 2013, http://www.thecrimson.com/article/1927/1/19/barr-to-lecture-ptomorrow-afternoon-at/; Lynes, *Good Old Modern*, 178.

35 Steven Watson, *Prepare for Saints: Gertrude Stein, Virgil Thomson, and the Mainstreaming of American Modernism* (New York: Random House, 1998), 80, 86. On Rindge's teaching appointments, see *Annual Catalogue of Vassar College, 1924–1925* (Poughkeepsie, NY: Vassar College [1924]), 101–3; *Annual Catalogue of Vassar College, 1925–1926* (Poughkeepsie, NY: Vassar College [1925]), 97–99; "Reappointments for 1925–1926," *Vassar Miscellany News*, June 15, 1925, 9.

36 *Hound & Horn* drew its name from Ezra Pound's poem "The White Stag": "'Tis the white stag, Fame, we're a-hunting, Bid the world's hounds come to horn!"

37 Henry Russell Hitchcock Jr., "The Decline of Architecture," *Hound & Horn: A Harvard Miscellany* 1, no. 1 (September 1927): 28–35; Searing, "Henry-Russell Hitchcock: Architectura et Amicitia," 3–4; Helen Searing, "Henry-Russell Hitchcock: Formative Years," *Skyline* (December 1982): 10–11. See also Leonard Greenbaum, *Hound & Horn: The History of a Literary Quarterly* (The Hague: Mouton, 1966); Phyllis Lambert, "Kirstein's Circle: Cambridge, Hartford, New York, 1927–1931," in *Autonomy and Ideology: Positioning an Avant-Garde in America*, ed. R. E. Somol (New York: Monacelli Press, 1997), 32–39; Kantor, *Alfred H. Barr, Jr.*, 140–45.

38 Jere Abbott, "Four Photographs," *Hound & Horn: A Harvard Miscellany* 1, no. 1 (September 1927): opp. p. 36.

39 Austin's watercolors, *The Old City: Carcassonne* and *La Cimiteria: Venice*, were illustrated in *Hound & Horn: A Harvard Miscellany* 1, no. 3 (March 1928): opp. p. 228. Austin was then associate director of the Wadsworth Atheneum in Hartford, Connecticut.

40 "John McAndrew," *Harvard Class of 1924 25th Anniversary Report* (Cambridge, MA: Harvard University, 1949), 555.

41 On Embury's work, see Peter S. Kaufman, *Designing the Moses Era: The Architecture and Engineering of Aymar Embury II* (Hempstead, NY: Hofstra Museum, 1988).

42 Philip Johnson to family, [August 13] 1929 (Box 25, Philip Johnson Papers, © J. Paul Getty Trust. Getty Research Institute, Los Angeles [980060]; hereafter cited as PJP, GRI).

43 Johnson to family, [August 13] 1929 (Box 25, PJP, GRI).

44 Johnson to family, [August 13] 1929 (Box 25, PJP, GRI).

45 Johnson to family, [August 13] 1929 (Box 25, PJP, GRI).

46 Philip Johnson to his mother, Louise Johnson [Mrs. Homer H. Johnson], September 22 [1929] (Box 25, PJP, GRI).

47 Johnson to Alfred Barr, October 16 [1929] (Alfred H. Barr Jr. Papers [AAA: 2164; 218]. The Museum of Modern Art Archives, New York; hereafter cited as MoMA Archives, NY).

48 Johnson to Barr, October 16 [1929] (AHB [AAA: 2164; 218]. MoMA Archives, NY).

49 Johnson to Louise Johnson, September 22 [1929] (Box 25, PJP, GRI]).

50 Johnson to Louise Johnson, September 22 [1929] (Box 25, PJP, GRI).

51 Johnson to Louise Johnson, September 22 [1929] (Box 25, PJP, GRI); Johnson to Barr, October 16 [1929] (AHB [AAA: 2164; 218]. MoMA Archives, NY).

52 Philip Johnson to Louise Johnson, October 3 [1929] (Box 25, PJP, GRI).

53 Johnson to Louise Johnson, October 3 [1929] (Box 25, PJP, GRI).

54 Johnson to Louise Johnson, October 3 [1929] (Box 25, PJP, GRI). The following summer Johnson suggested that his family hire Oud to design a house on their property at Pinehurst, North Carolina. Oud agreed to accept the commission in June 1931. Philip Johnson to Louise Johnson, June 20, 1930; J. J. P. Oud to Philip Johnson, November 12, 1930; Philip Johnson to J. J. P. Oud, March 17, 1932 (Registrar's Archive, Museum of Modern Art, New York), quoted in Terence Riley, *The International Style: Exhibition 15 and the Museum of Modern Art* (New York: Rizzoli, 1992), 35, 204n19, n20. Johnson featured the Oud project in *Modern Architecture: International Exhibition* (New York: Museum of Modern Art, 1932), 97–98, 108, 109.

55 Johnson to Louise Johnson, October 14 [1929] (Box 25, PJP, GRI).

56 Johnson to Barr, October 16 [1929] (AHB [AAA: 2164; 218]. MoMA Archives, NY); Johnson to Louise Johnson, October 14 [1929] (Box 25, PJP, GRI).

57 Johnson to Louise Johnson, October 14 [1929] (Box 25, PJP, GRI).

58 Johnson to Louise Johnson, October 3 [1929] (Box 25, PJP, GRI).

59 McAndrew, quoted in Lynes, *Good Old Modern*, 178; Philip Johnson, postcard to Mrs. H. H. Johnson, October 18, 1929 (Box 25, PJP, GRI). Ruhtenberg, a Latvian-born architect (of Swedish parents), was a private student of Mies van der Rohe in Berlin in 1929. In 1933, under Johnson's sponsorship, he would emigrate from Sweden to America. Cammie McAtee, "Alien #5044325: Mies's First Trip to America," in *Mies in America*, ed. Phyllis Lambert (New York: Harry N. Abrams in association with Canadian Centre for Architecture, Montreal, 2001), 137.

60 Johnson to Barr, October 16 [1929] (AHB [AAA: 2164; 218]. MoMA Archives, NY). See Howard Dearstyne, *Inside the Bauhaus*, ed. David Spaeth (New York: Rizzoli, 1986), 28–29.

61 McAndrew made the comment to Johnson. Johnson to Barr, October 16 [1929] (AHB [AAA: 2164; 218]. MoMA Archives, NY).

62 Johnson to Barr, October 16 [1929] (AHB [AAA: 2164; 218]. MoMA Archives, NY). Philip Johnson, fragment of letter [to Louise Johnson] [dated between October 14 and 26, 1929] (Box 25, PJP, GRI).

63 Johnson, fragment of letter [to Louise Johnson] [dated between October 14 and 26, 1929] (Box 25, PJP, GRI). Johnson later loaned the lighting fixtures, as well as plates, an ashtray, and other Bauhaus objects, for a Harvard Society for Contemporary Art exhibition on the Bauhaus (December 1930–January 1931). Nicholas Fox Weber, *Patron Saints: Five Rebels Who Opened America to a New Art, 1928–1943* (New York: Alfred A. Knopf, 1992), 118–19.

64 Johnson to Barr, October 16 [1929] (AHB [AAA: 2164; 218]. MoMA Archives, NY).

65 Johnson to Louise Johnson, October 26, 1929 (Box 25, PJP, GRI).

66 Johnson to Barr, October 16 [1929] (AHB [AAA: 2164; 218]. MoMA Archives, NY).

67 Kazys Varnelis, ed., *The Philip Johnson Tapes: Interviews by Robert A. M. Stern* (New York: Monacelli Press, 2008), 34. Christopher Isherwood, the British novelist who lived in Berlin during the early 1930s, chronicled its residents, his experiences there, and prewar culture in *Christopher and His Kind, 1929–1939* (New York: Farrar, Straus & Giroux, 1976).

68 Varnelis, *Philip Johnson Tapes*, 50.

69 Philip Johnson to family, November 18, 1929 (Box 25, PJP, GRI).

70 Riley, *International Style*, 12–18.

71 Franz Schulze gives an account of that period in his *Philip Johnson: Life and Work* (New York: Alfred A. Knopf, 1994), 104–46.

72 Julien Levy, *Memoir of an Art Gallery* (New York: G. P. Putnam's Sons, 1977), 13.

73 Levy, *Memoir of an Art Gallery*, 13–14.

74 Aymar Embury II to John McAndrew, October 5, 1931 (John McAndrew Papers, WCA).

75 "John McAndrew," *Harvard Class of 1924 25th Anniversary Report*, 555.

76   Referring to Austin's show, called *Newer Super-Realism*, McAndrew told Austin that "Our Super-Realist Show [at the Levy Gallery] is going to be just a little stepchild of yours." John McAndrew to A. Everett Austin, January 6, 1932 (A. Everett Austin Papers, Box 8, Folder 7, WAAHC). John McAndrew to A. Everett Austin, October 14, 1931 (A. Everett Austin Papers, Box 16, Folder 11, WAAHC).

77   Levy, *Memoir of an Art Gallery*, 59, 86. During the gallery's first years Levy exhibited Lynes's work in a group exhibition held January 9–29, 1932; a joint exhibition (with Evans) held February 1–19, 1932; and group shows from May 2 to June 11, 1932, and October 15 to November 5, 1932. Ingrid Schaffner and Lisa Jacobs, *Julien Levy: Portrait of an Art Gallery* (Cambridge, MA: MIT Press, 1998), 173–74.

78   The Levy Gallery exhibited Evans's photographs in a 1932 joint exhibition with Lynes (see previous note) and in group shows from May 2 to June 11, 1932, and April 23 to May 7, 1935. Schaffner and Jacobs, *Julien Levy*, 174, 177; Oral history interview with Julien Levy, May 30, 1975, 15 (Archives of American Art, Smithsonian Institution; the Jean and Julien Levy Foundation for the Arts).

79   George Platt Lynes to Monroe Wheeler, 1931, quoted in Anatole Pohorilenko, "The Expatriate Years, 1925–1934," in *When We Were Three: The Travel Albums of George Platt Lynes, Monroe Wheeler, and Glenway Wescott, 1925–1935* (Sante Fe, NM: Arena Editions, 1998), 75–76.

80   Pohorilenko, "Expatriate Years," 79–80.

81   In 1934 George Platt Lynes also photographed his brother Russell, with his head emerging from fern fronds, but it lacked the eroticism of the McAndrew portrait. See Pohorilenko, *When We Were Three*, fig. 157.

82   "Students Found New Art Society," *Harvard Crimson*, December 13, 1928, accessed December 31, 2012, http://www.thecrimson.com/article/1928/12/13/students-found-new-art-society-plast/?pri.

83   Watson, *Prepare for Saints*, 88–91.

84   On Mongan's informal role in the Harvard Society, see Kirstein, *Mosaic*, 170–71; Weber, *Patron Saints*, 35–37. Both Rindge and Mongan were students in Sachs's Museum Course. Lynes, *Good Old Modern*, 22. On Rindge's return to Vassar College, see "W. Van Ingen Wins Carnegie Fellowship," *Vassar Miscellany News*, May 2, 1928, 6.

85   Alfred Hamilton Barr Jr., "Contemporary Art at Harvard," *Arts* 15 (April 1929): 267. See also Watson, *Prepare for Saints*, 90.

86   "A Summary of the Activities of Its First Year," Harvard Society for Contemporary Art, Annual Report second year, February 1930. See also Kantor, *Alfred H. Barr, Jr.*, 202–7.

87   Edward Warburg to Sybil Gordon Kantor, August 15, 1984, quoted in Kantor, *Alfred H. Barr, Jr.*, 197, 415n25. Nelson Rockefeller may also have considered the Harvard Society as the precursor to the Museum of Modern Art. Bernice Kert, *Abby Aldrich Rockefeller: The Woman in the Family* (New York: Random House, 1993), 291.

88   Kantor, *Alfred H. Barr, Jr.*, 210–11.

89   On October 3, 1930, Marie Harriman opened her gallery on East Fifty-Seventh Street with an exhibition of works by Paul Cézanne, Paul Gauguin, Auguste Renoir, Pablo Picasso, André Derain, Vincent Van Gogh, and Henri Matisse. "Mrs. W. A. Harriman Opens Art Gallery," *New York Times*, October 4, 1930, 17. The John Becker Gallery opened on Madison Avenue in January 1930. "About Town: Van Konijnenburg, Two Frenchmen, and Others," *New York Times*, February 2, 1930, 117. In October 1931 Pierre Matisse, son of Henri Matisse, opened his new gallery in the Fuller Building. "Art News in Brief," *New York Times*, October 25, 1931, X12. Julien Levy opened his gallery in November 1931 with an exhibition of American photography (Paul Strand, Charles Sheeler, Edward Steichen, Clarence White, Gertrude Käsebier, Alfred Stieglitz) "assembled with the cooperation of Alfred Stieglitz." Edward Alden Jewell, "Art: Synthetic View on Photography," *New York Times*, November 3, 1931, 35. In 1927 F. Valentine Dudensing changed the name of his gallery on East Fifty-Seventh Street to the Valentine Gallery of Modern Art. "Exhibitions and Art News Briefly Noted," *New York Times*, November 20, 1927, X12. On Joseph Brummer's exhibitions see, for example, *Constantin Brancusi* (New York: Brummer Gallery, 1926).

90   In the spring of 1937 the MoMA galleries and storage rooms moved underground to the concourse of the Time-Life Building at 14 West Forty-Ninth Street and its offices to the fifteenth floor.

91   Recalling his three years of attending the Askew salons, Houseman gives a longer roster of guests. John Houseman, *Run-Through: A Memoir* (New York: Simon & Schuster, 1972), 97–98. For Levy's recollections, see his *Memoir of an Art Gallery*, 104–7. See also Lynes, *Good Old Modern*, 108–9.

92   Houseman, *Run-Through: A Memoir*, 98–99.

93   McAndrew, interview by Silverman, November 4, 1974 (WAAHC).

94   Thomson, quoted in Watson, *Prepare for Saints*, 188.

II. THE ART LIBRARY AND MCANDREW'S MODERNIST VISION

MCANDREW ARRIVES AT VASSAR

In 1932 John McAndrew set out to reach his academic goal by prevailing upon Agnes Rindge (later Claflin), then an associate professor in the Art Department at Vassar College, to act as his intermediary and advisor in helping him to secure a position at her institution. To McAndrew a Vassar appointment offered an ideal opportunity. During the 1920s, several Harvard modernists served on the Vassar faculty, including Alfred Barr (1923–24); Henry-Russell Hitchcock (1927–28, the year he was made a contributing editor to *Architectural Record*); and Margaret (Margherita) Scolari, who was a graduate student, an Italian instructor (1925–30), and later Barr's wife.[1] Since 1911 the Art Department had been under the leadership of Oliver Samuel Tonks, a Harvard-trained classicist who had previously taught on the faculty at Princeton University.[2] He had been the guiding force in expanding both the faculty and the curriculum.[3] During the winter of 1932 McAndrew enlisted Rindge's support, urging her to "put in lots of good words for me with Dr. Tonks."[4] In an effort to offset his lack of credentials—he had neither a graduate degree in the fine arts nor a master of architecture degree—and teaching experience, McAndrew pressed Chick Austin for a letter: "Will you do me a tremendous favor by writing, on impressive [Wadsworth] Atheneum Stationery, some sort of letter of recommendation which I can flaunt at the Art Department of Vassar. If you could work in that you once recommended me as your successor as assistant to Mr. Forbes in his course (you did) it would sound very impressive, as my total lack of pedagogical experience is bad, and the fact that I have had a few offers might help."[5] Rindge's efforts, bolstered by letters from Austin and from McAndrew's former Harvard professors, were successful.[6] In the spring of 1932, McAndrew was notified of his appointment as an instructor in the Art Department, and he joined Rindge on the faculty the following fall. He would continue to stay in touch with his circle of avant-garde friends in New York, often accompanying Rindge to Museum of Modern Art openings and Kirk and Constance Askew salons, but Vassar would become the focus of his new academic life.

In hiring McAndrew, Tonks brought to campus a faculty member who would not only teach the history of art and architecture but also campaign for modern architecture. During his first academic year (1932–33) McAndrew taught the history course Art 270:

Architecture and Art as well as one in architectural drafting emphasizing "theory and practice," Art 370: Domestic Architecture and Interior Decoration. In his second year (1933–34) he added Art 360: Studies in Post-Renaissance Architecture, and by 1936–37 he was also teaching Art 210: Greek and Roman Art and Art 387: Studies in Spanish Art.[7] McAndrew was photographed on campus by George Platt Lynes for the yearbook, *Vassarion*, in 1935, the year he was appointed assistant professor in the Art Department (fig. 2.1). Considered a popular teacher, McAndrew received enthusiastic student reviews. In the spring of 1935 one student described his Art 270: Architecture course (now taught without Art) as "Graphic, lucid....Architecture made aesthetically significant and exciting, combined with vivid scientific approach. Architecture brought into vital relationship with entire culture of period."[8] McAndrew had the ability to plumb the aesthetic, technical, and cultural dimensions of architecture. Vassar students understood his strengths while, at the same time, finding weaknesses in such courses as Professor Tonks's Art 340a: Modern Painting, which they faulted for its lack of a "complete enough analysis of the difficult problem of contemporary work."[9] Although anecdotal, the criticism suggests that students were eager to parse the meaning of contemporary art and the role of modernism, which had long defined the Art Department's mission.

MODERNISM AT VASSAR COLLEGE

What McAndrew discovered on his arrival at Vassar was a vital site for modern art. It had been shaped first by Tonks, who was responsible for expanding the course offerings of the Art Department and the exhibitions of the Taylor Art Gallery (also known as "Taylor Hall gallery"), and then subsequently by Rindge. As early as 1912 Tonks set up a division of Modern Art (along with Ancient Art) within the department. He promoted interdisciplinarity through affiliations with other disciplines in the humanities as well as faculty exchanges.[10] In addition to hiring faculty committed to modern art, he increased the Taylor Art Gallery acquisitions of recent works of art, supported exhibitions on modernism, and, notwithstanding student assessments, even gave insightful lectures on modern painting.[11]

The *International Exhibition of Modern Art*, held in New York in early 1913 and known as the "Armory Show," sparked a keen interest in modernism at the college. *The Vassar Miscellany*, the campus literary review, carried a timely report on the exhibition and encouraged students to visit it.[12] With over two thousand works by American and European artists, the exhibition provoked lively debate at Vassar, as it did in the press at large. One student in the class of 1914 stressed the "strength and vitality" of the new art, especially in the work of Paul Cézanne, Vincent van Gogh, Paul Gauguin, Francis Picabia, and the cubists.[13] Another classmate left the exhibition in a "tumult," recognizing the art's claim on "subjective expression" and its power to reverse previously held ideas.[14] On the eve of World War I, Vassar women were confronting the art of their time. They grasped both its exhilaration and its provocation. Moreover, their sensitivity to contemporary art, the new aesthetic authority it commanded, and its preoccupation with a culture of the *present* allowed them to understand the essence of modernity.[15]

Interest in modern art increased after the war. At Vassar, outside lecturers were brought in to speak on the modern movement, most notably Princeton professor Frank Jewett Mather on the "Newest Movements in Painting" in January 1922 and Philadelphia art critic and curator Christian Brinton on "The Modern Spirit in Contemporary Painting" in February 1923.[16] Walter Pach, an American artist, critic, and prime mover of the 1913 Armory Show exhibition, also lectured, on "The Classical Element in Modern Art" in April 1927.[17] Among these lecturers, Brinton would turn out to be the most significant influence in shaping Vassar's upcoming exhibitions of modern art. His visit to Vassar in early 1923 led him to suggest to Tonks that the college might host a show of modern art from the collection of the Société Anonyme, an organization founded in 1920 by Katherine Dreier along with artists Man Ray and Marcel Duchamp. Dreier endorsed Brinton's idea because it fit with the Société Anonyme's mission to act as a "circulating museum."[18] Brinton, the chairman of the Société Anonyme's membership committee, had assisted with its first major public exhibition, in 1921 at the Worcester Art Museum, for which he wrote his seminal essay, "Modernism in Art," promoting the idea that modern art evolved through an international movement of expressionism by virtue of discrete national developments.[19]

The invitation resulted in Taylor Hall hosting two Société Anonyme loan shows: *Exhibition of Paintings by Modern Masters of Spain, Germany, France, Russia, Italy, Belgium and America* (April 4–May 12, 1923) and *Paintings by Wassily Kandinsky* (November 1923).[20] *Paintings by Modern Masters* introduced Vassar students to different genres of abstraction in the works of European artists—Alexander Archipenko, Georges Braque, Albert Gleizes, Georg Muche, Francis Picabia, Pablo Picasso, Jacques Villon, and others—and the American painters Marsden Hartley and (Italian-born) Joseph Stella. Vassar College printed its own catalogue in the form of an exhibition list.[21] The show's most provocative painting was Picabia's *Prostitution Universelle* (Universal Prostitution) of 1916–17, a Dadaist piece rendered both mechanistic and metaphorical. But there were other significant works, including Stella's homage to modern American infrastructure, *Brooklyn Bridge* (1918–20). In two lectures coinciding with the exhibition in the spring of 1923, Oliver Tonks led a critical discussion emphasizing not only Picabia's Dadaism, but also the varied forms of expressionism in the art of Picasso, Villon, and Archipenko. There he described the development of modern painting using the word "modernism," an early use of that term in reference to art (see Preface).[22] However, Tonks regretted that Vassar's first

Société Anonyme loan show did not include the Russian abstract painter Wassily Kandinsky because a solo exhibition of his work had been held in New York that spring at the Société Anonyme galleries at 19 East Forty-Seventh Street.[23] Therefore, in November of that year Kandinsky's art was shown in Vassar's Taylor Hall in the form of a solo exhibition of fifteen paintings and watercolors organized by the Société Anonyme. The show featured the artist's *Composition No. 1* of 1921, later known as *Bright Circle* and still later as *Multicolored Circle* (fig. 2.2). The arrival of Kandinsky's paintings on campus introduced students to the artist's bold abstractions as well as to Bauhaus principles. But the show sparked controversy. Professor Tonks explained that the spirited canvases were a "logical inevitable result" of an "evolutionary process" in modernist painting.[24] Yet their very newness was debated in the campus press, where editors expressed appreciation for the artist's need for self-expression even though his method appeared to them quite obscure.[25] The exhibition gave Alfred Barr, who was teaching at Vassar in the fall of 1923, a firsthand experience of Kandinsky's art, although he was not involved in curating it.[26]

Barr responded with mixed criticism, applauding Kandinsky's use of color but faulting the artist's compositions for their lack of rhythm, loss of decorative effect, and failure to evoke demonstrable emotion.[27] He was even reported to have mocked the work as "hashish."[28] Vassar College was forward thinking in exhibiting the artist's controversial work and encouraging open debate about it. In a fictional interview with Kandinsky published in the *Vassar Miscellany News*, the editors imagined the artist's response to the campus as "cunning" and "*vieux jeu*" [old hat], belying "that quaintly emotional strain," which he claimed to be "typical of the American college girl of today." The editors even envisioned the campus as if Kandinsky had remodeled its buildings in a more expressive color palette invoking Vassar's school colors: "rose-of-dawn against a background of cloudy-grey" for the red-brick and quasi–Tudor Gothic North Hall (built by Pilcher and Tachau in 1907; now Jewett House).[29]

In 1927 Kandinsky's paintings were again the subject of intense interest at Vassar on the occasion of the *Exhibition of Modern European Art since 1900* (April 8–28, 1927) in Taylor Hall.[30] Comprised of works on loan from a number of galleries, including the Société Anonyme, the show displayed Kandinsky's *Abstract Interpretation* (formerly *Abstract Variations*) of 1925 and *Small Yellow* of 1926.[31] The exhibition also presented the work of Jean (Hans) Arp, Giorgio de Chirico, Max Ernst, El Lissitzky, László Moholy-Nagy, Jacques Villon, and Gino Severini, among others.[32] As with the two 1923 Société Anonyme loan exhibitions, Vassar students continued to debate the merits of modernism, concluding that these artists were Expressionists who used their intellect to analyze emotion. But the abstract character of Kandinsky's paintings, like those of Moholy-Nagy, still posed a challenge.[33] During a lecture he delivered on the 1927 exhibition, Walter Pach left the students with the provocation, "Do you believe in any art for expressing modern times?" He responded himself: "Modern art."[34]

It was not until the following decade that Barr would grasp the significance of Kandinsky's originality by featuring the artist's paintings and watercolors in a number of Museum of Modern Art exhibitions.[35] For MoMA's fifth-anniversary show, *Modern Works of Art in 1934*, Barr exhibited Kandinsky's painting *The Blue Circle* of 1922, on loan from Dreier's collection, which he now valued as "a kind of abstract expressionism embodying perfectly the romantic ideal of vaguely lyrical spontaneity."[36] For his landmark MoMA exhibition *Cubism and Abstract Art* in 1936, Barr situated Kandinsky squarely within the canon of modern painting. Exhibiting five of the artist's works, Barr featured *Composition No. 1 (Multicolored Circle)* of 1921, which he had first seen at Vassar in 1923.[37] Like Barr, Vassar students would also come to reassess the artist's work. In *Variety in Abstraction*, a Taylor Hall exhibition in 1944, which featured an early Kandinsky painting called *The Waterfall* (1909), they found a new appreciation for his "profusion of brilliant colors and dynamic energy."[38]

In addition to presenting the work of Kandinsky and other modern European artists, Taylor Art Gallery shows during the late 1920s and 1930s favored that of modern French painters and living American artists (see A Complete List of Exhibitions Held at the Vassar College Art Gallery, 1923–1940). Vassar's exhibition history supports the view that its gallery stood at the vanguard of American art institutions. Of course, Barr's early leadership was instrumental. Joining Professors Tonks and Rindge to guide many of the early exhibitions was another Art Department faculty member, Clarence Chatterton, who taught at Vassar between 1915 and 1948.

A painter and student of Robert Henri at the New York School of Art, Chatterton assisted with exhibitions of the work of Henri (1924, 1925) as well as those of fellow Henri students, including Rockwell Kent (1924), George Bellows (1927), and Edward Hopper (1928).[39] During the mid-to-late 1920s, interest in American art at the college increased. This paralleled a shift in direction among American artists away from Europe and back to the United States and, more specifically, to New York. Sensing the end of an era, the critic Henry McBride observed in April 1929 that "Paris is no longer the capital of Cosmopolis. All the intelligence of the world is focused on New York; it has become the battleground of modern civilization."[40] Six months later the discourse on modernism intensified when the Museum of Modern Art in New York opened its doors. In retrospect, the close match between Vassar's exhibitions of the 1920s and MoMA's early ones suggests that the Taylor Art Gallery joined with the Harvard Society for Contemporary Art to serve as precursors to the Museum of Modern Art.[41]

When Agnes Rindge returned to Vassar in 1928 with her PhD from Radcliffe and a keen interest in the art of the present, which had been kindled in the Sachs circle (see Chapter One), she took up the modernist cause on campus.[42] The following year she published her book *Sculpture*, which was based on her dissertation and written from "the contemporary point of view."[43] Recognized for her erudition in the field of sculpture and her knowledge of contemporary art, Professor Rindge became the Art Department's "vibrant center" and "guiding force."[44]

When McAndrew joined the faculty in 1932, he brought modern architecture to the college as a discipline. Earlier it had been the effort of such students as Elizabeth Bauer (later Mock, then Kassler), class of 1932, who was the sister of city planner and public housing advocate Catherine Bauer, class of 1926. In the spring before McAndrew's arrival, Elizabeth Bauer led a campaign in support of a modern gymnasium, rather than the proposed Collegiate Gothic project. She put forward her own plan, which called for athletic units with flat roofs and a swimming pool with an arched reinforced concrete roof, all grouped around an open solarium.[45] Although Bauer's ideas for the gymnasium did not gain traction at Vassar, they stimulated an interest in modern architecture on campus. They also helped to determine her own career path, which would later lead her to join McAndrew on the staff of the Museum of Modern Art in 1937 (see Chapter Three).

Together Rindge and McAndrew promoted the new art and architecture in their respective courses and lectures and by inviting visiting lecturers and facilitating loan exhibitions. They drew on several important resources, most especially the traveling exhibitions sponsored by the Museum of Modern Art and such New York galleries as Julien Levy's, as well as the circle of Harvard modernists now pursuing professional careers. Vital to the campaign for modernism at Vassar was its proximity to the great metropolis, where Vassar women could explore art museums and exhibitions. In 1932 MoMA offered educational memberships to students for two dollars, which enabled

them to preview its exhibitions.[46] Among them was MoMA's *Modern Architecture: International Exhibition* (February 10 to March 23, 1932), curated by Henry-Russell Hitchcock, Philip Johnson, and Alfred Barr, which introduced visitors to such modern houses as Le Corbusier's Villa Savoye at Poissy-sur-Seine, France (1929–31), by means of photographs and a model (fig. 2.3). In that landmark show, accompanying catalogue, and subsequent book by Hitchcock and Johnson, *The International Style: Architecture since 1922*, the curators promoted the concept of a transnational movement called the "International Style," a term used beginning in the late 1920s by Hitchcock, Barr, and Jere Abbott, among others within the Harvard modernist circle.[47] In his foreword to the exhibition catalogue, Barr advanced a set of aesthetic principles for an International Style, ones that Hitchcock and Johnson would explain in their book: volume rather than mass; structural supports that encouraged regularity rather than a reliance on Beaux-Arts symmetry; fine proportions, technique, and elegant materials rather than applied decoration.[48] McAndrew later surmised that the exegesis reflected "Barr's thinking."[49] Notwithstanding the formalist methodology underscoring their notion of style at the expense of social meaning or political concerns, the new work did admit a range of personal expression, especially in the work of its four masters: Walter Gropius, Le Corbusier (Charles-Édouard Jeanneret-Gris), J. J. P. Oud, and Ludwig Mies van der Rohe.[50] In May 1932, following the close of the MoMA exhibition, Hitchcock returned to Vassar to give the lecture "Modern Architecture: Convergence Toward a Style."[51] Speaking at a time when most American architecture was shaped by such historical styles as Tudor and Romanesque, he noted, modern architecture offered a new direction embodied in "the international postwar house" and in the work of Erich Mendelsohn and Oud, who were already household names to McAndrew's students.[52]

Throughout the 1930s a dynamic synergy flowed between schools of higher education and such cultural institutions as the Museum of Modern Art to advance their respective educational missions.[53] By 1932 the museum offered a robust program of circulating exhibitions, as had the Société Anonyme before it. Vassar was an exceptional recipient because of the way in which it integrated these shows into its curriculum. In the spring of 1933 the Art Department hosted MoMA's traveling *Exhibition of Photographs of Modern Architecture* (May 11–29, 1933).[54] Consisting of plans in addition to photographs, the show was a scaled-down version of MoMA's earlier traveling *International Exhibition of Modern Architecture* of 1932.[55] The new architecture encouraged campus debate. One student reviewer appreciated the innovations of the new work but took issue, for example, with its conspicuously frank construction. All the same, she endorsed the idea that a dormitory designed by Mies, Le Corbusier, or the Swiss émigré architect William Lescaze could enhance the college's community life.[56]

During the spring of 1933, in conjunction with the *Modern Architecture* exhibition at Vassar, Philip Johnson, then chairman of MoMA's Department of Architecture, delivered a series of three lectures to McAndrew's Art 370: Domestic Architecture class, which were open to all students. McAndrew must have invited Johnson, their relations intermittently maintained on a professional level. Johnson used the occasion to explore the evolution of and influences upon contemporary architecture. Unlike Lewis Mumford, who traced modern architecture to British sources, Johnson looked to the Germanic tradition. He found in Karl Friedrich Schinkel and his circle a sense of restrained ornament, rationalist tendencies (e.g., expressing the nature of the interior on the exterior and the use of a regular bay system), and asymmetrical design that in varying ways presaged the work of Henry Hobson Richardson as well as Le Corbusier and Mies. However, Johnson was also influenced by Mumford's book *The Brown Decades* (1931) when he suggested a lineage in the development of skeletal construction from William Le Baron Jenney and Louis Sullivan in Chicago to the work of Frank Lloyd Wright. Johnson capped the series with a final lecture on the International Style, contrasting the "French formalist" Le Corbusier to the "German romantic" Mies.[57]

It was not long before Vassar hosted Le Corbusier's visit to campus in conjunction with a circulating exhibition of twenty-six photographs of his work (October 30–November 6, 1935), both sponsored by the Museum of Modern Art.[58] McAndrew facilitated the visit of the celebrated French-Swiss architect and purist painter. Most likely he had seen Le Corbusier's early work during three trips to France from 1929 to 1933.[59] He had also developed a deep understanding of the architect's theory of design and purist color palette,

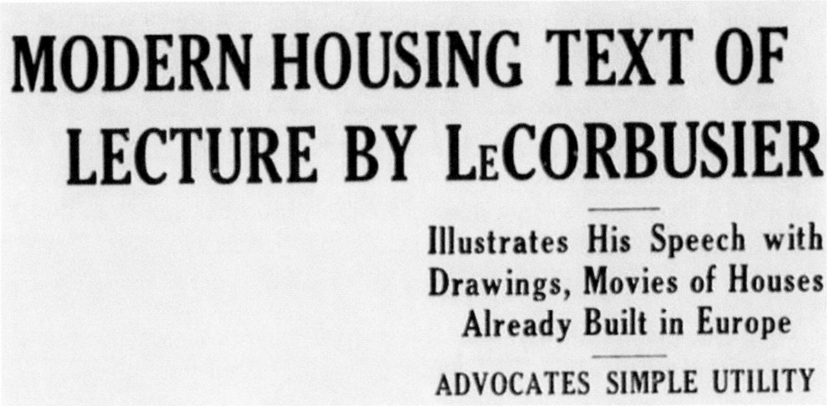

MODERN HOUSING TEXT OF LECTURE BY LeCORBUSIER

Illustrates His Speech with Drawings, Movies of Houses Already Built in Europe

ADVOCATES SIMPLE UTILITY

Figure 2.4
"Modern Housing
Text of Lecture by Le
Corbusier," *Vassar
Miscellany News*,
November 6, 1935, 1, 4

discussed below. He was personally invested in Le Corbusier's campus visit in the sense that it was an opportunity both to talk with the architect, whose work he had long admired, and to promote the students' understanding of his work and ideas. Moreover, McAndrew and Rindge considered the visit a signal event, giving Vassar the opportunity to host one of the fountainheads of European modernism.

Although Le Corbusier appeared at a dozen schools during his first lecture tour to the United States, he singled out his visit to Poughkeepsie as an unforgettable experience.[60] On November 1, he arrived at the college he described as situated "within a budding grove" (quoting Marcel Proust) in his account of the American tour, *When the Cathedrals Were White: A Journey to the Country of Timid People*.[61] Caught up in his own mixed emotions about Vassar, Le Corbusier was immediately struck by the young women he encountered. Before his lecture at Avery Hall, he had the opportunity to admire the "beautiful bodies" and athleticism of the students who were at work striking the previous evening's theater set. To him, four years at Vassar meant living in a "joyous convent."[62] That impression made his reception at the lecture all the more surprising. Le Corbusier had come to present his ideas on city planning, which meant retooling the contemporary city into what he called a *ville radieuse*, or radiant city. Dominated by "great obelisks" of glass skyscrapers spaced far apart on a grid, the resulting metropolis would have space, light, air, and order. To renew the decaying city center and eliminate the need for commuting to suburban houses, he proposed the construction of business towers and housing slabs. While Le Corbusier's lecture emphasized single-class urban housing blocks made from skeletal steel and concrete, he also showed students the suburban Villa Savoye and its salon by means of a short film by Pierre Chenal, *L'Architecture d'aujourd'hui* (1930) (figs. 2.3 and 2.4).[63]

Le Corbusier's lecture was in French. Would he be understood? If some audiences had been unresponsive to his talks, he assumed that it was because they did not understand French. But the Poughkeepsie audience was different. At a time when French was

Figure 2.5
Amelia Thompson
(Vose). Annotated
sketch (*la belle forme
pour l'apartment* [*sic*],
after Le Corbusier,
Y-shaped plan for
housing block, Vassar
College Lecture,
November 1, 1935
(Amelia Thompson
Vose family)

Figure 2.6
Le Corbusier. "Project
B," *Y*-shaped hous-
ing block for Bastion
Kellermann, Paris,
1937 (Le Corbusier
and Pierre Jeanneret,
*Oeuvre complète,
1934–1938*, ed.
Max Bill, Zurich:
Girsberger, 1939, 148;
Private collection ©
FLC-ADAGP, Paris /
Artists Rights Society
[ARS], New York 2017)

the language of art and architecture, Vassar students were celebrated for their fluency. Le Corbusier expressed surprise when he made a facetious remark and "they got it, everyone understood." This meant that Vassar women would be his "best propagandists."[64] The architect illustrated his lecture with colorful pastel drawings. As he talked, he sketched his ideas on long scrolls of paper stretched across the stage. Amelia Thompson (Vose), class of 1938, made her own sketches (after Le Corbusier), and annotated them in her college French. One sketch is particularly significant. She drew a *Y*-shaped plan for a superblock (later known as a "Cartesian skyscraper") and labeled it *la belle forme pour l'apartment* [*sic*] (fig. 2.5).[65] Le Corbusier had recently used the *Y*-shaped type, derived from José Luis Sert, for his Bastion Kellermann housing project (1934–35), which had been rejected for the 1937 Exposition Internationale des Arts et Techniques in Paris (fig. 2.6).[66] He had also used it for office buildings. Thompson's lecture notation, identifying the *Y*-shaped plan as "the beautiful form for the apartment block," confirms that the architect preferred this typology, rather than towers, for high-rise housing. Moreover, it suggests that he recast technical and functional problems into aesthetic solutions.

Le Corbusier may have felt understood by the Vassar students attending his presentation, but he was still unprepared for their response to it. Le Corbusier recalled how they rushed onto the stage, seized his improvisational drawings, and tore them into pieces. "Sign, sign," they cried. Using the satirical epithet with which Vassar women sometimes identified themselves, Le Corbusier despaired, "The Amazons reduced them to confetti!"[67] Yet, when conversing with the young women after the lecture, he was impressed by the "weight of their questions [on]…sociology, economics, psychology." Turning to sarcasm and humor, he countered, "You overwhelm me, you are too serious. I must be excused. I am going to join the people who are eating cookies!" In the end, among the dozen schools the architect visited on his American lecture tour, no campus enthralled him more than Vassar, with its intelligent, athletic, French-speaking, cigarette-smoking, and beguiling young women.[68]

According to Le Corbusier's interpreter Robert Jacobs, the Parisian was "very smitten" with one Vassar student in particular, a "statuesque, tall beautiful girl" named Alma Clayburgh in the class of 1936.[69] She was the daughter of a New York operatic singer known as "Madame" Alma Clayburgh, with whom the visitor later socialized. Le Corbusier found young Alma to be a "brilliant student" fluent in French but encumbered by her infatuation with Caravaggio, the sixteenth-century Italian artist whose predisposition was toward mannerism, which the architect and purist painter associated with surrealism.[70] By means of her classes with Professor Rindge, and also an important public lecture on baroque art in relation to mannerism by the renowned art historian Erwin Panofsky, young Alma learned about the painter.[71] "I always loved Caravaggio's work," she later recollected, because he was "so sensual."[72] But Le Corbusier thought that Caravaggio had a "very disquieting mentality" and that his work was suffused with a "funereal spirit" to which "troubled, youthful [American] hearts" were attracted.[73] To Le Corbusier, Alma's infatuation was a Freudian sign of an "unsatisfied heart" he hoped to win.[74] If the architect's psyche was wrapped up in such thoughts during his brief visit to Poughkeepsie and later encounters in Manhattan, he did not act on them, nor was Alma aware of any depth to his feelings.[75]

In addition to sponsoring Le Corbusier's lecture and exhibition, the Museum of Modern Art launched a loan program, which included the one-picture and three-picture exhibitions at Vassar (1934–36). There students saw Gauguin's *Tahitian Idyll* (1901) and Renoir's *Bal du Moulin de la Galette* (1876) as well as paintings by Cézanne and Henri Matisse.[76] Throughout the winter and spring of 1936 the Art Department featured MoMA's film series of American motion pictures, which examined their technical as well as artistic achievements.[77] The following year Vassar hosted MoMA's series of avant-garde European films. Among them, *The Cabinet of Dr. Caligari* (1919) "strived for greater and greater intensity of expression," as McAndrew explained in a review.[78] In spring 1936 MoMA also sent to Vassar an exhibition of posters by the prominent French designer A. M. Cassandre.[79]

Although the Museum of Modern Art was a principal resource for Vassar, it was not the only purveyor of modern art. By virtue of McAndrew's personal and professional association with Julien Levy, Vassar received a number of exhibitions originating from his New York gallery. In November 1932 Levy loaned works by the Russian-born surrealists Pavel Tchelitchew and Eugene Berman for an exhibition in the Taylor Hall gallery.[80] In the fall of 1934 Levy sent an exhibition of photographs by George Platt Lynes, who had already been seen on campus taking photographs for the 1935 spring yearbook, *Vassarion*.[81] In her review of the exhibition for the *Vassar Miscellany News*, reporter Aline Bernstein (class of 1935; later Aline

Louchheim Saarinen) emphasized the aesthetic achievement of
Lynes's photographs through their directness and "tactile quality"
while also conveying "the essentials of the subject."[82] In late 1934
the Art Department received a loan exhibition called *Eight Modes
of Modern Painting*, which had just been shown at the Julien Levy
Gallery under the sponsorship of the College Art Association, along
with a catalogue by Agnes Rindge.[83] Levy also loaned works from
his personal collection, as did Barr, Rindge, and McAndrew.[84]

In addition to inviting such renowned art historians as
Kenneth Conant and Walter Friedlander to give lectures on campus,
McAndrew and Rindge also asked many Harvard modernists to
speak, often in conjunction with exhibitions.[85] During the years from
1932 to 1937 these included Henry-Russell Hitchcock, Chick Austin,
Lincoln Kirstein, and Edward Warburg, along with Philip Johnson,
as previously discussed.[86] The French painter Jean Lurçat and the
architect William Lescaze also spoke at Vassar, both in 1934.[87] The
collector James Thrall Soby, later to become a curator at MoMA, gave
a lecture on "Photography and Modern Art," in conjunction with
a Man Ray exhibition in Taylor Hall.[88] The students recognized not
only the value of these lectures but also that McAndrew and Rindge
were responsible for bringing them to campus. For making possible a week of stimulating lectures in May 1934, the editors of *Vassar
Miscellany News* noted that McAndrew and Rindge "deserve all credit
for these excellent days. It was through their efforts and those of their
friends that the week was arranged."[89] McAndrew and Rindge may
have been initiators, facilitators, and lenders, but the intense student
engagement with the culture of modern art and architecture, and the
proximity of the institution to the vortex of the art world in New York
City, helped to define Vassar College as a leading site of modernism.

DESIGNING THE ART LIBRARY INTERIOR

An increased roster of art and architecture courses, swelling enroll-
ments, and the need to improve study conditions during the early
1930s compelled advocates of the Art Library to seek greater capacity
and new resources.[90] In the fall of 1934 the Art Department ordered
a topographic map of Vassar College from the Olmsted Brothers,
an indication of its intention to expand.[91] By late 1935, plans were
underway and ground was broken for the construction of a new
building connecting the main library with Taylor Hall as well as an
addition in back of the west wing. Charles Collens, of the firm of
Allen & Collens (later Allen, Collens & Willis), was commissioned to
design a contextual extension to Taylor Hall and the existing library
in order to provide for a new Art Library (1935–37) and renovated Art
Gallery (1935–37; demolished in 1991) (fig. 2.7). John McAndrew was
brought in to the project first as a consultant, but by early 1936 he
was responsible for drafting plans and drawings for the interior of the
Art Library, featuring a circulation desk, as well as the renovated Art
Gallery in Taylor Hall (figs. 2.8, 2.9, 2.10, 2.11).[92] Later McAndrew chose
to collaborate with the draftsman and interior designer Theodore Karl
Muller, who helped to execute McAndrew's ideas for interior finish-
ing and furniture.[93] Although McAndrew had little authority over the
Tudor Gothic exteriors of the Art Library and Art Gallery, he planned
to make their interiors designs of their time. Originally named after
Henry van Ingen (1833–1898), Vassar's first professor of art, the Van

Figure 2.8
John McAndrew
(with Theodore
Muller). Main Reading
Room, Art Library,
Vassar College,
1935–37, Vassar
College Libraries,
Steenson & Van Vlack,
Poughkeepsie, New
York (Archives and
Special Collections,
Vassar College
Libraries)

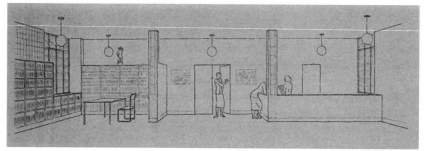

Ingen Library would soon be called simply the Art Library. It lays claim to be the earliest modern interior for an academic building on an American campus.[94]

In the spring of 1935 McAndrew, with assistance from Elinor Gordon (class of 1934), first brought modernism to campus with their design for a new Vassar Cooperative Bookshop (fig. 2.12). Shortly thereafter, McAndrew presumably renovated an office for Vassar's chief medical officer, Dr. Jane Baldwin, discussed below (fig. 2.49). Planned

on two levels for increased display, the bookshop featured pale blue walls, textured fabric on the north wall, cork on the east wall as well as on columns and tables, and terracotta-colored linoleum floors. French doors opened onto a terrace outfitted with bookshelves.[95] Fixtures and furniture introduced students to the most recent European modern design. White glass globes suspended from plain chromium stems derived from Bauhaus models. In *Vassar Miscellany News* Aline Bernstein noted that the bookshop featured Mies chairs of wicker and tubing, chairs "adapted from Le Corbusier," a desk and stools by Marcel Breuer, and "blue wood and tubing tables" for display purposes.[96] McAndrew's vision of modernism was distinctively pluralistic in the sense that it drew on many sources, both European and American. Unlike many of his European counterparts, he did not design the furniture, however. Rather, he ordered it from catalogues. His subsequent projects on the Vassar campus followed this pattern. Bernstein emphasized the good craftsmanship of its execution, which she considered important for modern architecture, concluding that the bookshop plan and interior design were both "relentlessly functional and aesthetically successful."[97] With its overt modernity and practical shelving for outdoor browsing, some cosmopolitan students boasted that "Vassar now rivals the Left Bank."[98]

With the completion of McAndrew's renovations to the Art Gallery, studio and art history classrooms, and faculty offices, the new facilities (and the existing lecture theater) were united for the first time in Taylor Hall under "one independent, fireproof roof" adjoining the new Art Library.[99] In her seminal essay, "The Art Department in New Quarters," published in the *Vassar Alumnae Magazine* in June 1938, Agnes Rindge analyzed the innovative components of the new

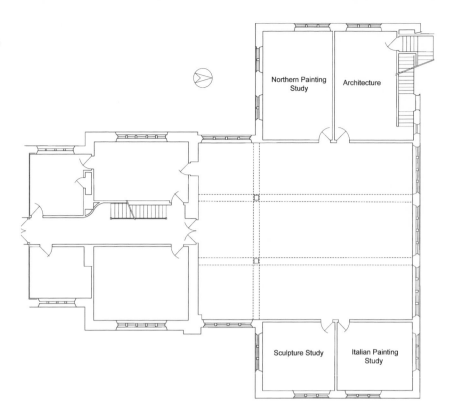

Northern Painting
Study

Architecture

Sculpture Study

Italian Painting
Study

headquarters with critical acumen enhanced by vivid description.[100] In doing so, she served as the Art Library and Art Gallery's chief interpreter, as she had been one of its principal agents in facilitating the project's completion. In designing the new Art Library interior, McAndrew was responsive to the Art Department's mandate for "better studying conditions" in conjunction with its signature method of instruction, which Rindge called "visual learning."[101] At Vassar, she maintained, art is "taught by seeing, not learning about things."[102] While both a distinctive and didactic practice at Vassar, "visual learning" paralleled to a degree the Harvard method, discussed in Chapter One. It was up to McAndrew, working with the head librarian, Fanny Borden, to determine how best to meet the needs of the Art Library— for, as Rindge pointed out, it served a strategic role, not merely as a repository of books, slides, and photographs but as a high-tech facility for the study and display of original works of art as well as "facsimile colour prints."[103] At a time when the use of microforms had recently become widely available and promised to transform the storage of and access to books as well as other forms of text and images, the new library would provide an optimal facility for its holdings.[104]

In consultation with Rindge, Borden, and other colleagues, McAndrew determined the Art Library program.[105] The new facility occupied the second and third floors of Taylor Hall with stacks below. The plan called for a main reading room (second floor) facing north with dedicated study rooms, two on either side (fig. 2.13). Architecture

Figure 2.14
John McAndrew (with
Theodore Muller).
Drafting room
for Architecture,
third floor, Taylor
Hall, 1935–37,
Wurts Brothers
(Archives and Special
Collections, Vassar
College Libraries)

and Northern Painting were situated in rooms on the northwest and southwest sides, respectively, while the Italian Painting and Sculpture rooms were located to the northeast and southeast. The Art Library's top (third) floor accommodated the Architecture room for drafting (northwest corner) (fig. 2.14; see Foreword, page 5, right). Students built models on modern furniture and sat on stools designed by Alvar Aalto (fig. 2.15). The Conference room for the Art 105 introductory course (southeast room) and several departmental offices were also on the third floor (fig. 2.16; see Foreword, page 5, right).

To observers today it comes as no surprise that an addition to a historic building, even one with a Tudor Gothic exterior defined by Beaux-Arts design principles (Beaux-Arts teaching offered a technique or method rather than a style), should have a modern interior. In 1935, however, this was a relatively new concept, which Rindge endorsed, later insisting that the interior need not conform to the exterior design but could be accepted on its own terms.[106] The idea of a modern interior inserted within a traditional Beaux-Arts exterior was not invented by McAndrew. In 1934 the Wadsworth Atheneum's Avery Court set a precedent for Vassar's Art Library. While Robert B. O'Connor, of the Beaux-Arts firm of Morris & O'Connor, designed the Avery exterior, fusing art deco and classical forms, Chick Austin designed the Avery Court interior, which looked to Bauhaus models (figs. 2.17, 2.18).[107] Given the audacious nature of Austin's design, it was inevitable that he should clash with O'Connor. As McAndrew later recalled, "Chick knew pretty much what he wanted and the architects knew what they wanted and they didn't agree entirely.... Finally it was more or less decided that Mr. O'Connor could have the outside

of the building if Chick could have the inside."[108] Whether or not
this was an entirely accurate account of Avery Court, it was how
McAndrew understood the design division for the Art Library and
it prepared him for future negotiations with Charles Collens. From
McAndrew's perspective, the Avery precedent meant that his modern
interior could have relatively little to do with Collens's Tudor Gothic
exterior. McAndrew maintained that the building should be planned
according to the functional needs of the interior—that is, designed
from the inside out. Ironically, this process conformed to Beaux-Arts
principles, which McAndrew knew well from his professional training
in architecture school. The orthogonal plan and the structure of the
Art Library with its bearing walls were restrictive, but the two large
supporting columns of the main reading room did enable a large
open space. However, there was no opportunity to bring into play a
curvilinear wall, a hallmark of the Levy Gallery. As a consequence,
McAndrew relied largely on applied color (as opposed to color
derived from materials) and also on materiality, notably the opacity
and transparency of glass bricks, discussed below.

By April 1936 the new Art Library was under construction.[109]
In executing his design of the interior, McAndrew was often at odds
with Collens. Even though he hoped to avoid "unnecessary wran-
gles," McAndrew opposed Collens's plans for cork on the south wall
of the main reading room, preferring instead "the wall to be all of
one homogenous surface," which he intended to have painted.[110]
McAndrew also fought off Collens's changes to his design for the
staircase of the main hall, insisting that it be "as simple and handsome
as possible."[111] Although McAndrew was obliged to adjust his design
of the main reading room to the Beaux-Arts symmetry of the plan and
facade, he was able to impose a slight shift in the placement of the
windows to accommodate the bookcases, which served as partitions
for the study alcoves and divided the open floor space (figs. 2.19, 2.20).
In the end, McAndrew won the support of Henry MacCracken,
Vassar's progressive president, for these and other decisions. By early
1937 he was given final approval over most of the interior design
details, especially the colors and lighting fixtures, discussed below.[112]

In her 1938 essay Rindge emphasized that the new design was both "functional," in that it maximized the exposure to sunlight, and "beautiful."[113] Like the Vassar bookshop, McAndrew's Art Library interior rejected historicism and academic ornament, allowing its materials, colors, furniture, and fixtures to announce its modernity. The main reading room broke new ground, its visual impact achieved through a simple geometric volume of open space with clerestory glass-brick walls and a cork floor (fig. 2.8). Tall steel bookcases painted "bright deep blue" defined the reading spaces (fig. 2.19).[114] Industrial fabrication involving new manufacturing processes for materials, such as steel for bookcases and glass for brick walling, were now readily available during the interwar period, which Lewis Mumford had first called the "Machine Age."[115] The library was also fully air-conditioned. This was rare among pre–World War II buildings and especially school libraries.[116] Like the climate-controlled Rockefeller Center in New York (1927–40), the Art Library was a product of American pragmatism that signaled its contemporaneity.

McAndrew drew on at least two American sources for his library interior. The first was Chick Austin's design for the Avery Memorial Research Library at the Wadsworth Atheneum (1933–34), a light-filled room outfitted with built-in bookshelves and tubular Breuer and Bauhaus furniture (fig. 2.21).[117] Because McAndrew taught for two years at the Hartford Art School, then located in the Avery addition, he visited Austin frequently and would have used the library when it was new.[118] More significantly, McAndrew looked specifically to William Lescaze's design of the Wilbour Library of Egyptology at the Brooklyn Museum of Art (Howe & Lescaze, 1933–34), which he visited in the spring of 1937 to study its installation (fig. 2.22).[119] McAndrew, who admired Lescaze as "one of the few men in America who knows how to build," might have first learned of the inspired Wilbour design at the architect's Vassar lecture in 1934.[120] Opaque glass windows furnished the Wilbour's two-story space with diffuse

Figure 2.17
Morris & O'Connor; Robert B. O'Connor, designer. Avery Memorial, Wadsworth Atheneum, 1934 (Wadsworth Atheneum Archives, Hartford, Connecticut)

Figure 2.18
A. Everett Austin. Avery Court, Wadsworth Atheneum, 1934 (Wadsworth Atheneum Archives, Hartford, Connecticut)

light. Lapis-blue balcony walls enlivened an otherwise gray interior. Lescaze designed all the furniture and fixtures, including lights screened by ground-glass globes, tall steel bookcases painted gray, desktop reflector lights, and tubular-steel chairs.[121] McAndrew may also have known of Edward B. Green's modern design of the Reference Room (1933) within the Beaux-Arts Albright Art Gallery (now the Albright-Knox Art Gallery) in Buffalo, New York (1900–05), whose steel desks and bookcases, Thonet tubular metal chairs, and desktop reflector lights shared similar intentions (fig. 2.23).[122]

The two most striking features of Vassar's Art Library were the natural lighting and what Rindge called the "color areas."[123] McAndrew's lighting design made extensive use of translucent glass blocks or bricks, a newly reconceived building material in the 1930s that was recommended in place of conventional windows for air-conditioned buildings.[124] Glass blocks provided a practical solution. Stocked in retail shops, including the Vassar bookshop, these everyday blocks were sold individually to serve as bookends and components for shelving.[125] Clerestory glass-brick walls not only offered texture but also admitted light from the study rooms to the main reading room. McAndrew also designed an entire wall of glass brick as a light-transmitting but opaque partition to divide the Architecture and Northern Painting Study rooms (fig. 2.24). During

Figure 2.20
John McAndrew (with
Theodore Muller).
Alcove, Main Reading
Room, Art Library,
Vassar College, 1935–
37, Joseph T. Murphy,
Poughkeepsie, New
York (Archives and
Special Collections,
Vassar College
Libraries)

the 1930s American and European modernists made liberal use of square blocks of transparent, translucent, and opaque glass for both exterior infill walls and interior walls. Glass walling, made of solid or hollow vacuum blocks, was versatile. Lescaze used glass blocks or bricks for his Manhattan town house at 211 East Forty-Eighth Street, New York (1933–34), another building the architect most likely showed in his 1934 Vassar lecture (fig. 2.25). One manufacturer used a photograph of Lescaze against the glass-brick wall of his town house to promote the material's capacity to insulate against heat and cold, sound, sun, and dirt, and also to screen street views (fig. 2.26). While giving the illusion of a window and transmitting light, the glass-brick wall afforded privacy.[126] The versatility and functional properties of glass bricks made them effective components in commercial and utilitarian buildings. Raymond Hood & Associates used them for interior walls at 30 Rockefeller Plaza.[127] William and Geoffrey Platt's air-conditioned Corning Glass Building at 718 Fifth Avenue, New York (1937), which served as a showroom for Steuben glass, employed both exterior and interior walls of Pittsburgh Corning glass block (fig. 2.27).[128]

In addition to the use of glass brick for the main reading room and study rooms, the glazed ceilings of adjacent rooms provided diffuse light. The ceiling of the Art 105 Conference room on the third floor, which resembled the top-lit main gallery of Taylor Hall, channeled shadowless natural light onto the walls and table to promote optimal viewing conditions (figs. 2.9, 2.16). The Conference room continued to serve the Art Department, including one of Professor Linda

Left: Figure 2.21
A. Everett Austin.
Avery Memorial
Research Library,
Wadsworth
Atheneum, 1933–34
(*Architectural Forum*
61, no. 1 July 1934, 43;
Wadsworth Atheneum
Archives, Hartford,
Connecticut)

Right: Figure 2.22
Howe & Lescaze;
William Lescaze,
designer. Wilbour
Library of Egyptology,
Brooklyn Museum of
Art, Brooklyn, 1933–
34 (Brooklyn Museum
Archives. Photograph
Collection [S06])

Nochlin's classes in 1959 (fig. 2.28). Students in Art 105 were required
to demonstrate visual mastery of works of art, consonant with the Art
Department's mission. Its walls were rigged with molding strips for
hanging or otherwise propping up prints and photographs for study.
The new facility displayed Vassar's collection of both "art prints"
(original works) and "colored prints" (photographic reproductions).
Rindge claimed that "no other college makes it possible to see colored prints while we study."[129] She predicted that the immediate
availability of the material by virtue of the new library would precip-
itate an entirely new method of teaching fine arts. This study system
was drawn from both Oliver Tonks's pedagogy at Vassar and the
"hands-on" approach to works of art that Rindge had experienced in
Paul Sachs's course Museum Work and Museum Methods. But it goes
further to suggest an empiricism, most notably a special significance
given to common things, which had been integral to the Vassar teaching tradition associated with the distinguished history professor Lucy
Maynard Salmon (1853–1927). At the dedication of the Art Library
in October 1937 a memorial tablet commemorating Salmon gave
evidence of her importance as a historian and seminal influence governing Vassar's academic tradition and art pedagogy. Her approach to
history before and during World War I, as historians Nicholas Adams
and Bonnie G. Smith have shown, employed an "object-based episte-
mology," which anticipated many of the methods and ideas associated
today with both "new history" and material culture.[130]

The entry-level staircase adjacent to the Art Library entrance
served a functional role to lead students up to the classrooms and
also a symbolic role to provide an overture to the library's modernism
(fig. 2.29). Constructed of plastered brick and iron, its contoured form
suggested a purist moment such as those found in Le Corbusier's
villas near Paris around 1930. Rindge pointed out that its "rounded
wall mass in the midst of curved walls" facilitated the flow of traffic. A
granite sculpture, *Mother and Child* (1932–33), by John B. Flannagan
(1895–1942), was installed at the top of the staircase to announce
one's arrival there (fig. 2.30).[131]

McAndrew redesigned the Taylor Hall gallery in relation to the Art Library. With enhanced exhibition space, the college's permanent collection could now be expanded. Following Austin's precedent at Avery Court, Taylor's top-lit galleries allowed original works of art to be seen in natural light. As McAndrew later explained, the glass ceiling "kept light on walls, off visitors."[132] A muted color palette governed the walls of Taylor's main gallery (figs. 2.9 and 2.31). The long side walls were covered in "pinkish-beige" textured fabric.[133] The main gallery featured "screen walls" on either end to increase the spatial capacity for hanging pictures.[134] As indicated on the plan, the screens partitioned the main gallery from two adjacent gallery spaces (East Gallery and Jade Room) (fig. 2.32). The color of the two screen walls at one end (toward the East Gallery) was "warm grey" while the color of the single screen wall at the other end (toward the Jade Room) was a "neutralized" terracotta.[135] Assigning colors to walls helped to define spatial divisions, serve as a foil for the artworks, and prepare the visitor for the constructive use of color in the Art Library. The Jade galleries, as seen in a corner view, demonstrated McAndrew's concept of displaying the Asian pottery collection in glass cabinets flush with the wall and illuminated by light from above—a veritable glass box (fig. 2.33).

Left: Figure 2.23 Edward B. Green. Reference Room, Albright Art Gallery, Buffalo, New York, 1933 ("Albright Library Sounds Modern Note," *American Magazine of Art* 27, no. 1, January 1934, 44. © Albright-Knox Art Gallery, Buffalo, New York. Image courtesy Albright-Knox Art Gallery)

Right: Figure 2.24 John McAndrew (with Theodore Muller). Northern Painting Study room with glass-brick wall, Art Library, Vassar College, 1935–37, Wurts Brothers (Archives and Special Collections, Vassar College Libraries)

ART LIBRARY COLOR PALETTE

Two empirical sources document the original color scheme of the Art Library, which shares a similar theoretical underpinning with the Art Gallery but reveals a more resonant palette. First, in the late 1930s Rindge described the Art Library's "novel color concept" and its "various combinations" of colors "according to the character of the rooms," detailed below.[136] Second, in 2008 and 2009 a paint conservator working in conjunction with the architectural firm of Platt Byard Dovell White Architects (PBDW) took core samples, which largely confirmed Rindge's descriptions. The conservator then matched the original colors with contemporary Benjamin Moore paints.[137]

Rindge pointed out that the Art Library did not draw on "bright primary modernistic colors," such as those found in Gerrit Rietveld's Schröder House in Utrecht, Netherlands (1923–24).[138] Rather, the library employed what Rindge described as "subtler blends [that] are spread over 'large simple areas and shapes.'"[139] The main reading room and each of the study rooms adjacent to it was distinguished by a different scheme. According to Rindge, they were suitable for the subjects (and programmatic functions) to which they were dedicated.[140] In assigning colors to the rooms McAndrew relied on his "marvelous visual memory," as one curatorial colleague recalled.[141]

Recent spectrographic analysis of the main reading room shows the use of a "light yellow white" color (corresponding to Benjamin Moore [BM] color Natural Linen) for the north and south walls and a "light greenish blue" (BM Blue Lake) for columns and doors (fig. 2.34; see Preface, page 34). Rindge noted that the Italian Painting Study room was painted in "soft terra cottas and light blue in order to blend with the Italian color prints (fig. 2.35)."[142] Paint-color identification of the Italian Painting Study room revealed the use of a "pinkish orange" color for its east wall and north walls (BM Sweet 'n Sour) as well as yellowish brown for the south wall (BM Cimarron).[143] (Later the PBDW restoration joined together the Italian Painting and Sculpture Study rooms, using the original "pinkish orange" [BM Sweet 'n Sour] color in the Italian Painting Study room.) Although conservators found no physical evidence of a blue wall in their photomicrographs of the room, they did identify a "light bluish green" paint color (BM Blue Lake) on the outer face of the wood door leading from the main reading room.[144] Open, the door would have provided the Italian Painting Study room with a color plane perceived as Rindge's "light blue" or "soft blue." A view from the main reading room indicates that the color of the door matched the original "light bluish green" of the supporting columns (fig. 2.34). "Strong colour contrasts," Rindge reported, dominated the Sculpture Study room (fig. 2.36).[145] Spectrographic analysis turned up the use of "yellowish brown" for its south wall (BM Cimarron) and "light yellow" for its east, north, and west

Figure 2.28
Linda Nochlin
instructing a class
in the Art 105
Conference room,
third floor, Taylor Hall,
Vassar College, 1959
(Archives and Special
Collections, Vassar
College Libraries)

walls (BM California Hills and Bronzed Beige).[146] By contrast, the Northern Painting Study room, with its glass-brick wall, relied on a "neutral" palette to enhance the character of "brightly colored pictures" (fig. 2.37).[147] Paint analysis of that room shows the use of "light yellowish orange" for the south wall (BM Brunswick Beige) and "yellowish white" for the east and west walls (BM Ocean Beach).[148]

What might account for McAndrew's otherwise spare library interior whose walls were painted in a range of applied colors? On what sources and theoretical models did McAndrew draw for the color scheme of the Art Library? In the summer of 1934 McAndrew made his first trip to Mexico, where he was attracted to the festive colors and character of its urban architecture, especially in Puebla. In a letter to Rindge he described his arrival in that mid-seventeenth-century colonial city with its "hundreds of colored tile domes glistening in the low afternoon sun" looking like "a basket of Easter Eggs" or a "mirage of the Heavenly City."[149] That summer McAndrew had seen Juan O'Gorman's Rivera-Kahlo Studios in San Angel, Mexico City (1929–32), whose exterior walls picked up on such local colors as deep blue and "Indian" red, a pigment that recalled the *tezontle*, or volcanic stone of the region that had been used for building since the pre-Columbian period.[150] McAndrew was also drawn to the colonial color palette of North America, having visited the John D. Rockefeller Jr.–sponsored reconstruction of eighteenth-century Williamsburg (still in progress) as well as Southern plantation houses with Alfred and Margaret (known as "Daisy") Barr in the spring of 1936.[151] On another tack, during the 1920s and 1930s vibrant color was used as a design feature in automobiles and architectural interiors.[152] It was also a general trend in journalism and advertising during the 1930s. Magazines such as *Fortune* featured colorful covers and ads. When Russell Lynes served as Vassar's director of publications,

he reconceptualized such reviews as *Vassar Alumnae Magazine* through the use of solid colors and modern design. But such examples of polychromy explain neither McAndrew's choice of colors nor their abstract rendering for the Art Library interior. He left little record of his ideas and preferences except for his choice of "cinnamon," an earthy color associated with the vernacular, for the walls of his New York apartment in 1930. For the Vassar bookshop (1935) he had used the contrasting colors of blue (walls) and terracotta (floors) (fig. 2.12). The reappearance of such colors in the spectrographic analyses of the Art Library resonates with McAndrew's interest in nature as well as his concept of a "naturalized" or Americanized modernism, which he would later elucidate (see Chapter Three).

As the Art Library neared completion in the fall of 1937, McAndrew had already left Poughkeepsie to take a position as curator of the Department of Architecture and Industrial Art at the Museum of Modern Art, though he would remain on Vassar's Art Department faculty as a lecturer. McAndrew was diffident about his design for the Art Library. He made no attempts to publicize his work or assign importance to it. Although he signed his drawings, he seems to have considered himself an anonymous architect, as if he were working in an office on a New Deal building project.[153] While he later claimed authorship (with Theodore Muller) for the Taylor Art Gallery and included it in his *Guide to Modern Architecture* (1940), he omitted the Art Library interior, even though similar design ideas informed both projects (figs. 2.9, 2.31, 3.19).[154] Architecture critics failed to review the library. It was left to Agnes Rindge to provide astute criticism and clues to McAndrew's sources.[155] A Harvard modernist due to her

Right: Figure 2.31
John McAndrew (with
Theodore Muller).
Main Gallery, Taylor
Art Gallery, Vassar
College, 1935–37
(Archives and Special
Collections, Vassar
College Libraries)

studies with Sachs and association with his students, Rindge was known for her passionate enthusiasm for and deep understanding of modern art and architecture.[156] During the construction phase she had acted on behalf of the Art Department to ensure its interests. Until now, her review "The Art Department in New Quarters" has been the principal critical appraisal of the Art Library and Taylor Art Gallery interiors. Inexplicably, she failed to mention McAndrew as their designer or Muller's contributions. Although their relationship was complex and problematic, Rindge and McAndrew shared a commitment to promoting the culture of modernism on campus.[157] They were also close friends, attended social events together, and corresponded frequently with each other.[158] McAndrew's departure from Vassar in late 1937 must have left her with a sense of abandonment. Nonetheless, Rindge carried on to champion the Art Department's new modern interiors and the cause they shared (see Epilogue).

Rindge attributed the library's program and design to "functional thinking in architecture," whose association with modernism in general and Bauhaus teaching concepts in particular had been absorbed in the United States before Gropius's arrival in 1937.[159] She explained that the walls of each study room were treated as "plane surfaces" in order to appreciate the resulting "volume of light and air." Moreover, she considered the library an "abstract composition in architecture" by virtue of its colors, textures, and wall planes.[160]

Where does one find these concepts more broadly in modernism? McAndrew, like Johnson, had been drawn to J. J. P. Oud's use of applied color in his housing estate at the Hook of Holland (1924–27)

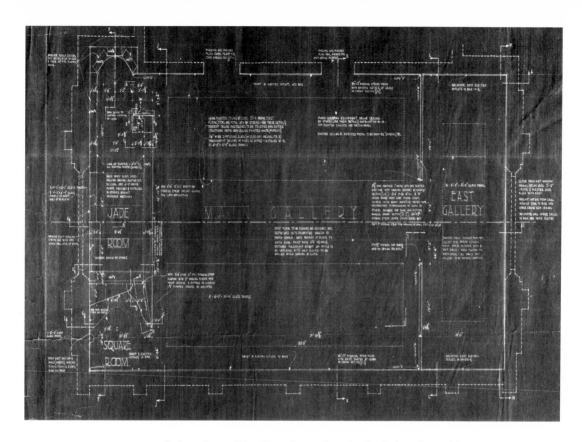

Figure 2.32
John McAndrew (with
Theodore Muller).
Plan of first floor,
Taylor Art Gallery,
Vassar College, 1937
(Courtesy Vassar
College Libraries)

and elsewhere. The Dutch modernist had developed his sense of color under the influence of De Stijl artists and architects, most notably Theo van Doesburg and Gerrit Rietveld. These artists sought to merge color with architecture and thereby render a total work of art. Through the conjunction of aesthetics and ethics, proponents of De Stijl aspired to create a pure form of art consonant with the new social order they envisioned. When collaborating with architects, many De Stijl artists used color as a way of emphasizing "architectural surfaces or structural divisions."[161] Van Doesburg's early work with Oud on the Potgieterstraat municipal housing project in the Spangen district of Rotterdam (1921), for example, shows how he wielded color to control certain building elements and achieve coloristic architecture.[162] Through his efforts to design a volume of space as a three-dimensional equivalent to abstract painting, van Doesburg sought "to place man within (instead of opposite) the plastic arts" and thus engage a work's humanist character.[163] However, even though Bauhaus designers picked up on van Doesburg's ideas, they did not adopt his overarching use of color to achieve fragmented wall planes and thereby manipulate spatial conditions. Further, their palette was less bold. For example, the color scheme of Bauhaus painting teacher Hinnerk Scheper for the wall surfaces of the director's office at the Dessau school (1925–26) was executed in varied tones of gray with an accent of pale ocher (fig. 2.38).[164]

90

Figure 2.33
John McAndrew (with
Theodore Muller).
Jade Galleries, Taylor
Art Gallery, Vassar
College, 1935–37,
Wurts Brothers
(Archives and Special
Collections, Vassar
College Libraries)

In 1929 the Austrian-born architect Frederick Kiesler realized De Stijl concepts with great panache in his Film Arts Guild Cinema (also Film Guild Cinema) on West Eighth Street in New York (fig. 2.39). For the cinema's foyer Kiesler employed an interlocking design of white walls and black Vitrolite glass. Its cement floor was painted an abstract pattern of red, gray, black, and white rectangles, which gave "the decoration a three-dimensional quality," according to architectural historian Laura McGuire.[165] McAndrew, living in New York during the late 1920s and early 1930s, undoubtedly knew the cinema firsthand as well as through published reviews.[166]

Chick Austin was among the first American designers to explore the De Stijl and Bauhaus concept of developing a volume of space as an abstract color composition. In 1930 Austin remodeled the director's office in the Morgan Memorial wing of the Wadsworth

Atheneum, the first of two offices he designed (fig. 2.40). He opened his first office to the public as if it were a modern "period room."[167] Austin's color scheme was audacious. He painted the walls and ceiling in a narrow range of colors from pink to deep reddish brown. A slender wall, a shelf, and built-in bookshelves were painted black.[168] According to Henry-Russell Hitchcock, Austin designed his office as "a free composition in colored planes rather than as a mere continuous background with applied accents."[169] Derived from De Stijl and Bauhaus thinking, his use of wall planes, each painted a different color to create an abstract three-dimensional composition, was still new to the American scene. Austin also appointed his first office with tubular-steel furniture, including a 1925 chair by Marcel Breuer (later called the "Wassily") designed at the Bauhaus. Knowing Austin's office well from his visits to the Atheneum, where he taught at the Hartford Art School, McAndrew absorbed its lessons.

Additional clues to account for McAndrew's use of applied color as a vehicle for abstraction lie in the path of McAndrew's curatorial work at MoMA under Barr's mentorship. That experience nurtured his understanding of modern art movements and the influence of art on architectural thinking, as well as the theory of modern architecture. McAndrew shared with Barr a special affinity for Le Corbusier and especially for his purist work. Using his given name, Jeanneret, Le Corbusier founded a movement with Amédée Ozenfant called purism toward the end of World War I. It was an effort to refine analytical cubism. The cubists thought of representation in terms of fractured forms, the objects having been broken down or "analyzed." By contrast, the purists offered a less fragmented and decorative form of representation. In their manifestos of the movement, *Après le cubisme* (1918) and "Le Purisme" (1921), Jeanneret and Ozenfant called for "logic" and "control" over intuition, richly textured surfaces, and ornamental effects.[170] They explained that "Purism offers an art that is perhaps severe, but one that addresses itself to the elevated faculties

of the mind."[171] In distancing themselves from the cubists, the purists were bent on reform through making a "logical choice of themes… not by deformation, but *by formation*."[172] Proponents regarded their painting as a constructed unit or an "association of purified, related, and architectural elements."[173] Moreover, purists revered classical antiquity and its principles. Caught up in Platonic idealism, they were preoccupied with a painting's essential geometric forms, often perceived as iconic forms, as well as a study of its formal structure or morphology.[174]

Le Corbusier (Jeanneret) admired precision in painting that could be associated with an aesthetic dimension of standardization, relationships among vernacular forms, and also classicism—objectives he also sought in his architecture. His *Still Life with a Stack of Plates* of 1920 represented such goals (fig. 2.41).[175] Its blues, ochers, pinks, and dark browns not only embodied the purist color palette but also layered the composition. By 1936 this purist painting had crossed the Atlantic. That year Barr featured *Still Life with a Stack of Plates* in his Museum of Modern Art exhibition *Cubism and Abstract Art*, along with Le Corbusier's model of the Villa Savoye, produced in the architect's Paris atelier (figs. 2.3 and 2.42).[176] In his exhibition catalogue Barr made two insightful observations that inextricably linked art and architecture. First, he suggested that purist paintings of the early 1920s were

Figure 2.35
John McAndrew (with Theodore Muller). Combined Italian Painting and Sculpture Study rooms, Art Library, Vassar College, 2009, orig. 1935–37, PBDW alteration 2009 (Photograph Andrew Tallon © 2017)

Figure 2.36
John McAndrew (with
Theodore Muller).
Sculpture Study room,
Art Library, Vassar
College, 1935–37,
Wurts Brothers
(Archives and Special
Collections, Vassar
College Libraries)

conceived "architectonically" and that their "sensitive adjustment of
subtle curves to straight lines" would mark the free ground plans of
Le Corbusier's later buildings.[177] When Barr paired *Still Life with a
Stack of Plates* with a black-and-white aerial view of the model of the
Villa Savoye, he suggested that Le Corbusier's painting and building shared a common morphology. In doing so, as the art historian
Stanislaus von Moos has recently observed, Barr designed the page
layout "as if to highlight the villa as a built still life and the still life
a piece of virtual architecture."[178] Second, and especially relevant
to McAndrew's Art Library, Barr observed how purist paintings
were "exercises in color which Le Corbusier was to use so subtly in
his architecture: light blues, pinks, and dark browns." [179] In pairing
Still Life with the Villa Savoye, Barr appreciated that the two works
shared similar colors. While there is some debate today about the
painting scheme and distribution of colors at the Villa Savoye, given
its several restoration projects, the original colors were drawn from
Le Corbusier's purist palette.[180] Barr was able to describe the blues,
pinks, and browns applied to the villa, having visited it in the summer
of 1930 with Hitchcock and Johnson.[181]

In addition to Barr's account of the Villa Savoye's color palette,
McAndrew knew of Hitchcock's description, emphasizing its pale rose
and pale blue.[182] McAndrew also saw the polychromed model as well
as the black-and-white photographs of the house on display at both
MoMA's *Modern Architecture: International Exhibition* in 1932 and its
solo exhibition of Le Corbusier's work in 1935. During McAndrew's
travels in Europe, including six months in 1932 and several months

Figure 2.37
John McAndrew (with
Theodore Muller).
View of the glass-brick
partition between
the former Northern
Painting Study room
and the Architecture
room on the west side
of the Art Library,
Vassar College,
1935-37 (Photograph
Andrew Tallon © 2017)

in 1933, he may well have visited the Villa Savoye.[183] As previously
mentioned, the house was featured in Chenal's film *L'Architecture
d'aujourd'hui*, which accompanied Le Corbusier's Vassar lecture.
McAndrew may also have drawn inspiration from the color scheme of
Le Corbusier's Salvation Army Building (Cité de Refuge) in Paris of
1929–33, about which he was certainly familiar and might also have
visited.[184] For both buildings, Le Corbusier used a selection of purist
colors, which were among those he had codified for the wallpaper

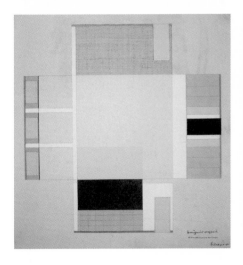 

company Salubra (Basel) in his celebrated "keyboard of colors" called *Claviers de couleur Salubra* (1931).[185]

In his essay of 1941, "Design in Modern Architecture," McAndrew echoed Barr's analysis when he also paired *Still Life with a Stack of Plates* with the Villa Savoye model. The comparison sought to underscore Barr's idea that Le Corbusier was important as both a painter and an architect and that his purist paintings and architectural compositions were inextricably related. McAndrew emphasized that Le Corbusier's buildings in general, and the Villa Savoye in particular, demonstrated the "interplay of curves and diagonals with the ever-present rectangles of architectural planning."[186]

One additional piece of evidence supports the argument that McAndrew's Art Library drew upon the purist color palette embodied in *Still Life with a Stack of Plates* (fig. 2.41). In the spring of 1937, while the Art Library was under construction but before its interior rooms were painted, McAndrew was offered a curatorial post at the Museum of Modern Art.[187] The offer would thrust him into the center of the modern art world in the United States as it was being framed by Alfred Barr and MoMA. His arrival at the museum that summer coincided with negotiations for the acquisition of *Still Life with a Stack of Plates*. The previous year McAndrew had seen Barr's exhibition *Cubism and Abstract Art* with its pairing of Le Corbusier's painting and Villa Savoye. Barr was so enamored of *Still Life* that he purchased it from the artist in November 1937 for $200.[188] It was a brilliant acquisition. *Still Life with a Stack of Plates* held a special significance for McAndrew. In 1941 he posed for a photograph in front of it, which Russell Lynes published in his book *Good Old Modern* (fig. 2.43).[189] For a second, more candid shot, a puckish McAndrew stood in front of the painting holding the Herbert Bayer–designed dust jacket to Sigfried Giedion's *Space, Time and Architecture* (1941), thus emphasizing the connection between *Still Life* and modern architecture (fig. 2.44). In doing so, he endorsed Giedion's observation that Le Corbusier's purist paintings were suffused with a "floating transparency" of objects whose

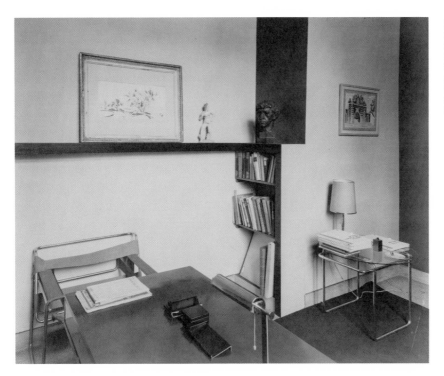

volumes and profiles produced what the painter called a "*mariage des contours*."[190] The play of volumes, light, shadow, and color in his architecture, Giedion observed, produced "great plastic sureness."[191] In May 1938 *Still Life with a Stack of Plates* arrived on the Vassar campus with other paintings on loan from MoMA to take center stage in *Abstract Art*, an exhibition aptly held in McAndrew's two new purist interiors.[192]

McAndrew's admiration for *Still Life with a Stack of Plates* leads us to speculate on the extent to which his color scheme for the Art Library follows a strategy aligned to Le Corbusier's purist palette and specifically to the keyboard of colors in *Salubra*. As Rindge had observed in her firsthand account, the library looked to "subtler blends," especially earthy colors. The polychromy of the main reading room appeared in the blue bookcases against white walls (fig. 2.19). The east and north walls of the Italian Painting Study room approached the color of terracotta, and those of the Sculpture Study room were of a yellowish brown "cimarron" hue juxtaposed with light yellow (figs. 2.35, 2.36). The library's earthbound polychromy contrasted with the monochromatic white color scheme of the staircase adjacent to the Art Library entrance. Le Corbusier featured these colors in his purist paintings and in the pattern cards, especially Velvet (*Velours*) I, in his *Salubra* book (fig. 2.45). Thus, in designing the library interior, McAndrew appears to have selected purist colors at the same time as he absorbed Le Corbusier's methodology and theory, which were embedded in "Le Purisme" (1921) as well as in his unpublished essay "Polychromie architecturale" (presumed to have been written in 1931 in conjunction with *Salubra*).

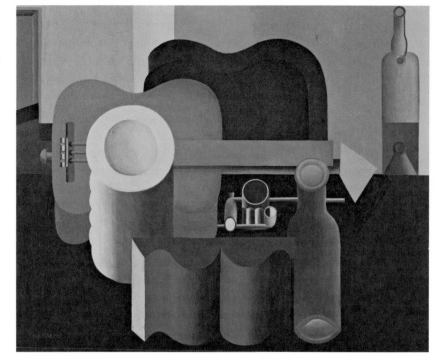

In "Le Purisme" Le Corbusier and Ozenfant distinguished three color groups, each of which was defined by a range of colors (*gamme*), along with their corresponding spatial properties. The "major scale" or range (*grande gamme*) was the principal group. Le Corbusier explained, "One can by hierarchy determine the *major scale* formed of ochre yellows, reds, earths, white, black, ultramarine blue, and, of course, certain of their derivatives; this scale is a strong, stable scale giving unity and holding the plane of the picture since these colors keep one another in balance. They are thus essentially constructive colors; it is these that all the great periods employed; it is these that whoever wishes to paint in volume should use."[193] Thus, the major scale was identified by its ocher yellows, reds, earth colors, and blues, along with white and black. Its colors were appropriate for use in architecture because of their "constructive" or architectonic properties. They defined spatial conditions. Moreover, Le Corbusier and Ozenfant assigned to color both physiological and psychological characteristics. Color also generated "sensory order."[194] In "Polychromie architecturale" Le Corbusier refined his theory of color with respect to these properties, emphasizing the architectonic character of the major scale.[195] Such constructive use of colors in the major scale meant that, for example, "blue and its green combinations create spaces" while "red (and its brown, orange, etc. combinations) fixes the wall" and serves as a stimulant.[196] As a vehicle for color, the wall plane may have an autonomous disposition but remains an integral component of a coherent space. Moreover, "the form of the room," Le Corbusier asserted, "will be totally maintained, revealed, if

Figure 2.42
Le Corbusier with
Pierre Jeanneret.
Model, Villa Savoye,
Poissy-sur-Seine,
France, 1929–31
(Alfred Barr, *Cubism
and Abstract Art*,
New York: Museum
of Modern Art, 1936,
165; © The Museum of
Modern Art/Licensed
by SCALA / Art
Resource, NY © FLC-
ADAGP, Paris / Artists
Rights Society [ARS],
New York 2017. Le
Corbusier © Artists
Rights Society [ARS],
New York/ADAGP,
Paris/FLC)

the ceiling is painted white."[197] The inherent contradiction between a
wall plane as autonomous, on the one hand, and as a constituent part
of a balanced composition, on the other, characterized Le Corbusier's
architecture, which suffused it with tension. For example, the picture
gallery of Le Corbusier's Villa La Roche in Paris (1923–25), according to architect Arthur Rüegg, displayed polychromed walls but still
affirmed its integrity as a "legible spatial unity," rather than collapsing
as a house of cards.[198] Moreover, Le Corbusier held that through the
use of color as "an incredibly effective triggering tool," the architect
had the ability to adjust "emotional, sensorial, and intellectual levels."[199] He maintained, for example, that the "blue acts on the body
as a calmative...at rest."[200] Such physiological and psychological
effects (i.e., functional roles assigned to color) were entwined with Le
Corbusier's vision and informed modern art and design.

The Art Library's architectonic polychromy underscores the
fact that McAndrew, an art historian and encyclopedic modernist,
had an exceptional understanding of not only color theory (and its
history going back to Goethe and Chevreul) but also Le Corbusier's
concept of purism, including one or more of the painter-architect's
pioneering studies on the topic. The main reading room of the Art
Library engages the "constructive color" of blue: ultramarine blue
for the bookcases and "light greenish blue" for the supporting columns (fig 2.34; see Preface, page 34). Bookcases rise to the level of the east
and west clerestory glass-brick windows and allow light and space to
flow above them (fig. 2.19). As with Le Corbusier and Lescaze (in the
Wilbour Library), McAndrew selected blue for its ability to expand
space. Producing a tranquil, peaceful effect, blue is an appropriate
color for reading and browsing. In contrast to the main reading room,

whose open plan and blue color enlarge the space, the four study rooms are confined rectangular volumes enclosed by bearing walls. Each has its own color ambience. The spatial effect is apparent in the original color schemes, notably those of the Italian and Sculpture Study rooms (fig. 2.36). Both of their south walls are painted the same dark yellowish brown color; they recede and thus anchor the space. In the case of the Sculpture Study room, the brown color of the south wall opposes the light yellow color of the other walls. Such light-dark color contrasts are consistent with the *Salubra* theory. In the original Italian room the use of "pinkish orange"—a shade of red—fixes and thereby affirms the east and north walls (fig. 2.35). As with Le Corbusier, McAndrew creates visual tension by means of the color "character" of each wall plane and its role in a coherent volume of space with a white ceiling unifying the whole. Similarly, the Taylor Art Gallery's "pinkish beige," "warm grey," and terracotta colors derive from purist painting in general and Le Corbusier's *Still Life* in particular, which help to assert the stable character of the walls and screen walls for exhibiting art works (figs. 2.9, 2.31).

The purist colors of Le Corbusier's *Still Life* and *Salubra* system were contemporary. They expressed modern life. Drawing on the

Figure 2.44
John McAndrew
standing in front of
Le Corbusier's *Still
Life with a Stack
of Plates* in 1941
holding the Herbert
Bayer–designed dust
jacket to Sigfried
Giedion's *Space, Time
and Architecture*
(Courtesy Peter J.
Fergusson © FLC-
ADAGP, Paris / Artists
Rights Society [ARS],
New York 2017)

general classification of purist color and its attributes, as well as on the formal geometry of purist painting, McAndrew transformed the Art Library into a three-dimensional work of purist vision. The unique color character of each room delivered an environment specific to its programmatic assignment and art discipline. McAndrew's knowledge of modernist color theory combined with his firsthand study of Dutch, Bauhaus, Bauhaus-inspired, and Corbusian buildings. In effect, he subscribed to the new theory of polychromy for modern architecture, which the German-born architect and historian Walter Curt Behrendt emphatically characterized in 1927: "The new architecture needs color, it needs it as a design tool to articulate the smooth surfaces of its walls, and it needs it in a *functional* sense to exploit color's chromatic values and valence and thereby express the tensional relationships of the spatial organism."[201] In executing what Behrendt described, McAndrew underscored the importance of color in North American modernism, as Kiesler and Austin had before him, which had been largely occluded by the International Style principles promoted by Hitchcock and Johnson. For, even though the two curators were aware of the distinctions between applied color and material color, as well as the significance of contemporary color theory, and

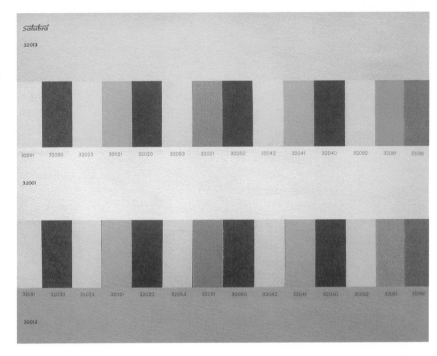

notwithstanding their sensitivity to the way in which architects used color on discrete wall planes to differentiate sections of a building's plan or program, they called for "restraint" of color in the service of their governing principle: "avoidance of applied ornament."[202] On the one hand, they appreciated that color "emphasizes strongly the effect of surface;" on the other hand, they recognized that "it breaks up the unity of volume," one of their cardinal principles.[203] Thus, as a form of ornament, color needed to be reined in.[204] Johnson later recalled his own reaction to the polychromy of the Villa Savoye on his visit in 1930: "To me the colors weren't necessary for the architecture, and they could mar the architecture."[205] His view on the role of color suffused the legacy of the International Style in opposition to McAndrew's thinking.

The infusion of purist polychromy in the Art Library and Art Gallery established them together as a key site in affirming the role of color in international modernism, and confirmed McAndrew as a critical interpreter of modernist color in the United States. Moreover, McAndrew upheld the functional role of color—its constructive character as well as the physiological and psychological effects assigned to it—as Le Corbusier had before him. And finally, when McAndrew advanced the correspondence between art and architecture and the idea of a 3-D color environment, he followed another burgeoning Corbusian path, which called for an alliance of painting, sculpture, and architecture. Known as a "Synthesis of the Arts," Le Corbusier would not fully develop that project until after World War II.[206]

ART LIBRARY FURNITURE AND FIXTURES

McAndrew's modernist vision for the Art Library required unity of expression. If the color scheme was intended to be didactic, so were the library's furniture and fixtures. As with the Art Gallery and the Cooperative Bookshop, McAndrew's library incorporated the latest design ideas as expressions of modern life on campus. The 1930s, the era of the Great Depression, was the first decade in which designers and producers sought a broad audience for modern design.[207] With Theodore Muller's assistance, McAndrew selected space-saving steel bookcases and tabletops supplied by the Art Metal Construction Company. Library tables were either circular or oblong and, according to Rindge, "mounted on chromium legs, finished with natural wood and covered with linoleum of putty grey, soft blue, or deep rust."[208] The library was equipped with tubular-steel furniture derived from Bauhaus models, which Breuer had first developed in 1925–26. By the 1930s such furniture was being sold in the United States. The library's principal rooms featured a chair designed, according to the curator and design historian Christopher Wilk, by the Dutch architect, furniture designer, and Bauhaus teacher Mart Stam; McAndrew and Muller ordered the chair from the American Thonet Brothers, Inc., catalogue **(fig. 2.46)**.[209] This cantilevered chair of tubular steel rested on two legs, maximizing its strength through a minimal amount of material. Although mass-produced, it employed a wood seat and ergonomically curved back to provide support and comfort. The selection of this Bauhaus model, now available for the American consumer, reflected McAndrew's interest in combining industrial design with natural materials and organic forms. Grouped around library tables, these lightweight cantilevered chairs helped to create freer and more open interior spaces in the main reading room and in smaller rooms such as the Sculpture Study room **(figs. 2.8, 2.36)**.

McAndrew and Muller equipped several of the Art Library offices, most notably a faculty office in the remodeled Taylor Hall (1937), with tubular steel furniture by Thonet Brothers after designs by Stam and Breuer **(fig. 2.47)**. In addition to the Stam chairs, that office featured Breuer's chrome-plated tubular steel desk with top and sides of lacquered wood known as "B465," available in America from the Thonet catalogue **(fig. 2.48)**.[210] A similar Breuer desk, known as "ST5283" and featured in Thonet catalogues, as well as a Breuer chair and another tubular chair (most likely a Howell Chromsteel model), distinguished the yellow and blue office of Dr. Jane Baldwin, Vassar's chief medical officer, in Ely Hall (1936; now Alumnae Gymnasium) **(fig. 2.49)**.[211] Presumably, such lightweight, open-framed furniture met the functional and aesthetic needs of both the art faculty and Vassar's head clinician. Modernism's association with progressive ideas meant that it could effectively serve an institution in step with the most up-to-date medical practice. Although no designer was credited with the Baldwin office, it was first published at the same time as the Vassar Cooperative Bookshop and resembled the Taylor Hall faculty office,

Figure 2.46
Mart Stam. Chair, No. ST 263 (Gebrüder Thonet, *Catalog no. 53*, New York: Thonet Brothers, 1938, 57; Courtesy Avery Architectural and Fine Arts Library)

both by McAndrew (figs. 2.12, 2.47). In the faculty office, tubular design appeared at a smaller scale in a desk lamp similar to the Luxus model 6631 in the Kaiser Idell series by Bauhaus designer Christian Dell (ca. 1934), possibly manufactured in the United States by the General Lighting Corporation.[212] Its bowl-shaped, metal shade hung from an arched support resting on a coiled base. The lamp added a whimsical note to the room. In calling for Bauhaus-designed furniture fabricated by Thonet Brothers, McAndrew followed the lead of Chick Austin, who had installed Breuer and Bauhaus furniture not only in the director's offices in the Morgan Memorial (1930) and in Avery Memorial (1934) but also in the Avery Memorial Research Library (1933–34) at the Wadsworth Atheneum (figs. 2.21, 2.40).[213] William Lescaze also drew on Breuer and Bauhaus models when he designed the furniture, most notably the chairs, for the Wilbour Library and the Philadelphia Saving Fund Society (PSFS) Building in Philadelphia (1929–32) (fig. 2.22).[214]

McAndrew and Muller also looked to Bauhaus design when they planned the Art Library's program of indirect and diffuse artificial lighting. It complemented the natural lighting supplied by the library's windows and glass-brick walling. Kurt Versen Lamps, Inc., of New York supplied the fixtures, which were largely based on

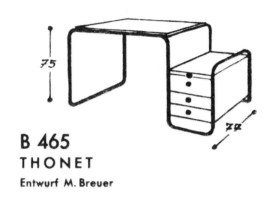

B 465
THONET
Entwurf M. Breuer

Bauhaus prototypes. A leading lighting expert, Kurt Versen designed, manufactured, and sold his own fixtures. Like the architect William Muschenheim, who called upon Versen to supply lighting for many of his buildings, McAndrew admired the fixtures for their design and efficiency.[215] As with the Vassar bookshop, McAndrew chose Bauhaus-inspired spherical glass globes for the entry and circulation desk of the main reading room, the Northern Painting Study room, and entry-level hall adjacent to the staircase (figs. 2.10, 2.24, 2.29, and 2.50). Drawn from Bauhaus design ideas, these fixtures transmitted "shadowless lighting."[216] A ceiling light with satin chromium stem and white opal glass bowl provided several study rooms, including the Italian Painting and Sculpture Study rooms, with Versen indirect illumination (fig. 2.36). Each spherical pendant fixture directed light onto the white ceiling. Marketed as the "Lucette" model, it was based on a Bauhaus ceiling light by Christian Dell and manufactured in 1932 by Kaiser & Co. (fig. 2.51).[217] Library tables in the main reading room alcoves were equipped with brushed chromium reflector lights, also supplied by Versen (fig. 2.20).[218]

McAndrew did not articulate his views on European and American modernism until after the completion of the Art Library and Taylor Art Gallery following his departure for the Museum of Modern Art in the summer of 1937. However, his Vassar designs evinced the originality and direction of his thinking. Like his fellow architects Raymond Hood and Edward Durell Stone, McAndrew was trained in Beaux-Arts principles but adopted modern ones. His knowledge of European modernism was firsthand. Moreover, his position on modernism was not merely based on aesthetics but on contemporaneous art theory, as well as on Mumford's cultural assumptions—themes explored in Chapter Three. On the one hand, McAndrew's predispositions and designs, like those of European modernists, challenged International Style orthodoxy. On the other hand, his views were not burdened by European attachments to political ideology or the need to embody *Sachlichkeit* (factualness or matter-of-factness). McAndrew's Art Library interior joined

Left: Figure 2.48 Marcel Breuer. Chrome-plated tubular steel desk, B465, ca. 1934 (Thonet B465, in Christopher Wilk, *Thonet: 150 Years of Furniture*, Woodbury, NY: Barron's, 1980, 102, fig. 134)

Right: Figure 2.49 Office of Dr. Jane Baldwin, Ely Hall (now Alumnae Gymnasium), Vassar College, 1936, Margaret DeM. Brown (Archives and Special Collections, Vassar College Libraries)

"Lucette"

kurt versen, inc. • new york, n. y.   6

Left: Figure 2.50
John McAndrew (with
Theodore Muller).
Entry and circulation
desk, Art Library,
Vassar College, 1935–
37, Platt Byard Dovell
White Architects
(Photo © Jonathan
Wallen)

Right: Figure 2.51
Kurt Versen Company,
after design by
Christian Dell.
"Lucette" model
lamp, 1937 (Kurt
Versen Lamps, Inc.,
*Contemporary
Lighting: Indirect
Illumination*, New York:
Corporation [1938],
6. Courtesy Avery
Architectural and Fine
Arts Library)

together American pragmatism (air conditioning, glass brick, indirect lighting) and European avant-garde theory (purism, De Stijl, Bauhaus) as he deployed architectonic colors to layer space.[219] The rooms were rich in the materiality, using glass, cork, and wood, which were associated with organic life and the vernacular, as well as metal, associated with industrial production. The library demonstrated design ideas that McAndrew had taught in his architecture classes, ideas that would later inform his concept of a naturalized or Americanized modernism. As his Art Library and Art Gallery interiors showed, he viewed the influence of European modernism through the lens of American principles and practice. The Art Library especially introduced to the United States something it had not seen before: an interior that drew on purist thinking about the relationship between color and space. At the same time, in its use of glass blocks to maximize light, cork floors to dampen sound and soften textures, linoleum-topped wooden tables with chromium legs, metal bookcases, strip molding to secure photographs and prints, and air conditioning, the library expressed the latest pragmatic American design ideas. This was the kind of transatlantic synthesis that exemplified his vision of modernism, one that he would define in his exhibitions and essays for the Museum of Modern Art (see Chapter Three).

When Agnes Rindge was left to carry on the campaign for modernism at Vassar in the Art Department's new headquarters, she turned to modern sculpture and called upon the resources of MoMA. She helped to sponsor its loan exhibition of abstract art which, in addition to Le Corbusier's *Still Life*, featured the work of the Russian constructivist sculptor Naum Gabo along with a lecture by him.[220] Those events soon precipitated an anonymous gift to the college of Gabo's *Construction* (1937), a small model for one of the sculptures in the exhibition.[221] The new Art Gallery facilitated the expansion of the collection through the acquisition of new works.[222] Together the Art Library and Taylor Art Gallery served as a "teaching agent" for students to study works of art in interiors suggesting the latest design ideas.[223] The new Art Department headquarters thus empowered Rindge to believe that the "history of art [had] continuity" at Vassar College.[224] McAndrew envisioned another linkage too, one that was geocultural: The Art Library and the Art Gallery embodied a vision of modernism that embraced the continuity of avant-garde developments between Europe and the United States. They forged a long-held alliance between modernism and optimism by reconstituting the heroic confidence of Corbusian purism and modern design. For Vassar students these avant-garde interiors captured the spirit of their time.

1   Barr was appointed an instructor. "Appointments, 1923–24," *Vassar Miscellany News*, June 15, 1923, 10; Margaret Scolari Barr, "Our Campaigns," *New Criterion*, Special Issue (Summer 1987): 5–6. Hitchcock held the post of assistant professor. "Faculty Notes," *Vassar Miscellany News*, January 14, 1928, 2; Henry-Russell Hitchcock, "Modern Architecture—A Memoir," *Journal of the Society of Architectural Historians* 27, no. 4 (December 1968): 231. Scolari received her master of arts degree from Vassar in 1927. "1927 Become Bachelors of Art," *Vassar Miscellany News*, June 10, 1927, 1; Oral History Interview with Margaret Scolari Barr concerning Alfred H. Barr, February 22–May 13, 1974 (Archives of American Art, Smithsonian Institution; hereafter cited as AAASI).

2   Tonks received his PhD from Harvard University in 1903. At Princeton he held the post of preceptor (equivalent to associate professor) in the Department of Art and Archaeology from 1905 to 1911 and served as chair of the Art Department from 1911 to 1943. "New Appointments," *Vassar Miscellany* 40 (June 1, 1911): 719; Susan Donahue Kuretsky and Nicholas Adams, "The History of Art at Vassar College," http://art.vassar.edu /about/history.html.

3   Pamela Askew, "The Department of Art at Vassar: 1865–1931," in *The Early Years of Art History in the United States*, ed. Craig Hugh Smyth and Peter M. Lukehart (Princeton, NJ: Department of Art and Archaeology, Princeton University, 1993), 63.

4   John McAndrew to Agnes Rindge, undated [before February 20, 1932] (Agnes Rindge Claflin Papers 11.141, Archives and Special Collections, Vassar College Libraries; hereafter cited as ASC, VCL).

5   John McAndrew to Chick Austin, March 3, 1932 (A. Everett Austin Papers, Box 8, Folder 7, Wadsworth Atheneum Archives, Hartford, Connecticut; hereafter cited as WAAHC).

6   McAndrew did apply formally to Tonks. Among the letters he received from McAndrew's Harvard professors was one from George Harold Edgell. See also George H. Chase [John E. Hudson Professor of Archaeology in the Department of Fine Arts at Harvard] "To Whom It May Concern" [Tonks], March 8, 1932 (John McAndrew Papers, Courtesy of Wellesley College Archives; hereafter cited as John McAndrew Papers, WCA); John McAndrew to Agnes Rindge, undated [before March 12, 1932]; John McAndrew to Agnes Rindge, "Income Tax Day" [April 15, 1932] (Agnes Rindge Claflin Papers 11.141, ASC, VCL).

7   "Curriculum to Have Many New Additions," *Vassar Miscellany News*, April 22, 1933, 1; *Bulletin of Vassar College* 23 (Poughkeepsie, NY: Vassar College, 1932– 1933), 70, 72. See also *Bulletin* vols. 24 (1933–1934), 25 (1934–1935), 27 (1936–1937).

8   "News to Publish Course Survey by Ranking Students," *Vassar Miscellany News*, April 20, 1935, 2.

9   "News to Publish Course Survey by Ranking Students," 2.

10   Oliver S. Tonks, "Departmental Correlation," *Vassar Miscellany* 41 (May 1912): 610–11.

11   For example, Tonks gave a lecture on modern painting on April 18, 1923, and another, "The Modernist Movement in Painting," on November 1, 1923, in conjunction with an exhibition of Wassily Kandinsky's work at Vassar. "Traces Evolution of Modern Painting," *Vassar Miscellany News*, April 21, 1923, 1, 6; "Calendar," *Vassar Miscellany News*, October 31, 1923, 6.

12   "Outlying Fields," editorial, *Vassar Miscellany* 42 (February 1, 1913): 313–14.

13   Marjorie Newcomb Wilson, "The Outlook: The International Art Exhibit," *Vassar Miscellany* 42 (May 1, 1913): 578.

14   Margaret M. Armstrong, "The Outlook: What Is Art?," *Vassar Miscellany* 42 (May 1, 1913): 578–79.

15   On the search for a culture of the present in the construction of modernism, see Preface, note 2.

16   "Art Professor on Newest Movement in Painting," *Vassar Miscellany News*, January 11, 1922, 3; "Mr. Brinton Speaks on Modern Painting, *Vassar Miscellany News*, February 28, 1923, 2, 6.

17   "Walter Pach to Speak on Modern Painting," *Vassar Miscellany News*, April 16, 1927, 1.

18   Katherine S. Dreier to Oliver Tonks, March 5, 1923 (Katherine S. Dreier Papers, Series I, Correspondence, Box 35, Folder 1040, Vassar College 1923–32, Société Anonyme Archive, Yale Collection of American Literature, Beinecke Rare Book and Manuscript Library, Yale University; hereafter cited as SAA, YCAL, BRBML, YU).

19   Andrew J. Walker, "Critic, Curator, Collector: Christian Brinton and the Exhibition of National Modernism in America, 1910–1945" (PhD diss., University of Pennsylvania, 1999), 134, 137, 143. Christian Brinton, "Modernism in Art," *Exhibition of Paintings by Members of the Société Anonyme* (Worcester, MA: Worcester Art Museum, 1921), unpaged. Brinton continued to collaborate with Dreier, serving as special deputy for foreign art for the Société Anonyme exhibition at the Philadelphia Sesqui-Centennial International Exposition in 1926, writing its catalogue text. Christian Brinton, *Modern Art at the Sesqui-Centennial Exhibition* (New York: Société Anonyme, 1926). Christian Brinton, *The Archipenko Exhibition: Under the Auspices of the Société Anonyme* (New York: Kingore Gallery, 1924).

20   Robert L. Herbert, Eleanor S. Apter, and Elise K. Kenney, eds., *The Société Anonyme and the Dreier Bequest to Yale University: A Catalogue Raisonné* (New Haven, CT: Yale University Press, 1984), 777. I wish to thank Molly

Nesbit, professor of art at Vassar College, for assisting me with Société Anonyme documents, especially those relating to Vassar College exhibitions.

21 *Exhibition of Paintings by Modern Masters of Spain, Germany, France, Russia, Italy, Belgium and America* (Poughkeepsie, NY: Vassar College, 1923) (Katherine S. Dreier Papers, Series VIII, Société Anonyme: Public Programs, Box 89, Folder 2304, SAA, YCAL, BRBML, YU).

22 Francis Picabia, *Prostitution Universelle* (Universal Prostitution), 1916–17, Yale University Art Gallery, Gift of Collection Société Anonyme; Herbert, Apter, and Kenney, *Société Anonyme and the Dreier Bequest at Yale University*, 526–28, 632–34, cat. nos. 550, 651; "Expressionism Takes Varied Form," *Vassar Miscellany News*, April 14, 1923, 2; "Traces Evolution of Modern Painting," 3.

23 In preparation for the New York show, Dreier visited Kandinsky in his Bauhaus studio in Weimar, where the artist taught the Wall Painting Workshop and Preliminary Course. Herbert, Apter, and Kenney, eds., *Société Anonyme and the Dreier Bequest at Yale University*, 355, 359–60, 777, cat. no. 375; announcement, *New York Times*, April 15, 1923, 10. Dreier wrote a brochure for the first exhibition. Katherine Sophie Dreier, *Société Anonyme: Kandinsky* (New York: Société Anonyme, 1923).

24 "Modernist Movement in Painting Outlined," *Vassar Miscellany News*, November 7, 1923, 1.

25 "Kandinsky," *Vassar Miscellany News*, November 7, 1923, 2.

26 Letter, Alfred Barr to Katherine Dreier, May 9, 1950, Katherine S. Dreier Papers, Société Anonyme Archive, Yale Collection of American Literature, Beinecke Rare Book and Manuscript Library, Yale University, quoted in Sybil Gordon Kantor, *Alfred H. Barr, Jr. and the Intellectual Origins of the Museum of Modern Art* (Cambridge, MA: MIT Press, 2002), 31, 32, 385n47.

27 "Kandinsky Discussed," *Vassar Miscellany News*, November 14, 1923, 2.

28 "Lectures on Modern Art," *Poughkeepsie Star*, November 3, 1923, n.p., quoted in Kantor, *Alfred H. Barr, Jr.*, 32, 386n49.

29 "Kandinsky Plans to Remodel Vassar," *Vassar Miscellany News*, November 17, 1923, 5; Karen Van Lengen and Lisa Reilly, *Vassar College: Campus Guide* (New York: Princeton Architectural Press, 2004), 80–81.

30 "Art Exemplifies Expressionism," *Vassar Miscellany News*, April 13, 1927, 1; Herbert, Apter, and Kenney, *Société Anonyme and the Dreier Bequest at Yale University*, 778.

31 Herbert, Apter, and Kenney, *Société Anonyme and the Dreier Bequest at Yale University*, 362, 364, cat. nos. 377, 379.

32 "Exhibition of Modern European Art," checklist of the exhibition, Taylor Hall Art Gallery, April 8–28 [1927] (Katherine S. Dreier Papers, Series I, Correspondence, Box 35, Folder 1040, Vassar College 1923–32, SAA, YCAL, BRBML, YU).

33 "Art Exemplifies Expressionism," 1.

34 "Classic Elements Are Present in All Art," *Vassar Miscellany News*, April 23, 1927, 1.

35 Rona Roob, "From the Archives: Kandinsky and The Museum of Modern Art," *MoMA* 19 (Spring 1995): 24.

36 Alfred H. Barr Jr., "Modern Works of Art," in *Modern Works of Art: Fifth Anniversary Exhibition* (New York: Museum of Modern Art, 1934), 14, 30, cat. no. 90.

37 Alfred H. Barr Jr., *Cubism and Abstract Art* (New York: Museum of Modern Art, 1936), 68, 69, 212, fig. 53 (105).

38 Belle Krasne and Nina Wild, "Speaking of Art," *Vassar Chronicle*, December 9, 1944, 7.

39 On Chatterton, see "Clarence K. Chatterton," Vassar Encyclopedia, https://vcencyclopedia.vassar.edu/faculty/.

40 Henry McBride, "Modern Art," *Dial* 86 (April 1929): 353–55, quoted in Maria Morris Hambourg and Christopher Phillips, *The New Vision: Photography between the World Wars* (New York: Metropolitan Museum of Art, 1989), 46, 282n174.

41 In November 1929 MoMA launched its first exhibition with a loan show, *Cézanne, Gauguin, Seurat, van Gogh*. Alfred H. Barr Jr., *First Loan Exhibition: Cézanne, Gauguin, Seurat, van Gogh* (New York: Museum of Modern Art, 1929). MoMA's second exhibition was devoted to paintings by nineteen living American artists, including Hopper and Kent. Alfred H. Barr Jr., *Paintings by Nineteen Living Americans* (New York: Museum of Modern Art, 1929). For a list of the Vassar College Art Gallery exhibitions, see A Complete List of Exhibitions Held at the Vassar College Art Gallery, 1923–1940.

42 "New Faculty Members Appointed for 1928–1929," *Vassar Miscellany News*, October 3, 1928, 1.

43 Agnes Millicent Rindge, introduction to *Sculpture* (New York: Payson and Clarke, 1929); Agnes Millicent Rindge, "The Art of Sculpture: An Analysis of the Aesthetics of Sculpture" (PhD diss., Radcliffe College, 1928).

44 Kuretsky and Adams, "History of Art at Vassar College."

45   Elizabeth L. Bauer, "Vassar Buildings, A Modern Gymnasium," *Vassar Miscellany News*, May 14, 1932, 7.

46   M. Sloane, "Student Rates Offered by Modern Art Museum," *Vassar Miscellany News*, January 9, 1932, 3.

47   Alfred H. Barr Jr., foreword to *Modern Architecture: International Exhibition* (New York: Museum of Modern Art, 1932), 13. Abbott, for example, employed the term "International Style" in an account of his trip to Russia with Barr in 1928. "Notes from a Soviet Diary," *Hound & Horn: A Harvard Miscellany* 2 (Spring 1929): 263. On the origin of the term "International Style," see Kantor, *Alfred H. Barr, Jr.*, 167, 292–93, 409n76, 439n65. See also Terence Riley, *The International Style: Exhibition 15 and the Museum of Modern Art* (New York: Rizzoli, 1992), 89–93; Henry-Russell Hitchcock Jr. and Philip Johnson, *The International Style: Architecture since 1922* (New York: W. W. Norton, 1932).

48   Barr, foreword to *Modern Architecture: International Exhibition*, 14–16; Hitchcock and Johnson, *International Style: Architecture since 1922*.

49   In his interview with Russell Lynes, McAndrew speculated: "The clarity of the exposition, the ideas in it of the International Style—volume not mass, asymmetry not symmetry—all that was Alfred's thinking." John McAndrew, interview by Russell Lynes, Venice, October 1971 (Russell Lynes Papers, 1935–1986, Archives of American Art, Smithsonian Institution). Barr later attributed the "exposition" chiefly to Hitchcock. A. H. B. Jr. [Alfred H. Barr Jr.] to Lewis Mumford, February 27, 1948, reproduced in *Museum of Modern Art Bulletin* 15, no. 3 (Spring 1948): 21.

50   Barr, foreword to *Modern Architecture: International Exhibition*, 15–16.

51   "H. R. Hitchcock to Lecture on Modern Architecture," *Vassar Miscellany News*, May 18, 1932, 1.

52   "Russell Hitchcock Talks on Modern Architecture," *Vassar Miscellany News*, May 25, 1932, 1, 7.

53   On MoMA's educational mission, see [Alan Blackburn] *Present Status and Future Direction of the Museum of Modern Art: Confidential Report to the Executive Committee* (1933), 2–6 (Rockefeller Family Archives, Folder 197, Box 20, Record Group 2, Office of the Messrs. Rockefeller, Cultural Interests Series, Rockefeller Archive Center).

54   "Lectures to Elucidate Architecture Exhibit," *Vassar Miscellany News*, May 6, 1933, 1; Margaret Miller, "Current Art Exhibitions: Modern Architecture," *Vassar Miscellany News*, May 24, 1933, 2.

55   *International Exhibition of Modern Architecture*, MoMA's first circulating exhibition, consisted of ten models and seventy-five photographs and plans and reached fourteen venues in nearly two years. Because universities and small art galleries required a less extensive (and expensive) exhibition, the museum organized a more modest second show, *Photograph Exhibition of Modern Architecture*, which included the same photographs and plans but substituted large photographs for the models. Elodie Courter, "Circulating Exhibitions," *Bulletin of the Museum of Modern Art* 1, no. 7 (March 1934): 2; Elizabeth Mock, memorandum, The Museum of Modern Art, May 26, 1944, reprinted in Riley, *International Style*, Appendix 5, 222.

56   Miller, "Current Art Exhibitions," 2, 4.

57   Johnson delivered three lectures in Taylor Hall in conjunction with MoMA's circulating exhibition on modern architecture in May 1933: on the influence of Schinkel and others on contemporary architecture (May 16), on American architecture and the Chicago School in the 1880s (May 17), and on American architecture since World War I (May 18). "Lectures to Elucidate Architecture Exhibit," 1; "Calendar," *Vassar Miscellany News*, May 17, 1933, 4; "Johnson Traces Modern Trends in Architecture," *Vassar Miscellany News*, May 20, 1933, 1, 3, 4; "P. Johnson Ends Series of Talks on Architecture," *Vassar Miscellany News*, May 24, 1933, 1.

58   "Le Corbusier, Famed French Architect, to Speak Here Friday," *Vassar Miscellany News*, October 30, 1935, 1; "Modern Housing Text of Lecture by Le Corbusier," *Vassar Miscellany News*, November 6, 1935, 1, 4.

59   John McAndrew, curriculum vitae [1941] (Bio File, John McAndrew Papers, WCA).

60   Vassar College paid an honorarium of $100 for the lecture. Vassar's payment was made to the Museum of Modern Art, which collected the lecture receipts, deducted its expenses, and, at the conclusion of the lecture tour, turned the balance over to Le Corbusier. Thomas Dabney Mabry Jr. to Le Corbusier, December 2 and 13, 1935; "Le Corbusier Lecture Tour Statement of Receipts and Expenditures"; "Expenditures for Publicity on Le Corbusier Lecture Tour" (FLC U3 [18], 71, 75, 127, 128, Fondation Le Corbusier, Paris). See also "Le Corbusier to Speak Here," *Poughkeepsie Eagle-News*, October 30, 1935, 9. For Le Corbusier's account of his visit to Vassar College, see Le Corbusier, *When the Cathedrals Were White: A Journey to the Country of Timid People,* trans. Francis E. Hyslop Jr. (New York: Reynal & Hitchcock, 1947), 135–38. For a discussion of Le Corbusier's American lecture tour, see Mardges Bacon, *Le Corbusier in America: Travels in the Land of the Timid* (Cambridge, MA: MIT Press, 2001), 59–124.

61   Le Corbusier, *When the Cathedrals Were White*, 136. In the original French edition, Le Corbusier uses the expression *"collège des 'jeunes filles en fleurs.'"* (*À l'ombre des jeunes filles en fleurs* is the title of the second volume of Marcel Proust's novel *À la recherche du temps perdu*.) Le Corbusier, *Quand les cathédrales étaient blanches: voyage au pays des timides* (Paris: Librairie Plon, 1937), 203.

62   Le Corbusier, *When the Cathedrals Were White*, 136–37.

63 "Le Corbusier, Famed French Architect, to Speak Here Friday," 1; "Le Corbusier Gives Opinions on Mussolini, Vassar, N.Y.C.," *Vassar Miscellany News*, November 6, 1935, 1, 3.

64 Le Corbusier, *Quand les cathédrales étaient blanches*, 205; Le Corbusier, *When the Cathedrals Were White*, 137.

65 Amelia Thompson Vose, annotated sketches on note cards (Amelia Thompson Vose family).

66 On the Bastion Kellermann housing project, see Le Corbusier, *When the Cathedrals Were White*, 21–24; Le Corbusier and Pierre Jeanneret, *Oeuvre complète, 1934–1938*, ed. Max Bill (1939; repr., Zurich: Girsberger, 1964), 148–51.

67 Le Corbusier's drawings from his Vassar lecture have not survived. "Le Corbusier Gives Opinions on Mussolini, Vassar, N.Y.C.," 3; Le Corbusier, *When the Cathedrals Were White*, 137. See also "Modern Housing Text of Lecture by Le Corbusier," 1, 4. On Vassar "Amazons," see "Princeton Men Branded as Sissies by Vassar Amazons," *Vassar Miscellany News*, November 23, 1932, 1; I wish to thank Nicholas Adams, Professor of Art on the Mary Conover Mellon Chair at Vassar College, for sharing this reference with me. For an earlier use, see "The Acid Test," *Vassar Miscellany News*, May 22, 1920, 4.

68 Le Corbusier, *When the Cathedrals Were White*, 136–38.

69 Robert Allan Jacobs, interview by the author, Pawling, New York, November 21, 1984.

70 Le Corbusier, *When the Cathedrals Were White*, 138.

71 Panofsky delivered an illustrated public lecture, "What Is Baroque?," on May 3, 1935. "Prof. Panofsky Lectures Here About Baroque," *Vassar Miscellany News*, May 8, 1935, 1, 7; "Lectures—Goal for the Future," *Vassar Miscellany News*, May 8, 1935, 2.

72 Alma Clayburgh Grew, interview by the author, Boston, December 12, 1987.

73 Le Corbusier, *When the Cathedrals Were White*, 145.

74 Le Corbusier, *When the Cathedrals Were White*, 147.

75 In a letter congratulating Clayburgh on her recent marriage to James Hooper Grew, a diplomat who would serve as ambassador to Japan in the 1940s, Le Corbusier described her as "*la plus belle femme du monde.*" Le Corbusier to Mrs. James Hooper Grew [Alma Clayburgh Grew], July 25, 1938 (Fondation Le Corbusier, Paris). Alma Clayburgh Grew, interview by the author, December 12, 1987.

76 See "Tahitian Idyll by Gauguin in Taylor Hall Exhibit," *Vassar Miscellany News*, December 12, 1934, 1; "Cézanne Portrait of Wife Now to Be Seen in Taylor," *Vassar Miscellany News*, January 16, 1935, 1. See also illustration of Matisse's *Interior with a Violin Case* and

article by Alice Dannenberg, "Three Modern Masters," *Vassar Miscellany News*, January 15, 1936, 1, 2.

77 "Up from the Nickelodeon," editorial, *Vassar Miscellany News*, May 16, 1936, 2; calendar notices for the Museum of Modern Art Film Series in *Vassar Miscellany News*, January 15, 1936, 8; February 12, 1936, 6; March 11, 1936, 6; April 15, 1936, 8; April 29, 1936, 6.

78 John McAndrew, "McAndrew Reviews 2nd Film in Series," *Vassar Miscellany News*, February 10, 1937, 1. See also John McAndrew, "Museum of Modern Art Presents Second Series of Growth of Motion Pictures," *Vassar Miscellany News*, March 4, 1936, 1, 6.

79 Alice Dannenberg, "Posters by Cassandre," *Vassar Miscellany News*, April 4, 1936, 2.

80 Claire Fisk, "Tchelitchew and Berman," *Vassar Miscellany News*, November 12, 1932, 2, 4.

81 Aline Bernstein, "The Taylor Hall Art Gallery, Redecorated, Opens with Two Exhibitions," *Vassar Miscellany News*, October 17, 1934, 1, 6.

82 Aline Bernstein, "Arts and Exhibitions: Photographs by George Platt Lynes," *Vassar Miscellany News*, October 27, 1934, 3, 4.

83 Agnes Rindge, *Eight Modes of Modern Painting: A College Art Association Exhibition* (New York: [College Art] Association, 1934); Aline Bernstein, "Eight Modes of Painting," *Vassar Miscellany News*, December 15, 1934, 2, 4. On Levy's exhibitions of Lynes's photographs and *Eight Modes of Modern Painting* at Vassar, see Ingrid Schaffner and Lisa Jacobs, *Julien Levy* (Cambridge, MA: MIT Press, 1998), 176–77.

84 Barr loaned Russian posters to the Vassar exhibition *Russian Art*, January 10–31, 1934. "Russian Art and Theatre," *Vassar Miscellany News*, January 10, 1934, 1. Rindge and McAndrew loaned works to *Exhibition of Paintings and Drawings by Eugene Berman and Pavel Tchelitchew*, November 6–December 4, 1932. Fisk, "Tchelitchew and Berman," 2, 4. For a Taylor Hall exhibition Rindge loaned from her collection a small oil painting by Georges Rouault of *Pierrot*. "Art Notes," *Vassar Miscellany News*, December 5, 1936, 2. See also *An Exhibition in Memory of Agnes Rindge Claflin, 1900–1977: Professor of Art and Director of the Vassar Art Gallery* (Poughkeepsie, NY: Vassar College Art Gallery, 1978), 22.

85 *Requisitions Account Book, 1936–37* (Art Department, Vassar College).

86 In addition to his lecture in 1932, Hitchcock spoke on "Romantic Gardens" in 1937. Calendar, *Vassar Miscellany News*, May 19, 1937, 8. During Art Week in May 1934, Austin gave a talk on contemporary painting (May 8), Lurçat on contemporary French artists and the School of Paris (May 9), Lescaze on contemporary American architecture (May 9), Warburg on Gaston Lachaise and contemporary sculpture (May 10), and Kirstein on the history of ballet (May 10). "Austin

Discusses Dying Art and Values in Stein," "Week of Brilliant Art Events Stirs College Enthusiasm," and "Kirstein Traces History of Ballet to its Present Form," *Vassar Miscellany News*, May 12, 1934, 1, 4, 6.

87   "Lectures to Elucidate Architecture Exhibit," "Messieurs Austin, Lurçat, and Lescaze Express Opinion on the Relation of Art to Propaganda," and "Good Modern Architecture Rare Says William Lescaze," *Vassar Miscellany News*, May 12, 1934, 1, 3.

88   Alice Dannenberg, "Art Notes," *Vassar Miscellany News*, April 27, 1935, 3, 4.

89   "Making Art a Tradition," *Vassar Miscellany News*, May 12, 1934, 2.

90   See McAndrew statement in "MacCracken and Tonks Discuss Advantages Offered by Planned Additions to Taylor Hall and Library," *Vassar Miscellany News*, December 7, 1935, 1, 3.

91   *Requisitions Account Book, 1934–35* (Art Department, Vassar College).

92   Ground was broken on December 9, 1935. "McAndrew Gets Help as He Drafts Plans," *Vassar Miscellany News*, February 20, 1936, 3; "Planning Van Ingen," *Vassar Alumnae Magazine* 21 (May 15, 1936): 2. McAndrew and Muller's renovated Taylor Hall galleries were demolished to accommodate the construction of new headquarters for Vassar's Art Department in conjunction with the Frances Lehman Loeb Art Center, both designed by Cesar Pelli & Associates (1991–93).

93   Muller received his master of arts degree from Columbia University in 1915. During McAndrew's leave from teaching in the spring term 1936 while he worked on designs for the Art Library and Taylor Art Gallery, he hired Muller to teach Art 370: Domestic Architecture. McAndrew described him as a "draftsman from Ed Stone's office." In 1936 Muller served on the faculty of the Bauhaus-inspired Design Laboratory (name changed to Laboratory School of Industrial Design in 1938) in New York. He specialized in interior design. *Catalogue of Officers and Graduates of Columbia University, 16th edition* (New York: Columbia University, 1916), 1019; John McAndrew to President MacCracken, December 14, 1936 (Henry Noble MacCracken Papers, 1907–1968, Series II. Buildings and Grounds, Folder 18.20, ASC, VCL); Russell Lynes, *Good Old Modern: An Intimate Portrait of the Museum of Modern Art* (New York: Atheneum, 1973), 178; "Design Laboratory, New York," *American Magazine of Art* 29 (February 1936): 117. To assist with McAndrew's Art 370 course, John Coolidge, who was pursuing architectural studies first at Columbia University and then at the Institute of Fine Arts, New York University, was brought to Vassar to give lectures on modern architecture. He returned to Vassar to teach during the academic year 1937–38. "McAndrew Gets Help as He Drafts Plans," 3. On the Design Laboratory, see Shannan Clark, "When Modernism Was Still Radical: The Design Laboratory and the Cultural Politics of Depression-Era America," *American Studies* 50, no. 4 (Fall/Winter 2009): 35–61.

94   The Van Ingen Library kept its name until the retirement of its head librarian, Fanny Borden. "Miss Borden Retires; Head of VC Library Since 1928," *Vassar Miscellany News* 29 (Commencement Issue, 1945): 2.

95   "New Rooms for Old," *Vassar Alumnae Magazine* 21 (February 15, 1936): 6; Aline Bernstein, "Art Notes: New Book Shop Reviewed," *Vassar Miscellany News*, May 1, 1935, 2; "New Terra-Cotta and Blue Co-op Will Contain Furniture by Europe's Best Modern Architects," *Vassar Miscellany News*, April 6, 1935, 1.

96   Bernstein, "New Book Shop Reviewed," 2.

97   Bernstein, "New Book Shop Reviewed," 2.

98   "Opening of New Bookshop Attended by Large Crowd," *Vassar Miscellany News*, May 1, 1935, 1.

99   Askew, "Department of Art at Vassar," 62.

100 Agnes Rindge, "The Art Department in New Quarters," *Vassar Alumnae Magazine* 23 (June 1, 1938): 2–9. See also "Dr. Keppel Will Dedicate Van Ingen October 15th," *Vassar Miscellany News*, October 6, 1937, 1, 3; *Vassar College Art Gallery, 1939* (Poughkeepsie, NY: [The Gallery] 1939).

101 "MacCracken and Tonks Discuss Advantages," 3; Rindge, "Art Department in New Quarters," 3.

102 "Planning Van Ingen," 2.

103 Rindge, "Art Department in New Quarters," 3.

104 "Vassar Dedicates Her New Library," *New York Times*, October 16, 1937, 10.

105 On the program and design development, see [John McAndrew] "Suggestions regarding Progress Prints of January 4, 1935"; "Library Addition," "allocation of rooms" [undated; ca. 1936]; "Suggested Amendments to Process Prints of 12–10–35"; and [Henry Noble MacCracken] to Charles Collens, December 18, 1935 (Henry Noble MacCracken Papers, 1907–1968, Series II. Buildings and Grounds, Folder 18.11, ASC, VCL).

106 Rindge, "Art Department in New Quarters," 4.

107 Morris & O'Connor, "Architecture and the Role of the Avery Memorial"; Henry-Russell Hitchcock Jr., "The Avery Memorial," *Bulletin of the Wadsworth Atheneum* 12, no. 1 (January–March 1934): 6–13; "Modern Museum of Art," *Architectural Forum* 61, no. 1 (July 1934): 37–44.

108 John McAndrew, interview by Jill Silverman, November 4, 1974 (WAAHC).

109 "Growth in Art Meets Praise," *Poughkeepsie Eagle-News*, April 4, 1936, 2.

110 John McAndrew to Dr. [Henry N.] MacCracken, November 13, 1936 (Henry Noble MacCracken Papers,

1907–1968, Series II. Buildings and Grounds, Folder 18.13, ASC, VCL)

111 McAndrew to MacCracken, November 13, 1936. See also Charles Collens to Henry N. MacCracken, October 26, 1936 (Henry Noble MacCracken Papers, 1907–1968, Series II. Buildings and Grounds, Folder 18.13, ASC, VCL).

112 Henry Noble MacCracken to Keene Richards [general manager and consulting engineer], January 12 [1937] (Henry Noble MacCracken Papers, 1907–1968, Series II. Buildings and Grounds, Folder 18.13, ASC, VCL).

113 Rindge, "Art Department in New Quarters," 3–4.

114 Rindge, "Art Department in New Quarters," 4.

115 Lewis Mumford, "The City," in *Civilization in the United States*, ed. Harold E. Stearns (New York: Harcourt, Brace, 1922), 11. Richard Guy Wilson defines the "Machine Age" in his essay "America and the Machine Age," in *The Machine Age, 1918–1941*, ed. Richard Guy Wilson, Dianne H. Pilgrim, and Dickran Tashjian (New York: Brooklyn Museum, 1986), 23–29.

116 It was not until 1946 that the Charles Hayden Memorial Library at MIT by Voorhees, Walker, Foley & Smith was built with an air conditioning system. "University Libraries," *Architectural Record* 100, no. 5 (November 1946): 100, 107.

117 "Modern Museum of Art," 43.

118 McAndrew remembered that "beginning about '33 or '34, for two years I used to go over to Hartford on Friday afternoons. Because I gave a course in the Hartford Art School that [the] Austins had persuaded me to do....And I often used to stay at the Austins' house." McAndrew, interview by Silverman, November 4, 1974 (WAAHC). See also Eugene R. Gaddis, *Magician of the Modern: Chick Austin and the Transformation of the Arts in America* (New York: Alfred A. Knopf, 2000), 176.

119 Rindge reported to President MacCracken, "Mr. McAndrew went to Brooklyn Museum yesterday to see about installation and photographs of their recent remodeling." Agnes Rindge to Mr. [Henry N.] MacCracken, May 12, 1937 (Henry Noble MacCracken Papers, 1907–1968, Series II. Buildings and Grounds, Folder 18.13, ASC, VCL).

120 "Good Modern Architecture Rare Says William Lescaze," 1.

121 "The Wilbour Library, Brooklyn Museum, Brooklyn, New York," *American Architect* 147 (December 1935): 14–15; Christian Hubert and Lindsay Stamm Shapiro, *William Lescaze*, Institute for Architecture and Urban Studies Catalogue 16 (New York: Rizzoli, 1982), 84. McAndrew included the Wilbour Library in his *Guide to Modern Architecture, Northeast States* (New York: Museum of Modern Art, 1940), 59.

122 "Albright Library Sounds Modern Note," *American Magazine of Art* 27, no. 1 (January 1934): 43–44. I thank Nicholas Adams for pointing out the Albright Art Gallery Library's Reference Room as a possible precedent for the Vassar Art Library. McAndrew visited Lescaze's Wilbour Library, which remains the most significant model for the Vassar Art Library. However, it is important to note that he would have known the published source for the Albright Reference Room and also that Rindge gave a lecture at the Albright Art Gallery on April 16, 1934.

123 Rindge, "Art Department in New Quarters," 4.

124 George Herrick, "A Glass-faced Building, New York," *Builder* 153 (August 20, 1937): 314.

125 Rindge, "Art Department in New Quarters," 4.

126 See Structural Glass Corporation advertisement showing Lescaze in profile against the glass-brick wall of his house at 211 East Forty-Eighth Street, New York, in *Architectural Forum* 61, no. 6 (December 1934): [14–15]. See also "House of William Lescaze, New York," *Architectural Forum* 61, no. 6 (December 1934): 389; Lewis Mumford, "The Sky Line," *New Yorker*, September 15, 1934, 101. On Lescaze's town house, see Hubert and Shapiro, *William Lescaze*, 80–83.

127 "Rockefeller Center, New York," *Architectural Glass* (Corning, NY: Architectural Division, Corning Glass Works [1935]), unpaged.

128 "Building for Corning Glass Works, New York City," *Architectural Forum* 67, no. 6 (December 1937): 457–60; Herrick, "A Glass-faced Building, New York," 314–15. On the wide use of glass brick, see Harold Donaldson Eberlein, *Glass in Modern Construction* (New York: Charles Scribner's Sons, 1937).

129 McAndrew was reported to have claimed that Vassar's collection of art prints was "the oldest in any American college, except Bowdoin." "MacCracken and Tonks Discuss Advantages," 3.

130 Nicholas Adams and Bonnie G. Smith, introduction to *History and the Texture of Modern Life: Selected Essays / Lucy Maynard Salmon*, ed. Nicholas Adams and Bonnie G. Smith (Philadelphia: University of Pennsylvania Press, 2001), 9; Nicholas Adams, "Lucy Maynard Salmon: A Lost Parent for Architectural History," *Journal of the Society of Architectural Historians* 55, no. 1 (March 1996): 4.

131 Rindge, "Art Department in New Quarters," 4; *Vassar College Art Gallery, 1939*, 65, 118, fig. 71. Flannagan would be given a solo exhibition at MoMA in 1942. Dorothy C. Miller, ed., *The Sculpture of John B. Flannagan* (New York: Museum of Modern Art, 1942).

132 McAndrew, *Guide to Modern Architecture, Northeast States*, 84.

133 Rindge, "Art Department in New Quarters," 9.

134 "Planning Van Ingen," 2.

135 Rindge, "Art Department in New Quarters," 9.

136 "Dr. Keppel Will Dedicate Van Ingen October 15th," 1; Rindge, "Art Department in New Quarters," 4.

137 Serena Losonczy, associate, Platt Byard Dovell White Architects, email to Nicholas Adams, July 31, 2009.

138 "Dr. Keppel Will Dedicate Van Ingen October 15th," 1.

139 "Dr. Keppel Will Dedicate Van Ingen October 15th," 1, 3.

140 "Dr. Keppel Will Dedicate Van Ingen October 15th," 3.

141 Oral History Interview with Eleanor M. Garvey, February 28–June 13, 1997 (Archives of American Art, Smithsonian Institution).

142 "Dr. Keppel Will Dedicate Van Ingen October 15th," 3. Rindge also described the colors of the Italian Painting Study room as "soft blue and dull terra cotta with white." Rindge, "Art Department in New Quarters," 4.

143 SuperStructures Engineers + Architects, "Summary Findings, Van Ingen Library Finishes, Vassar College, Poughkeepsie, NY/ Super No. 04023R01/75–77" (Vassar College).

144 Compare Sample Number #35 "Outer face of door, Room no. 3" and Sample Number #37 "Column face, Column no. 2, no. 1," "Van Ingen Library Interior Finishes," SuperStructures Engineers + Architects, "Paint Color Identification Report, Van Ingen Library, Vassar College," Project no. 04023R01, March 25, 2008 (Vassar College).

145 Rindge, "Art Department in New Quarters," 4.

146 "Summary Findings," in "Paint Color Identification Report, Van Ingen Library, Vassar College," SuperStructures Engineers + Architects.

147 "Dr. Keppel Will Dedicate Van Ingen October 15th," 3.

148 "Summary Findings," in "Paint Color Identification Report, Van Ingen Library, Vassar College," SuperStructures Engineers + Architects.

149 John McAndrew to Agnes Rindge, June 30, 1934 (Agnes Rindge Claflin Papers, 11.141, ASC, VCL). Several colonial buildings in Puebla, including the polychromed churrigueresque Casa del Alfeñique (1790) by Antonio de Santa María Incháurregui, would be featured in McAndrew's MoMA exhibition *Twenty Centuries of Mexican Art*. See *Twenty Centuries of Mexican Art* (New York: Museum of Modern Art, 1940), 82, fig. 51.

150 Edward R. Burian, "The Architecture of Juan O'Gorman: Dichotomy and Drift," in Edward R. Burian, ed., *Modernity and the Architecture of Mexico* (Austin: University of Texas Press, 1997), 136–38.

151 "McAndrew Will Speak to Arts Association," *Poughkeepsie Eagle-News*, April 8, 1936, 8; "Faculty Notes," *Vassar Miscellany News*, April 11, 1936, 6. Margaret Barr recalls the year (incorrectly) as 1937. Barr, "Our Campaigns," 49. During his visit to Colonial Williamsburg McAndrew might have seen the "colonial" blue walls of the Raleigh Tavern (1769; rebuilt in 1930–31 in conjunction with Colonial Williamsburg) or the salmon-colored living room walls of Sabine Hall in nearby Richmond County, Virginia (1733–42).

152 See Jeffrey L. Meikle, *Twentieth Century Limited: Industrial Design in America, 1925–1939* (Philadelphia: Temple University Press, 1979), 12–13, 15; Kristina Wilson, *Livable Modernism: Interior Decorating and Design during the Great Depression* (New Haven, CT: Yale University Press, 2004), 19, 116–17.

153 See "Alphabets and Architects," *American Architect* 168 (January 1936): 18–19, as cited in Gwendolyn Wright, *USA: Modern Architectures in History* (London: Reaktion, 2008), 116.

154 McAndrew, *Guide to Modern Architecture, Northeast States*, 84.

155 "Dr. Keppel Will Dedicate Van Ingen October 15th," 1, 3.

156 Steven Watson, *Prepare for Saints: Gertrude Stein, Virgil Thomson, and the Mainstreaming of American Modernism* (New York: Random House, 1998), 80, 86; Richard Krautheimer, "'And Gladly Did He Learn and Gladly Teach,'" in *Rome: Tradition, Innovation and Renewal; A Canadian International Art History Conference, 8–13 June 1987* (Victoria, BC: University of Victoria, 1991), 101.

157 In the summer of 1933, a Vassar-affiliated party of ten explored northern Spain in two touring cars. In the town of Oviedo, McAndrew was at the wheel of a Ford, while Russell Lynes drove the second car. As McAndrew descended a steep grade while following a bend in the road, one wheel rolled over the edge, turning the car over and landing it upside down. Rindge's mother, Mrs. Minaus Rindge, fifty-eight years old, was killed. Both McAndrew and Rindge suffered serious contusions. On the accident, see President Henry MacCracken to Leila Barber, August 29, 1933 (Henry Noble MacCracken Papers, 1907–1968, Series III, Faculty, Box 37); Claude S. Bowers, US Ambassador to Spain, to President Henry MacCracken, August 14, 1933 (Henry Noble MacCracken Papers, 1907–1968, Series III, Faculty, Box 39, ASC, VCL); "Mrs. Rindge Killed While Touring Spain," *New York Times*, August 9, 1933, 10; "Vassar Motor Party in Crash," *Poughkeepsie Eagle-News*, August 10, 1933, 1; Pamela Askew, "A History of the Art Department and Art Gallery Vassar College," unpublished manuscript. I wish to thank Susan Donahue Kuretsky, Professor of Art on the

Sarah Gibson Blanding Chair at Vassar, for generously providing me with a copy of this manuscript. I thank the late George P. Lynes II and Elizabeth Hollander for their recollections of the accident, as told to them by their father, J. Russell Lynes, and mother, Mildred Akin ('32) Lynes, both in the travel group. George P. Lynes II, email to the author, April 28, 2014.

158 During McAndrew's trip to Mexico in the summer of 1934, the two colleagues exchanged warm letters. Rindge was recovering from the car accident but feeling better (see previous note), while McAndrew negotiated the streets of Mexican cities with a walking cane. McAndrew to Rindge, June 30, 1934, and John McAndrew to Agnes Rindge, undated [Summer 1934] (Agnes Rindge Claflin Papers, 11.141, ASC,VCL). In a letter to McAndrew during his tenure at MoMA, most likely written in 1938 because it coincided with McAndrew's Aalto exhibition that spring, Rindge signed her letter "Affectionately Agnes." Agnes Rindge to John McAndrew, Easter Eve [April 16, 1938] (Registrar Exhibition Files, Exh. #75. The Museum of Modern Art Archives, New York).

159 Gropius first toured the United States in 1928. "Gropius Praises Efficiency Here," *New York Times*, May 27, 1928, 31. On the early reception of the Bauhaus and Bauhaus pedagogy in the United States, see Milton D. Lowenstein, "Germany's Bauhaus Experiment," *Architecture* 60 (July 1929): 1–6. In addition to the Harvard Society for Contemporary Art's exhibition on the Bauhaus from December 30, 1930 to January 1931, the John Becker Gallery held its Bauhaus exhibition in February 1931 and produced a catalogue on the school. "Adventures of Pioneering Bauhaus," *New York Times*, January 25, 1931, X13.

160 Rindge, "Art Department in New Quarters," 4.

161 Nancy Troy, "The Abstract Environment of De Stijl," in *De Stijl, 1917–1931: Visions of Utopia*, ed. Mildred Friedman (Oxford, UK: Phaidon, 1982), 167, 169.

162 For the color scheme envisioned in van Doesburg and Oud's project for the Potgieterstraat, see Troy, "Abstract Environment of De Stijl," 179, figs. 158, 159.

163 Theo van Doesburg, "Notes on Monumental Art," in *De Stijl, 1917–1931: The Dutch Contribution to Modern Art*, ed. and trans. Hans L. C. Jaffé (Amsterdam: J. M. Meulenhoff, 1956), 103, quoted in Troy, "Abstract Environment of De Stijl," 182.

164 Barry Bergdoll, "Bauhaus Multiplied: Paradoxes of Architecture and Design in and After the Bauhaus," in *Bauhaus, 1919–1933: Workshops for Modernity*, ed. Barry Bergdoll and Leah Dickerman (New York: Museum of Modern Art, 2009), 40–41, 187, cats. 20, 235.

165 Laura M. McGuire, "A Movie House in Space and Time: Frederick Kiesler's Film Arts Guild Cinema, New York, 1929," *Studies in the Decorative Arts* 14, no. 2 (Spring–Summer 2007): 49.

166 See William Rendell Storey, "Picture Theatres Made to Fit Our Day," *New York Times*, June 9, 1929, SM8, 14.

167 Gaddis, *Magician of the Modern*, 173; Helen Searing, "From the Fogg to the Bauhaus: A Museum for the Machine Age," in *Avery Memorial Wadsworth Atheneum*, ed. Eugene R. Gaddis (Hartford, CT: Wadsworth Atheneum, 1984), 21.

168 Gaddis, *Magician of the Modern*, 173.

169 Henry-Russell Hitchcock Jr., "An Office in the Contemporary Style," *Bulletin of the Wadsworth Atheneum* 8, no. 2 (April 1930): 25, 27.

170 Amédée Ozenfant and Charles-Édouard Jeanneret, *Après le cubisme* (Paris: Éditions des Commentaires, 1918); "Le Purisme," *L'Esprit nouveau* 4 (January 1921), translated in *Modern Artists on Art*, ed. and trans. Robert L. Herbert (Englewood Cliffs, NJ: Prentice-Hall, 1964), 71. See also Kenneth E. Silver, *Esprit de Corps: The Art of the Parisian Avant-Garde and the First World War, 1914–1925* (Princeton, NJ: Princeton University Press, 1989), 378.

171 Ozenfant and Jeanneret, "Le Purisme," trans. Herbert, 66.

172 Ozenfant and Jeanneret, "Le Purisme," trans. Herbert, 65.

173 Ozenfant and Jeanneret, "Le Purisme," trans. Herbert, 67.

174 Silver, *Esprit de Corps*, 383–84.

175 In 1920 Le Corbusier (Jeanneret) executed two versions of *Still Life with a Stack of Plates*. In addition to the version at MoMA, a second version, formerly in the collection of Raoul La Roche, is currently in the Kunstmuseum Basel. For an illustration of the latter, see Stanislaus von Moos, *Le Corbusier: Elements of a Synthesis* (Rotterdam: 010 Publishers, 2009; revised and expanded edition), 50, fig. 45.

176 Le Corbusier's model of the Villa Savoye has resided at MoMA since its inclusion in *Modern Architecture: International Exhibition* in 1932. The museum purchased the model in 1941. Barr, *Cubism and Abstract Art*, 164–65, figs. 178, 180.

177 The reference is to Le Corbusier's development of the "five points" (1925–26) and most especially to his "free plan." Barr, *Cubism and Abstract Art*, 166.

178 Von Moos, *Le Corbusier: Elements of a Synthesis*, 269.

179 Barr, *Cubism and Abstract Art*, 166.

180 Jacques Sbriglio, *Le Corbusier: The Villa Savoye* (Basel: Birkhäuser in association with Fondation Le Corbusier, Paris, 2008), 77. Although records of the paint colors of the Villa Savoye are sparse, there is documentation for the use of blue on the walls of the

salon. See bill from the painter Celio, July 10, 1931, FLC 279–284, as cited in Tim Benton, "Villa Savoye and the Architects' Practice," in *Le Corbusier*, ed. H. Allen Brooks (Princeton, NJ: Princeton University Press, 1987), 92. See also Arthur Rüegg, "On Color Restoration of the Villa Savoye," *A & U: Architecture & Urbanism* 3, Special Issue (March 2000): 198–201.

181 Philip Johnson to Louise Johnson, Pentecost, June [8], 1930 (Box 25 Philip Johnson Papers, © J. Paul Getty Trust. Getty Research Institute, Los Angeles [980060]).

182 Hitchcock wrote a vivid description of the Villa Savoye in the catalogue to *Modern Architecture: International Exhibition*. He pointed out the villa's color contrast of "dark green below and cream above with dark chocolate window trim." He also noted how "the pale rose and pale blue emphasize the adjustment of the curved and straight planes." Henry-Russell Hitchcock Jr., "Le Corbusier," in *Modern Architecture: International Exhibition*, 77.

183 John McAndrew, curriculum vitae [1941] (Bio File, John McAndrew Papers, WCA).

184 "Cité de refuge de l'Armée du salut; Le Corbusier et P. Jeanneret, archs," *L'Architecte* 11, new series (August 1934): 81–84, pls. 43–44. For recent color photographs of the interior of the Salvation Army Building, see Kenneth Frampton, *Le Corbusier: Architect of the Century* (New York: Harry N. Abrams, 2002), 5.56, 5.57, 5.59–5.63.

185 Le Corbusier, *Claviers de couleur Salubra* (Basel: Éditions Salubra, 1931).

186 John McAndrew, "Design in Modern Architecture," in *Art Education Today* (New York: Teachers College, Columbia University, 1941), 45.

187 "Rails, Boards and Wire Netting Form Barricades in New Van Ingen Library," *Vassar Miscellany News*, April 17, 1937, 5; Lynes, *Good Old Modern*, 178.

188 Alfred Barr to Le Corbusier, November 27, 1937 (FLC, C1–2, 243; Fondation Le Corbusier, Paris).

189 Lynes, *Good Old Modern*, opp. p. 238.

190 Sigfried Giedion, *Space, Time and Architecture: The Growth of a New Tradition* (Cambridge, MA: Harvard University Press, 1941), 408.

191 Giedion, *Space, Time and Architecture*, 412.

192 "Le Corbusier *Still Life* (1920), Exhibition History," Department of Painting and Sculpture, Museum of Modern Art, New York; "Art Notes," *Vassar Miscellany News*, June 17, 1938, 2. Although *Still Life with a Stack of Plates* was included in the traveling exhibition of Barr's *Cubism and Abstract Art* in 1936 and 1937, the show did not come to Vassar presumably because renovations to Taylor Art Gallery and Van Ingen Library were not yet completed.

193 Ozenfant and Jeanneret, "Le Purisme," trans. Herbert, 70. See Arthur Rüegg's discussion of *Grande gamme* in his essay "Le Corbusier's Polychromie Architecture and His Color Keyboards from 1931 and 1959," in *Polychromie architecturale*, ed. Arthur Rüegg (Basel: Birkhäuser, 1997), 43. See also Barbara Klinkhammer, "After Purism: Le Corbusier and Color," *Preservation Education & Research* 4 (2011): 20–21.

194 Ozenfant and Jeanneret, "Le Purisme," trans. Herbert, 70.

195 Le Corbusier, "Polychromie architecturale" (manuscript written circa 1931 but published for the first time in 1997 in French with translations in English and German), in Rüegg, *Polychromie architecturale*, 95, 101. See also Jan de Heer, *The Architectonic Colour* (Rotterdam: 010 Publishers, 2009), 149.

196 Le Corbusier, "Polychromie architecturale," in Rüegg, *Polychromie architecturale*, 113, 115. As Jan de Heer points out, the concept of architectonic colors derives not only from purism but also from the special relationship between painting and architecture in Charles Blanc's *Grammaire des arts du dessin* (1867), on which Le Corbusier drew. De Heer, *Architectonic Colour*, 149.

197 Le Corbusier, "Polychromie architecturale," in Rüegg, *Polychromie architecturale*, 119.

198 Rüegg, "Le Corbusier's Polychromie architecture and his Color Keyboards," in Rüegg, *Polychromie architecturale*, 24.

199 Le Corbusier, "Polychromie architecturale," in Rüegg, *Polychromie architecturale*, 99.

200 Le Corbusier, "Polychromie architecturale," in Rüegg, *Polychromie architecturale*, 115.

201 Walter Curt Behrendt, *The Victory of the New Building Style*, trans. Harry Francis Mallgrave (Los Angeles: Getty Research Institute, 2000); originally published as *Der Sieg des neuen Baustils* (Stuttgart, Germany: Akademischer Verlag Wedekind, 1927), 129. On the functional capacity of color, Behrendt cites Ewald Dülberg, "Die Farbe als funktionelles Element der Architektur," *Der Neubau* 20 (May 24, 1924): 105–16, 121f.

202 Hitchcock and Johnson, *International Style: Architecture since 1922*, 75.

203 Hitchcock and Johnson, *International Style*, 76.

204 See Mark Wigley's discussion of "surface" in *White Walls, Designer Dresses: The Fashioning of Designer Dresses* (Cambridge, MA: MIT Press, 1995), 349–51.

205 Kazys Varnelis, ed., *The Philip Johnson Tapes: Interviews by Robert A. M. Stern* (New York: Monacelli Press, 2008), 51.

206 See Arnoldo Rivkin, "Synthèse des Arts: Un double paradoxe," in *Le Corbusier, une encyclopédie*, ed. Jacques Lucan (Paris: Centre Georges Pompidou, 1987), 386–91.

207 Wilson, *Livable Modernism*, 16.

208 Rindge, "Art Department in New Quarters," 4.

209 Christopher Wilk, "On Modernism," lecture at Vassar College, September 12, 2009. Wilk (Vassar class of 1976), is Keeper, Furniture, Textiles and Fashion Department at the Victoria and Albert Museum in London. See also No. ST 263 in Gebrüder Thonet, *Catalog no. 53* (New York: Thonet Brothers, 1938), 56.

210 *Gebrüder Thonet Stahlrohrmöbel* (ca. 1934). The Breuer desk B465 is illustrated in Christopher Wilk, *Thonet: 150 Years of Furniture* (Woodbury, NY: Barron's, 1980), 102, fig. 134.

211 Breuer desk No. ST5283 appears in Gebrüder Thonet, *Catalog no. 53* (New York: Thonet Brothers, 1938), 60 (Avery Architectural and Fine Arts Library). "New Rooms for Old," 6. For illustrations of the 1930 Thonet catalogues (*Salon 1930* [tubular steel], 1930, and *Thonet Stahlrohrmobel* [tubular steel], ca. 1930), see Wilk, *Thonet*, 98–99, figs. 127, 128. See also *Modern Chromsteel Furniture by Howell*, manufacturer's catalogue (Geneva, IL.: Howell Company, 1933); Wilson, *Livable Modernism*, 23, 35, 37–40.

212 For a similar postwar table lamp by the General Lighting Corporation, see Mary Roche, "Home: New Design," *New York Times*, June 23, 1946, SM20.

213 For an illustration of the Director's Office, Avery Memorial, Wadsworth Atheneum (1934), see Gaddis, *Magician of the Modern*, 240.

214 "The Wilbour Library, Brooklyn Museum, Brooklyn, New York," 14–15.

215 John McAndrew to Dr. [Henry N.] MacCracken, undated [April 1936] (Henry Noble MacCracken Papers, 1907–1968, Series II. Buildings and Grounds, Folder 18.19, ASC, VCL). Versen designed a series of lighting fixtures for Muschenheim's Solomon R. Guggenheim Foundation, New York (1937). For drawings of the Guggenheim light fixtures (1939), which resemble those of Vassar's Art Library, see Muschenheim Digital Archive, Bentley Historical Library, University of Michigan, AWM01381, accessed April 5, 2014, http://quod.lib.umich.edu/b/bhl2ic ?from-index; med=1;size=20;sort=relevance;start =21;type=boolean;view=thumbnail;rgn1;ic _all;q1=guggenheim.

216 "Alumnae Hold Conference on Teaching Art," *Vassar Miscellany News*, April 8, 1936, 1.

217 Kurt Versen Lamps, Inc., *Contemporary Lighting: Indirect Illumination* (New York: Corporation [1938]), 6; "Contemporary Lighting," Kurt Versen, Inc., November 27, 1936 (Henry Noble MacCracken Papers,

1907–1968, Series II. Buildings and Grounds, Folder 18.19, ASC, VCL).

218 Kurt Versen to Keene Richards, October 2, 1937 (Henry Noble MacCracken Papers, 1907–1968, Series II. Buildings and Grounds, Folder 18.19, ASC, VCL).

219 On the meaning of the term *Sachlichkeit* with its root in *Sache* (fact), see Francesco Passanti, "The Vernacular, Modernism, and Le Corbusier," *Journal of the Society of Architectural Historians* 56, no. 4 (December 1997): 442, 448–449n18, n19.

220 "Exhibition of Abstract Art; Gabo's Work Represented," *Vassar Miscellany News*, May 7, 1938, 1–2; Anne Cleveland, "'Absolute' Art Discussed Here by Naum Gabo," *Vassar Miscellany News*, May 7, 1938, 1, 4.

221 Esther Gordon, "Abstraction Added to V.C. Collection," *Vassar Miscellany News*, December 7, 1938, 1, 4.

222 Holdings in the modern field increased significantly in 1939 with the acquisition of the Dexter Mason Ferry Collection. Agnes Rindge, "Acquisitions of the Vassar College Art Gallery from June 1938 to June 1939," *Vassar Miscellany News*, June 14, 1939, 5, 6.

223 Agnes Rindge, "The Character and Purpose of the Collection," in *Vassar College Art Gallery, 1939*, 25.

224 Rindge, "Art Department in New Quarters," 9.

III. CONSTRUCTING A "NATURALIZED" MODERNISM AT THE MUSEUM OF MODERN ART

CURATORSHIP

When John McAndrew stepped into his new position in July 1937 as curator of Architecture and Industrial Art at the Museum of Modern Art, he pursued his vision of modernism through a more public platform.[1] But the museum's job offer had been completely unexpected. As McAndrew later recalled, he had been invited to give lectures at the Institute of Fine Arts in New York that spring.[2] Unbeknownst to him, it was a chance to be "looked over" by the architect and MoMA trustee Philip L. Goodwin and others at the museum.[3] McAndrew already knew Alfred Barr well, having spent the summer of 1935 in Rome with him and his wife, Margaret (Daisy); they had also traveled together to Williamsburg, Virginia, in the spring of 1936, as discussed in Chapter Two. McAndrew speculated that he might have been brought in as a kind of sounding board for Barr, whose method of "thinking and working," he believed, involved talking to other people.[4] Joining the museum reunited him with a core group of Harvard modernists. His appointment, Russell Lynes later observed, "kept the Sachs-Barr-Abbott-Hitchcock-Johnson line...unbroken."[5] If McAndrew was engaged as Barr's agent, he would not remain in that capacity for long; he soon asserted his persona and framed his own views on modernism as curator and designer. Nonetheless, throughout his tenure at MoMA, he would remain Barr's mentee.

McAndrew's leadership of the Department of Architecture from 1937 to mid-1941 brought stability to a period of shifting curatorships. Since 1930 its exhibitions had been dominated by the curatorial direction of Philip Johnson (and Henry-Russell Hitchcock from outside the institution).[6] Although Johnson had left his position as chairman of the Department of Architecture in late 1934 to pursue the right-wing politics of Huey Long, by the spring of 1935 he had returned home to Ohio, from where he informally directed the Le Corbusier exhibition at MoMA that summer under the curatorship of Ernestine Fantl, who assumed the leadership of the Department of Architecture and Industrial Art as curator the following year.[7] In 1935 and 1936 the department sponsored a number of ambitious exhibitions, most notably one assembled and supervised by Hitchcock on the architecture of Henry Hobson Richardson, accompanied by his monograph on the architect's work.[8] But Fantl's tenure was short lived.[9] By the time McAndrew was on board, Barr was already planning a major Bauhaus exhibition.

McAndrew's arrival also occurred at a critical juncture in the history of the museum. In the fall of 1937 Philip Goodwin and Edward Durell Stone were in the throes of designing a new headquarters on West Fifty-Third Street.[10] Barr, who had wanted a European modernist to design the building and had held out for Ludwig Mies van der Rohe, was not consulted in the final decision.[11] Instead, it was made by Stephen C. Clark, chairman of the Building Committee; Nelson Rockefeller, who was treasurer of the museum; and A. Conger Goodyear, who was the museum's president. Initially, Barr had been a member of the Building Committee, but with Stone's appointment, he resigned.[12] As plans unfolded, Barr regretted his decision.[13] From Barr's perspective, his absence on the committee was an additional reason to hire McAndrew, whose professional training in architecture meant that he could provide "technical supervision of the museum's new building."[14] In effect, McAndrew served as Barr's representative at committee meetings.[15] A former classmate of Stone's at the Harvard School of Architecture, McAndrew shared Stone's conversion from Beaux-Arts theory and design to modernism, and knew his work.[16] The new curator now found himself spending about half of his time on the Building Committee.[17] That role also gave him the opportunity to insert his own design ideas.

The museum employed structural steel and reinforced-concrete floor slabs with an envelope of stainless steel, Georgia marble, plate glass, and glass brick.[18] Its structure and open floor plan allowed for moveable partitions to accommodate changing installations.[19] According to Margaret Barr, McAndrew introduced three innovative design ideas that helped to define the character of the Goodwin-Stone building: the *S*-curve of the entrance marquee with its fin on the Fifty-Third Street side, the lobby, and the "cantilevered canopy of the penthouse terrace" (fig. 3.1).[20] These design elements became the focus of Lewis Mumford's enthusiastic review in the *New Yorker*. Mumford pointed out that the curved marquee offered both a functional and aesthetic introduction to the building because it defined an outside lobby for those waiting to enter the museum and also announced the judicious use of curved forms within its interior.[21] Mumford also endorsed the terrace on the top floor, which let visitors sit outdoors.[22] Its reinforced-concrete canopy featured a row of eleven round skylights, each with a diameter measuring five feet—what *Fortune* called a "Swiss cheese roof," architecture critic Ada Louise Huxtable later described as the "'cheese hole' canopy," and still later Johnson tagged as the "cheese holes."[23] McAndrew may have drawn this playful motif from the cantilevered pergola of André Lurçat's Maison Guggenbühl in Paris (1927).[24] Although originating with Le Corbusier, the motif was also reinterpreted and popularized during the 1930s by many designers, including Alvar Aalto and Jean Prouvé.[25]

The lobby, dominated by an information desk, provided something new. Its sweeping curve offered a welcome gesture. In keeping

Figure 3.2
Philip Goodwin and
Edward Durell Stone.
Library, The Museum
of Modern Art, New
York, 1936–39 (© The
Museum of Modern
Art/Licensed by
SCALA / Art Resource,
NY)

with MoMA's institutional mission to promote modern art, the
desk displayed an impressive collection of exhibition catalogues
whose publication served to enhance the museum's "national and
international reputation."[26] McAndrew also assisted in designing
and furnishing other interior spaces, most notably the museum
library (fig. 3.2).[27] Like Vassar's Art Library, it too was equipped
with a Pittsburgh Corning Glass block wall (now curved), bookcases supplied by the Art Metal Construction Company, oblong
linoleum-topped wood tables, and Mart Stam–designed tubular
steel and wood chairs. Lighting was also similar. Like Vassar's library,
the museum library employed reflector lights (hanging, in this case)
supplied by Kurt Versen, and its Architecture room used Bauhaus-
inspired spherical glass globes.[28] Further, McAndrew collaborated
with Barr on the design of the members' lounge, which featured
Bruno Mathsson wood chairs whose curvilinear forms conveyed their
Scandinavian character but distanced them from the geometrical
rigor of Bauhaus models.[29]

SCULPTURE GARDEN

McAndrew's greatest contribution to the Museum of Modern Art's
new headquarters was the design of its first sculpture garden (1939)
located on the north-facing West Fifty-Fourth Street (fig. 3.3). Barr
assisted with the project and shared the credit, but McAndrew was
the lead designer.[30] McAndrew's garden holds a seminal place in the
history of landscape architecture, although it was later replaced by
five subsequent gardens: in 1942 by Philip Goodwin; in 1953 with the

inauguration of the Abby Aldrich Rockefeller Sculpture Garden by
Philip Johnson; in 1963–64 by Johnson again; in 1982–84 by Cesar
Pelli; and in 2004 by Yoshio Taniguchi. In his 1940 *Guide to Modern
Architecture, Northeast States,* McAndrew described the sculpture garden
as "the only large modern garden in US."[31] More recently, architectural
and landscape historian Mirka Beneš, who has published extensive
studies of the museum's early sculpture gardens, distinguished the
1939 garden as "the first attempt anywhere to build a sculpture garden according to modernist principles of garden and architectural
design."[32] It was to last through McAndrew's tenure at the museum,
to be replaced in 1942 by a restaurant garden designed by Goodwin.[33]
Although McAndrew later submitted proposals for a new west wing
and sculpture garden (ca. 1946–48), they were not executed.

Formed in 1938, the Museum Garden Committee, which
included Barr, McAndrew, and Goodwin, opted for a permanent

garden that would serve the purpose of an "outdoor sculpture gallery."[34] Under the influence of other committee members, notably the trustee Mrs. Stanley Resor and Joseph Hudnut, dean of Harvard's Graduate School of Design, an emphasis was placed on the relationship between sculpture and an enclosed setting.[35] The selection of designers for the project emerged from within the committee. There was no competition. McAndrew's original assignment had been to design a small garden on a narrow strip of land extending 130 feet along the building's north side and seventy-five feet from the rear of the building. But in late April 1939, shortly before the May 10 opening of the museum's new building and its tenth anniversary exhibition, *Art in Our Time*, McAndrew was able to take advantage of a large plot of land along the Fifty-Fourth Street side—now loaned to MoMA by John D. Rockefeller Jr.—on which to build an extensive garden measuring 380 feet long by 100 feet deep.[36] While the sculpture in the garden served the *Art in Our Time* exhibition, the site would serve as a "permanent" garden for the next four years.[37] The 1939 garden achieved two purposes. First, it functioned as a sculpture garden not only for the museum's permanent collection but also for future exhibitions. Second, it provided views from the plate-glass windows of the museum's rear wall, thereby connecting interior and exterior spaces. In his critical review of the building, Mumford noted the rewards of beholding the garden from deep within the museum's interior.[38]

A grand garden design had never been planned, since there was no provision in the budget for one. With limited funds, therefore, the two curators needed to be resourceful about the cost of the project as well as mindful of the speed with which it could realistically be executed. McAndrew recalled, "Alfred and I sat up all one night, and I made a model of the whole garden with steel-wool trees while Alfred placed sculptures where they could be seen best."[39] Museum curator Elizabeth Bauer Mock (Kassler) later remembered that Barr "had everyone including himself make scale reminders of the sculpture he wished to show, then figured how each might best be displayed— whether for a near view or a near-and-far view, and whether against a background or set out free, easy to walk around."[40] The large rectangular space of the resulting garden was partitioned through the use of lightweight walls and fencing of plywood, stripped saplings, woven wood, and corrugated transite (asbestos cement). Some partitions ran perpendicular to the museum building and created static spaces, like those of the Taylor Art Gallery (see fig. 2.31). Other partitions were designed either on a diagonal or as curvilinear free forms, inspired by the artist Hans Arp. Its dynamic spatial flow contrasted not only with the orthogonal character of the museum's rear facade and the Manhattan grid, as Barr later pointed out, but also with the Vassar Art Gallery and Art Library.[41] The plan of the sculpture garden shows how it fanned out from the museum's rear terrace, forming discrete spaces bounded largely by convex and concave screens to the north, east, and west (fig. 3.4). Benches and two plywood pavilions provided

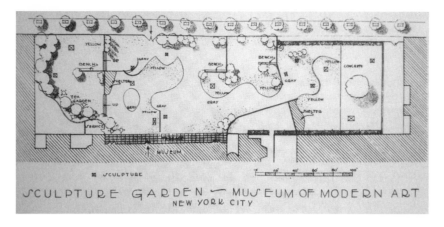

SCULPTURE GARDEN — MUSEUM OF MODERN ART
NEW YORK CITY

shade. Shrubs and trees—especially white birches, gingkoes, pines, and cypresses—helped to mold the space and create a natural setting for sculpture. According to one authoritative account, the ground plane was covered in yellow and gray pebbles laid out in flowing mosaic patterns.[42] Mumford, however, viewed the colored pebbles slightly differently. He described them as ocher and blue, colors that suggested earth tones (with a modernist preference for complementary ones) and aligned the garden palette with that of the Vassar Art Library.[43] McAndrew most likely had looked to the pebble gardens of Mexico, disposed in similar patterns of varying colors, as well as to the monochromatic pebble gardens of Colonial Williamsburg, which he and Barr had recently visited. In arranging the pebbles in organic free forms, McAndrew also drew more generally on garden design of the 1930s.[44]

McAndrew and Barr conceived of the outdoor sculpture gallery as an open plan with partitions, paralleling Barr's earlier determination that the building plan be open. In fact, during its planning phase, the director had supported the nomination of Mies van der Rohe as consulting architect, recognizing that "he has made special studies in installation problems, [and] is a master in flexible space compositions."[45] McAndrew remembered that planning discussions addressed the question of "how to make the frame of a building that could have concrete-slab floors with no beams so that partitions could be moved around."[46] It had been Stone's idea to use flat-slab construction, to "build a loft with columns in which there were no permanent walls."[47] Such "movable interior walls" meant that gallery spaces could be configured in different sizes and shapes.[48] As with the interior partitions, some of the outdoor fences of the sculpture garden would be redesigned over time to display outdoor sculpture in conjunction with future exhibitions, as discussed below.

Beneš astutely points out that McAndrew's plan of the sculpture garden bears a close resemblance to Stone's project for a garden intended for *Outdoor Exhibitions* as part of his design for a competition for a Smithsonian Gallery of Art proposed for the Mall in Washington, DC, on which he was working in the spring of 1939

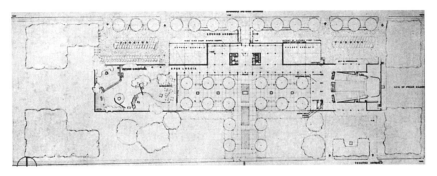

Figure 3.5
Edward Durell
Stone. Project
for an "Outdoor
Exhibitions" garden,
Smithsonian Gallery
of Art competition,
Washington, DC, 1939
("Smithsonian Gallery
of Art Competition,"
Architectural Forum
7, no. 1, July 1939, XVI)

(fig. 3.5).[49] Stone's design captured a third prize in the competition won by the firm of Eliel and Eero Saarinen with Robert Swanson.[50] It responded to the program drawn up by Joseph Hudnut, advisor to the jury, which called for the "exhibition of sculpture" and encouraged "some garden treatment for enclosed or partly enclosed areas."[51] Stone's plan situated sculpture in semi-enclosed spaces of various configurations formed by plantings as well as walls and screens—curved, straight, and diagonal. Although the results of the Smithsonian competition were not made public until June 1939, McAndrew must have known about Stone's Smithsonian plan, even from Stone himself, with whom he was working on the Museum Building Committee.

For MoMA's inaugural installation, about a third of the *Art in Our Time* collection was exhibited in the garden. While most of the sculpture was figurative, some pieces were abstract, by both European and American sculptors.[52] As Barr had prescribed, sculpture was exhibited in its own discrete outdoor setting. Beneš maintains that McAndrew and Barr adopted Miesian notions of "architectural, sculptural, and garden elements...freely arranged in an interconnected, overall composition," and of "free-standing statues playing a spatial or architectural role."[53] To this one must add that McAndrew also drew on what he considered to be Frank Lloyd Wright's foundational and "revolutionary" contributions. These included Wright's conception of interior space, which flowed freely from one room to another and from interior to exterior. As with "organic form," McAndrew would later emphasize, Wright's designs "unfold similarly from within."[54] McAndrew and Barr's larger vision may also have looked to the precedents of such architects as Paul Nelson and landscape architects, notably Christopher Tunnard and Garrett Eckbo, who pioneered the integration of modern sculpture with outdoor gardens during the 1930s.[55]

Aside from the garden's spatial conceptualizations and placement of sculpture in the open air, which drew upon the visions of other modernists, its use of ordinary everyday materials suggested a new direction. On the one hand, low-cost materials were dictated by necessity. On the other hand, the saplings, woven-wood fencing, and plywood sheds that McAndrew and Barr called for were materials of choice. Thus McAndrew and Barr's vision represents a hybrid view of modernism, with a spatial sophistication derived largely from Wright

Figure 3.6
John McAndrew. West
Wing and Sculpture
Garden, east eleva-
tion, The Museum of
Modern Art, New York.
Blueprint with colored
chalks, ca. 1946–48
(The Museum of
Modern Art Archives,
New York. © The
Museum of Modern
Art/Licensed by
SCALA / Art Resource,
NY Photograph
Courtesy Mirka Beneš)

and Mies and a reliance on both organic free forms and standardized techniques that used locally sourced vernacular materials. Defined by transnational design, the sculpture garden, like the Vassar interiors, fused European and American ideas through McAndrew's concept of "naturalization," or an Americanized modernism, discussed below.

McAndrew proposed designs for a new west wing and sculpture garden (ca. 1946–48), including north and east elevations as well as a plan and two section drawings in colored chalk on blueprint, after he had left his post as curator, settled in Mexico where he spent the war years, and returned north to take a teaching position at Wellesley College in 1946 (see Epilogue) (fig. 3.6). The drawings were submitted to the museum after Johnson had resumed his directorship of the Department of Architecture (in 1946), presumably during a period of detente between the two curators, but the project was never built. The designs for the building and garden drew inspiration from Latin America, giving rise to the idea that they would feel at home in one of its metropolitan centers, as Beneš has proposed.[56] Moreover, the draw-ings suggest that the structure of the building would be reinforced concrete. Its facade, dominated by a grid of brise-soleils, indicates that McAndrew followed Le Corbusier's example, not just his collaborative work with Lúcio Costa on the Ministry of Education and Health in Rio de Janeiro (1936–43) but more specifically his Unité d'habitation in Marseille (1945–53) at the moment that it was being constructed and published.[57] McAndrew's use of patterned walls on the north and east facades, as well as his inclusion of a totem pole in the garden, sug-gest a new Pan-Americanism. Clearly, he was drawing at once on the latest structural developments as well as on the art and architecture of the Americas, both modern and ancient. Thus, he may have looked to such Latin American precedents as Roberto Burle Marx's roof garden for the Ministry of Education in Rio and Luis Barragán's El Pedregal Gardens in Mexico City (begun in 1945), which he admired, as well as to the textured wall decoration, both molded and carved, of Mayan and other pre-Columbian architecture.[58]

During his four years as curator, McAndrew was instrumental in defining MoMA's institutional mission for architecture, as he had earlier defined the discipline and practice of architecture at Vassar.[59] His tenure at the museum would represent the most productive curatorship during the interregnum between Philip Johnson's two periods as director of the Department of Architecture: 1930–34 and 1946–54. As curator, McAndrew produced an astonishing run of thirteen exhibitions and eight circulating exhibitions, matched only by Barr's own record.[60] These ranged from the ambitious to the modest. He also helped to produce the film *The Evolution of the Skyscraper* (1939) and edited the landmark *Guide to Modern Architecture, Northeast States* (1940).

When McAndrew assumed his position, Barr and his museum colleagues had already defined a major task for painting and sculpture. The Museum of Modern Art was not merely an importer of avant-garde theory and design but a mediator between European and American theory and practice. Although initially Eurocentric, Barr's vision of modernism evolved to become purposely open-ended, pluralistic, and concerned with an all-embracing view that mined its intellectual and formal roots.[61] Barr's construction of modernism was formalist at the same time that it embraced cultural perspectives and the contemporaneity of modern forms from "high" to "low." Barr and his colleagues were also concerned that the museum be responsive to the broadest public constituency in a time of economic uncertainty during the Great Depression. Thus, working against the dominance of European modernism and its attending internationalism, a wide range of vernacular expression entered the discourse on modernism at the museum. Foremost was the need for cultural authenticity. Toward that objective Barr organized a number of early exhibitions devoted to the sources of European modernism, including postimpressionism (*Cézanne, Seurat, Gauguin, van Gogh*, 1929). Together with his assistant, Dorothy Miller, a specialist in American art, they interrogated the sources of American modernism in a number of exhibitions. Barr addressed multiculturalism and the Americas in group shows and in the work of Diego Rivera (1931). The museum promoted vernacular expression in folk art, especially after Holger Cahill was brought in to curate several North American exhibitions, including *American Folk Art: The Art of the Common Man in America, 1750–1900* (1932).[62] The origins of modernism in North America could also be found in indigenous traditions and ethnography, and to that end Cahill curated an exhibition of Aztec, Mayan, and Incan art called *American Sources of Modern Art* (1933).[63] Everyday forms of art, by virtue of film, photography, and industrial arts, had the capacity to evoke regional and national expression as well as local culture.[64] They also served as effective vehicles for tapping the public consciousness.

Barr viewed the mid-1930s as a watershed moment in abstract art. In his catalogue for the 1936 exhibition *Cubism and Abstract Art*, he identified the emergence of two streams of abstract art: one was "intellectual, structural, architectonic, geometrical, rectilinear, and classical in its austerity and dependence upon logic and calculation," while the other was "intuitive and emotional rather than intellectual; organic or biomorphic rather than geometrical in its forms; curvilinear rather than rectilinear, decorative rather than structural."[65] In contrast with the geometrical and mechanical current, organic forms such as those found in the work of Hans Arp and Joan Miró were "definitely in the ascendant," according to Barr.[66] He even considered the later work of Wassily Kandinsky "generally biomorphic."[67] The show included architecture, especially works by Le Corbusier, Berthold Lubetkin, and others, either to help reinforce the new tendencies in painting or to suggest parallel developments.[68]

Before 1937 the museum's quest for cultural authenticity in modern architecture engaged the vernacular largely through its recognition of a wide range of sources for American architects, engineers, and builders. For example, in its *Modern Architecture: International Exhibition* of 1932, Barr had identified Wright as a "pioneer ancestor."[69] Hitchcock and Johnson were influenced by Mumford's *The Brown Decades* (1931) and also *Sticks and Stones* (1924), the book on American architecture that related buildings to their respective urban or rural landscapes and signaled the importance of regional distinctions; as such, the two curators viewed the work of Chicago architects William Le Baron Jenney, Louis Sullivan, H. H. Richardson, Wright, and Burnham & Root as antecedents to the International Style. On another tack, these museum curators were also aware that European modernists, most notably Walter Gropius and Le Corbusier, had drawn on the example of American utilitarian and vernacular buildings as both sources for and exemplars of modern architecture.[70] Barr had even paid homage to the American industrial vernacular tradition in his review of the Necco candy factory in Cambridge, Massachusetts (1927), following its earlier publication in *Hound & Horn* (see Chapter One).[71] Further, Hitchcock drew parallels between the formal language of the International Style and that of American vernacular architecture a century before in an exhibition at Wesleyan University in 1934. Had McAndrew not seen Hitchcock's show, he certainly knew its brochure.[72]

When McAndrew joined the museum in 1937, he was initially predisposed to elucidate modernism through the lens of the International Style because he believed that its core principles had been Barr's and also because by then it had become a generic term. His arrival coincided with the closing months of the first traveling version of *Modern Architecture: International Exhibition*. While McAndrew continued to invest in International Style principles (see Chapter Two), he also dedicated himself to synthesizing them with other influences, thereby enriching an evolving modernism. Crafting his own agenda by broadening and refining MoMA's objectives, McAndrew curated exhibitions that advanced by turns six themes: First was a commitment to vernacular expression that embraced organic forms and materials, especially evident in the work of Frank Lloyd Wright in America, Le Corbusier in Europe, and Alvar Aalto and Marcel Breuer on both sides of the Atlantic.[73] Second was a critical position reconciling the formalism advanced by Barr, Hitchcock, and Johnson with the sociocultural and regionalist convictions held by Mumford. A third theme centered on the belief that architects were transforming the International Style through a process of naturalization, which resulted in a transatlantic synthesis of received ideas from Europe and American practice. Next was the significance of utilitarian buildings and the contributions of engineers. Fifth was a commitment to promoting the ethics of public housing and of the architect's social responsibility. Sixth was an acute awareness of the Americas and with it an exploration of Latin American expression and especially the native character, or "Mexicanness," of Mexican art.

McAndrew's vision of modernism can be understood in all its complexity by examining his MoMA exhibitions through the prism of these various themes. The work of "pioneer" Frank Lloyd Wright was the subject of two shows, marking the alpha and omega of McAndrew's exhibition record. The first, which was entirely devoted to Wright's Fallingwater, Bear Run, Pennsylvania (1934–37), signified to McAndrew that the architect had been "brought back to life" after a dormant period.[74] Although a Wright retrospective had been envisioned for the fall of 1936, it was subsequently postponed to 1939 and still later to 1940.[75] Once McAndrew joined the museum, he came up with the idea to mount a small exhibition devoted to Fallingwater. He then wrote to the owner Edgar Kaufmann Sr. requesting to visit the new house and received an invitation from Mrs. Kaufmann to join them in November 1937, when the house was being photographed by Hedrich-Blessing for a special issue of *Architectural Forum* (January 1938) devoted to Wright's work. McAndrew later recounted that he first knew of the house through Charles Allen Bernstein, a set designer in New York, whose sister Aline Bernstein Louchheim (later Saarinen) had been McAndrew's former student at Vassar.[76] The Bernsteins were related by marriage to the Kaufmann family. Upon meeting the young curator, Kaufmann sought Wright's endorsement for the Fallingwater show, telegraphing him that "McAndrew wants future exhibits and seems sincere."[77] Aside from his own inclination to promote Wright's work, McAndrew intended for the proposed show to help carry out Barr and Cahill's strategy to unearth the roots of modernism, as previously seen, in the work of its pathfinders extending back to the 1880s in Europe and the United States. At a time when Barr and McAndrew were preparing a Bauhaus exhibition, that strategy intersected with a directive from Nelson Rockefeller urging Hitchcock to support more American-born architects, as opposed to German modernists, and the institution's embarrassment over Philip Johnson's sympathy with Nazi activity in 1936 and 1937.[78] McAndrew, who welcomed more American subjects, had found an opportunity.

The monographic exhibition *A New House by Frank Lloyd Wright on Bear Run, Pennsylvania* opened on January 25, 1938. It was the first

A NEW HOUSE BY FRANK LLOYD WRIGHT

ON BEAR RUN
PENNSYLVANIA

THE MUSEUM OF MODERN ART · NEW YORK · 1938

Museum of Modern Art exhibition devoted to one building designed by a living architect. Although the show's catalogue presented twenty photographs and plans drawn from the *Architectural Forum* publication, it contained no critical essays by McAndrew and others, as originally intended (fig. 3.7).[79] Rather, it merely presented a brief explanatory text by Wright.[80] As architectural historian Neil Levine has suggested, the unprecedented character of Fallingwater prompted Wright to defend his work against alleged European influence; Wright offered the disclaimer, "The ideas involved here are in no wise changed from those of early work. The materials and methods of construction come through them here."[81] The house, which was cantilevered over a mountain stream, proved a dramatic example of what Wright continued to call "organic architecture," and it addressed facets of vernacular and regional engagement.[82] The museum's press release for the exhibition, most likely written by McAndrew, emphasized Wright's "genius for harmonizing the building with its natural setting" in which stone and bedrock from the site counterbalanced its cantilevered concrete terraces.[83] The show was immensely successful. Mumford was among its enthusiastic supporters, drawing attention in his *New Yorker* review not only to the house's stone construction "laid in irregular horizontal blocks…rugged and strong" but also to its infrastructural character, whereby Wright handled "great reinforced-concrete monolithic slabs…as cleanly as if he were building a dam for a hydroelectric works."[84] McAndrew's Fallingwater exhibition was largely responsible for launching Wright's second career.

By the late 1930s the formalism of International Style thinking and the creative vision of its protagonists in America were being challenged. Mumford had long objected to architecture based on "style."[85] Now Hitchcock, one of the movement's founders, would urge American architects to accept the precepts of the International Style even as he questioned their ability to achieve a level of "coherent modern expression" as had their European counterparts.[86] McAndrew sought a new destiny for contemporary architecture as a result of the distance it had traveled from orthodox International Style principles. It was a North American position, one that could account for the character of European as well as American architecture. He regarded the work of Alvar Aalto and his new generation in the 1930s as having evolved beyond the work of Gropius, Mies, J. J. P. Oud, and Le Corbusier in the 1920s. Although Aalto still retained the functional mandate and aesthetic principles of the older masters, McAndrew maintained that his architecture and furniture were informed by both his "personal sensibility" and the "national character" of his native Finland.[87]

McAndrew claimed that he initiated MoMA's solo exhibition of Aalto's architecture and furniture in the United States when he saw an Aalto chair illustrated in an issue of *L'Architecture d'Aujourd'hui*. From there he ordered Aalto furniture for the Goodwin-Stone building. McAndrew later recalled that Aalto was "one of the things that I had to push at the Museum."[88] Of course, the MoMA circle knew of Aalto's Finnish Pavilion at the 1937 Exposition Internationale des Arts et Techniques in Paris, Henry-Russell Hitchcock having given it a "first rank" standing in *Architectural Forum*.[89] *Alvar Aalto: Architecture and Furniture* (1938) introduced the American public to this new direction in European architecture. Only once before—in the case of Le Corbusier in 1935—had MoMA devoted its galleries to the major works of a single architect. The Aalto exhibition brought together a number of the architect's key buildings, including the Viipuri Library in Viipuri, Finland (now Vyborg, Russia; 1927–35), and the Finnish Pavilion, shown in photographs, air views, drawings, and models. In an effort to offset the severity and geometrical abstraction of the library's white prismatic forms, McAndrew emphasized the lecture hall's curved acoustic ceiling fabricated from Karelian pine.[90] Once rejected for their non-modern character, organic materials and curvilinear forms (as with Arp's painting) appeared in Aalto's work. To McAndrew, they embodied not only the architect's inventiveness but also a regional response.

McAndrew's exhibition featured Aalto's ergonomically designed bentwood chairs, their free forms sympathetically displayed on low-rise rounded platforms and skied on the wall to emphasize their profiles and laminated wood construction made possible by low-cost methods of mass production (fig. 3.8).[91] Aalto chairs even encouraged "relaxing," represented by a photo montage of a reclined woman hovering above her chaise longue, which was featured in both the show's press release and catalogue (fig. 3.9).[92] McAndrew called attention to

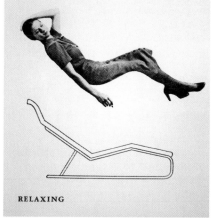

RELAXING

the fact that Aalto's furniture was inexpensive and thus more accessible to the consumer.[93] This observation, no less than the exhibition itself, encouraged Alvar and Aino Aalto to install their Artek store on Madison Avenue in the summer of 1940.[94] Like the curator, Mumford appreciated Aalto's liberation from rectangular forms through his use of curves, which he considered an expression of human need. Mumford also endorsed Aalto's application of functional design in response to different typologies. When Mumford claimed that "a modern material is any material one uses in a modern way" and affirmed that wood is represented in the architectural traditions of both Finland and the United States, he validated Aalto's modernism with its vernacular and regional affinities.[95]

McAndrew's full-throated curatorial voice and transatlantic modernist vision emerged in the MoMA exhibition *Trois siècles d'art aux États-Unis* (Three Centuries of Art in the United States) held at the Musée du Jeu de Paume in Paris in 1938, for which he served as curator of the Architecture section. The exhibition was sponsored by the French government and served as a firsthand introduction to North American art, architecture, and culture. In crafting the Architecture section McAndrew was assisted by two Vassar graduates who had recently joined his staff: Elizabeth Bauer Mock (see Chapter Two), who accompanied McAndrew to Paris to assist with the installation, and Janet Henrich, class of 1935.[96] The show was divided into four parts. First there was a chronological development of American architecture from the early European settlements through the neoclassical period, "arranged" by Mock.[97] Infrastructure as well as commercial and utilitarian building, including the evolution of the skyscraper, formed a second part (fig. 3.10). The curator viewed the third section through the lens of Mumford's Richardson-Sullivan-Wright lineage, much as he deployed it in *The Brown Decades*.[98] The last part presented a range of contemporary building, "arranged" by Henrich.[99]

Although McAndrew collaborated with his assistants on the design of the show, he was responsible for the conceptual framework of the exhibition and wrote the catalogue essay, "Architecture in the

Figure 3.10
Installation view of the
Architecture section,
*Three Centuries of
American Art*, Musée
du Jeu de Paume,
Paris, 1938; organized
by the Museum of
Modern Art, New York.
Gelatin-silver print,
4 1/2 x 7" (11.4 x 17.7
cm). (Photographic
Archive. The Museum
of Modern Art
Archives, New York.
© The Museum of
Modern Art/Licensed
by SCALA / Art
Resource, NY)

United States." There he suggested a dichotomy between European derivations in American architecture (from the early settlements to the twentieth century) and everyday vernacular building that expressed "a robust local style," especially "in the centers most isolated from Europe."[100] McAndrew and Mock represented the polemic in the installation. The visitor first experienced a sweeping chronological development of American architecture "showing a close relation to Europe" and then encountered a doorway labeled "but," which led to images of vernacular buildings such as Pennsylvania stone barns and New England farmhouses.[101] In his catalogue essay McAndrew further elucidated his position on contemporary buildings, maintaining that "European doctrines are being translated into American terms." He called this practice "naturalization." Just as other countries had borrowed forms and "naturalized" them, so the United States had localized foreign ones.[102]

The following year McAndrew, with the assistance of Mock and Henrich, restaged the Architecture section of *Trois siècles* for a New York exhibition called *Three Centuries of American Architecture*, held in MoMA's temporary quarters in the concourse of the Time-Life Building at Rockefeller Center.[103] To accompany that show he published a revised version of his *Trois siècles* catalogue essay, also called "Architecture in the United States," in which he presented a more nuanced view of his ideas.[104] He still held that vernacular expression had suffused the long history of American building as well as diverse streams of American modernism, their sources, and resulting trans-atlantic fusion. His critical position mediated between the formalism of Barr, Hitchcock, and Johnson and the sociocultural persuasion of Mumford, laid out in both *Sticks and Stones*—the book that had influenced McAndrew in architecture school—and *The Brown Decades*.[105] McAndrew's two essays elucidated his position on the naturalization, or Americanization, of forms. He argued that this process had long preceded the arrival of European modernism. He pointed to local conditions, including climate and materials (for example, wood in heavily forested North America); to forms derived from local practice, such as those that had inspired such ingenious cabinetmaker architects as Samuel McIntire; and to the grafting of verandas onto Virginia planters' houses, whose basic designs derived from British builders' manuals.[106] "Naturalizations" were also the result of cultural conditions, such as neoclassical temple fronts to symbolize the new American democracy.[107]

Together, both essays suggested four forms of vernacular expression, which intersected with the themes embodied in McAndrew's curatorial objectives. The first sought antecedents for modern architecture in America. Early on, Frank Lloyd Wright's work and ideas had been absorbed by Mies and other European architects.[108] Now McAndrew would instrumentalize Mumford's construction of the Richardson-Sullivan-Wright trilogy and carry both its organic tradition and Wright's formative role in the modern movement to the heart of the museum's project. Mumford himself applauded McAndrew's efforts to endorse that lineage, especially the "continuity between H. H. Richardson and Sullivan," which, like the American vernacular tradition, he emphasized, "gives depth and continuity" to the efforts of contemporary architects.[109] McAndrew understood how Barr, Hitchcock, and Johnson had designated Chicago architects of the 1880s and 1890s as ancestors to International Style practitioners, as previously discussed. He also appreciated how European modernists, especially Gropius and Le Corbusier, were among the first modernists to draw on American precedents. From the time of his studies in architecture school, McAndrew had absorbed Le Corbusier's appropriated images of American technology, including the grain elevators, daylight factories, and skyscrapers illustrated in *Vers une architecture*.[110]

The cultural authenticity of American utilitarian buildings embodied a second form of vernacular expression, in effect a technological vernacular. Late nineteenth-century commercial architecture in Chicago and examples of American infrastructure were prominently displayed in the MoMA exhibitions in both Paris and New York. To McAndrew such works expressed their function and structure with "unconscious candor" and "technical efficiency."[111] His task was to reestablish their significance, long recognized in Europe, as native contributions to American modernism.

The third form of vernacular expression in McAndrew's essays, which was related to the previous two, assumed a critical role in the naturalization of "European doctrines."[112] This Americanization implied an acculturation between received European ideas and long-standing local building traditions, which often favored organic materials. That process led to an American modernism and frequently to a regional modernism. If French, Spanish, and English architects as well as Mexican craftsmen had adapted imported styles, "naturalized" them to their respective locales, and synthesized them with indigenous forms, he suggested, so could North American architects.

During the 1930s, practitioners in the United States were divided in their objectives. Some, such as Goodwin and Stone, pursued the aesthetic formalism of the International Style for the new Museum of Modern Art building. The legacy of International Style design, McAndrew understood, could be most fully realized in North America by virtue of its technological superiority, as in the case of the new building whose glass walls were made viable through reliable US-manufactured heating and air-conditioning systems.[113] By contrast, other contemporary architects sought to Americanize and also regionalize modernism through an engagement with topography, climate, views, and access to sunlight, vernacular building traditions, and organic materials. McAndrew appreciated how "local materials and conditions had already fostered *regional* developments of genuinely modern building."[114] Such practitioners as Walter Gropius and Harwell Hamilton Harris were designing houses with stud-frame construction and clapboard sheathing reminiscent of American vernacular architecture in New England and California, respectively. Regional expression precipitated adjustments to climate and views, which appeared in Richard Neutra's California houses.[115]

In one sense, McAndrew's call for naturalization and Americanization attempted to reconcile European and American modernism. Imported European design had already drawn on the lessons of Wright's work and ideas. In 1932 Mumford took the position that "Europeans have moved nearer to Wright" and "have acquired some of Wright's love for natural materials, his interest in the site and the landscape, and his feeling for the region."[116] Europeans had also looked to American utilitarian building, infrastructure, and technique, as well as to Chicago buildings of the 1880s and 1890s and to the skyscraper as an American typology, whose local character for the most part had remained authentic. The repatriation of Wright (from Europeans), defining him as a native son, was a key objective of both Mumford and McAndrew. Moreover, the reappropriation of American building types and techniques as well as an attention to regional identity, which was invested in local practice and environment, also shaped McAndrew's transatlantic synthesis.[117] In another sense, this Americanizing tendency reflected the broader currents of regionalism in the arts and American culture, as well as the nationalism associated with Franklin D. Roosevelt's political agenda during the 1930s.

McAndrew identified a fourth stream of the vernacular that emerged in American housing, made possible by techniques of mass production and standardization, especially prefabricated building

Figure 3.11
A. Lawrence Kocher.
Plywood House, 1938.
*Town of Tomorrow
Exhibition*, New York
World's Fair, 1939
(*Architectural Forum*
71, no. 1, July 1939, 65)

components. Less efficient than the manufacture of American auto-mobiles, however, most factory-made shelter could not keep pace.[118] Nonetheless, the curator endorsed housing when industrially pro-duced components resulted in low-cost construction. For his Plywood House (1938) in the *Town of Tomorrow* exhibition at the New York World's Fair in 1939, A. Lawrence Kocher employed a plywood frame and surface along with flat roofs and strip windows (fig. 3.11).[119] Through the use of plywood and other forms of prefabrication, on the one hand, and the production of housing by the Public Works Administration (PWA), on the other, McAndrew maintained that con-struction costs could be managed to meet future needs.[120]

The French historian and critic Edmond Pauty appreciated McAndrew's insightful analysis of vernacular traditions but was critical of most modern American architecture, which he felt derived from European models. However, Pauty did find originality in "two distinct categories of indigenous productions": first, large wood constructions of a spreading horizontality, evident in the work of Frank Lloyd Wright; and second, utilitarian construction with a thrust toward verticality, ever present in the American skyscraper.[121] Yet the lack of a major Wright disciple, he held, meant that the path for-ward for American modernism in 1938 was dominated by European émigrés, notably Richard Neutra, William Lescaze, Walter Gropius, and Marcel Breuer. In the end, Pauty faulted (and misrepresented) McAndrew's concept of naturalization, concluding that modern American architecture was less original than either its own utilitarian construction or European modernism.[122] But on the eve of World War II there was a more important concern. Pauty endorsed McAndrew's view that the critical focus should not be "construction, function, esthetics nor naturalization of an imported style" but "the humanitar-ian and social problem" to provide better housing.[123]

Throughout McAndrew's first sixteen months at the museum, and while he was simultaneously working on other shows, he was deeply involved in the exhibition *Bauhaus: 1919–1928*, which was

Figure 3.12
Installation view of
Bauhaus: 1919–1928,
The Museum of
Modern Art, New
York, 1938–39
(Photographic
Archive. The Museum
of Modern Art
Archives, New York.
Photographer: Soichi
Sunami © The Museum
of Modern Art/
Licensed by SCALA /
Art Resource, NY)

initiated by Barr, who had visited the German design school in 1927. Of course, McAndrew and Johnson were also Bauhaus enthusiasts, having gone there together in 1929 and Johnson again on subsequent trips. Since the summer of 1937, Barr had relied on McAndrew's assistance with the show, although it was organized by both Gropius, the school's founding director, and Herbert Bayer, a former Bauhaus teacher. Opening in December 1938, the Bauhaus show was well timed (fig. 3.12). The school had been closed by the Nazi regime in 1933. Gropius and Bayer had recently immigrated to the United States. Since the spring of 1937 Gropius served as professor of architecture at Harvard University, where he transformed its architectural education through an infusion of Bauhaus pedagogy.[124] In the fall of 1937 László Moholy-Nagy founded the New Bauhaus in Chicago.[125] On November 9 McAndrew attended the school's dedication in conjunction with a lecture by Gropius titled "Education Toward Creative Design." On the streets of Chicago the curator joined Walter and Ise Gropius in search of buildings by Louis Sullivan and other proto-modernists, which Gropius had not appreciated on his first trip to Chicago in 1928 (fig. 3.13).[126] In the fall of 1938 Mies settled in Chicago, where he was appointed professor at the Armour Institute of Technology (now Illinois Institute of Technology) and reshaped the curriculum.[127] To distinguish their exhibition, Gropius and Bayer emphasized the school's Dessau period before their departure in 1928.[128] McAndrew helped them arrange the show, that assignment complementing his service as trustee of the Bauhaus-influenced Laboratory School of Industrial Design (formerly Design Laboratory), where Theodore Muller was a member of the faculty (see Chapter Two).[129]

The organizers of *Bauhaus: 1919–1928* sought to convey the curricular structure of the school and the character of its design

by devoting sections of the installation to the preliminary courses
of Johannes Itten, Josef Albers, and László Moholy-Nagy as well
as the painting courses of Paul Klee and Wassily Kandinsky, along
with their color experiments. The organizers also staged displays of
Bauhaus furniture, pottery, and weaving workshops as well as its
photography, painting, and architecture. If the organizers intended
for the show to be didactic, they also hoped that it would brand
Bauhaus products for American consumers. The *New York Times* welcomed this exhibition of "Nazi-banned art," a reference to both the

closing of the Dessau school and the 1937 *Degenerate Art Exhibition* in Munich.[130] Lewis Mumford was impressed with the show and hoped that the Bauhaus émigrés would be influential in recreating in North America the school's spirit with its "combination of imagination and logic."[131] However, many reviews were unfavorable. The industrial and product designer Jacques Levy, a member of the Laboratory School faculty, saw no evidence that the Bauhaus products on display demonstrated "a true exploitation of new materials" and "design possibilities inherent in mass production methods."[132] Moreover, another critic faulted the Bauhaus for producing "modernistic chairs," and another for its "streamlined fixtures…in banks and offices" and for providing "a major source of streamlined vision."[133] In doing so, these critics mistook Bauhaus production for design emanating from both the 1925 Paris Exposition Internationale des Arts Décoratifs et Industriels Modernes and the 1933 Chicago World's Fair, A Century of Progress. Barr took the criticism to heart, judging *Bauhaus: 1919–1928* a disaster and enlisting McAndrew's help to mount a defense of the 1938 show in the *Bulletin of the Museum of Modern Art*.[134] In his essay "'Modernistic' and 'Streamlined,'" McAndrew countered the criticism with orthodox Bauhaus philosophy: form determined by use, material, and process of manufacture. "Modernistic," he asserted, was a superficial term and a "sloppy substitute for modern." "Streamlined vision" and "streamlining," he further held, were associated with objects designed to "move efficiently at high speed" and had "almost nothing" to do with the Bauhaus. Rather, Bauhaus design, he concluded, was "free of both modernistic and streamlined aberrations."[135] In his foreword to *A Design Student's Guide to the New York World's Fair*, compiled by the Laboratory School of Industrial Design, McAndrew cautioned visitors to the 1939 fair. Much that they were about to see, he advised, was not modern but, like the 1925 Paris fair and the 1933 Chicago fair, "modernistic (zig-zags, rays, etc. Compare with your nearest Shoe Shoppe)." By contrast, "honest modern design," he pointed out, was "free of mannerisms" and reflected Bauhaus principles, which informed the Laboratory School curriculum.[136]

In two subsequent exhibitions McAndrew applied Bauhaus thinking to everyday American consumer goods: *Useful Household Objects under $5.00* (September 28–October 28, 1938) and *Useful Objects of American Design Under $10* (December 7, 1939–January 7, 1940). The idea for the *Useful Objects* shows had come from Barr. For a course at Wellesley College Barr had assigned a competition for a "Still Life," in which each student was to make an arrangement using local five-and-dime store products made from modern materials.[137] At MoMA Johnson first drew upon Barr's theme for two design shows: *Objects: 1900 and Today* (1933) and *Machine Art* (1934).[138] While industrial art played only a minor role in *Objects: 1900 and Today*, it occupied a central position in *Machine Art*. However, Johnson's principal concerns were still aesthetic. "The Exhibition," Johnson explained in the *Machine Art* catalogue, "contains machines, machine parts, scientific

instruments, and objects useful in ordinary life. There are no purely ornamental objects; the useful objects were, however, chosen for their aesthetic quality."[139] By contrast, McAndrew's two *Useful Objects* exhibitions reconciled utility with beauty. Both functional and well crafted, they embodied Bauhaus theory and design. Furthermore, unlike the products shown in the Bauhaus exhibition, those in the two *Useful Objects* shows employed methods of mass production and featured new materials. The first displayed "household articles of good modern design," available to middle-class consumers at retail shops **(fig. 3.14)**.[140] To carry out his plans McAndrew received the help of his friend Edgar Kaufmann Jr., whose family owned Kaufmann's Department Store in Pittsburgh and who had an exceptional knowledge of the trade and its customers.[141] By exhibiting industrially designed kitchen utensils and coat hangers obtained from five-and-dime stores along with Aalto stools and ceramics from department stores, McAndrew emphasized that these well-designed objects could be appreciated not only for their low cost and utilitarian use but also for their aesthetic character.[142] Making the added point that functional design could be sympathetic to both organic and abstract forms, McAndrew frequently chose objects and display tables that were curvilinear. Destined as traveling exhibitions, both *Useful Objects* shows relied on simplicity of display. However, *Useful Objects of American Design Under $10* deployed specially designed collapsible freestanding shelves and tables to facilitate their staging.[143] Arranged in conjunction with director of circulating exhibitions Elodie Courter and assisted by Mock, it displayed objects fabricated from such alluring new materials as pliable lucite and Plexiglas as well as fiberglass, only recently made available to the consumer.[144] The exhibition also

Figure 3.15
John Yeon. Watzek
House, Portland,
Oregon, 1936–38
(John Yeon Center,
University of Oregon)

emphasized American product design for the American market. Nevertheless, McAndrew's conceptual underpinning for both *Useful Objects* shows was cross-cultural because it represented a fusion of American and European ideas. In promoting what he called "form must follow function" criteria for design, based on purpose, materials, and manufacturing processes, and allowing for "aesthetic quality," McAndrew reconciled the homegrown theory of function, espoused in the nineteenth century by Horatio Greenough and Louis Sullivan, with Bauhaus pedagogy and practice.[145] Through his two innovative exhibitions McAndrew helped to kindle a burgeoning mass market for modern design, which encouraged MoMA to mount seven successive *Useful Objects* exhibitions until 1949.[146]

For the tenth anniversary *Art in Our Time* exhibition, inaugurating the new Goodwin-Stone building in the spring of 1939, McAndrew focused on housing. This was a radical departure from the 1932 *Modern Architecture: International Exhibition*, whose relatively small housing section was a concession to Mumford. Although the museum had staged two important housing exhibitions, in 1934 and 1936, it had relied on the assistance of housing experts Carol Aronovici and Catherine Bauer.[147] The extensive "Houses and Housing" exhibit for *Art in Our Time* was curated by McAndrew in conjunction with the United States Housing Authority (created in 1937) and its assistant director of informational services, Frederick Gutheim. In it the curators viewed avant-garde developments and the state of public housing in Europe and the United States through a Mumfordian prism, emphasizing such regional considerations as site conditions, climate, "humble materials," and an architect's "cultural climate."[148] Now they admired Le Corbusier's Villa Savoye for its ramp, wind screen, roof garden, and colors, not merely as a purist abstraction.[149] But they also celebrated the American character of the timber-frame Watzek House by John Yeon (credited to J. B. Yeon, A. E. Doyle & Associates), in Portland, Oregon (1936–38), which harmonized its modern design with a western landscape by means of an alignment with Mount Hood (fig. 3.15).[150]

"Houses and Housing" provided McAndrew and Gutheim with a platform for their predictions on future developments. Rather than factory-made and assembled houses, there would be increased production of prefabricated components and equipment for public as well as private housing. In the public sector they anticipated a large appropriation, made possible by the passage of the Wagner-Steagall Act in 1937. Influenced by the research of the International Congresses of Modern Architecture (CIAM) and by US housing policy, they offered recommendations: minimum spatial requirements for units, judicious site-planning to replace symmetrical planning, land-use calling for open spaces and gardens, and standardization to achieve more economical large-scale developments.[151] McAndrew and Gutheim proposed models for future building, including the English garden city and the European *Siedlung*, or housing community, with stores and communal services, in addition to American housing projects carried out by the PWA, most notably Oskar Stonorov and Alfred Kastner's Carl Mackley Houses in North Philadelphia (1931–35).[152] They supported the US housing policy governed by defederalization and, more specifically, the US Housing Authority's mission to delegate the selection of architects, choice of site, construction, and management of new projects to regulatory agencies. Moreover, they endorsed a new form of community-based planning that encouraged local housing authorities and their architects to experiment with new materials and new building methods specific to their area. The exhibition confirmed McAndrew's commitment to one of the principal tenets of European and American modernism: namely, to meet the need for social housing.

McAndrew's interest in vernacular and regional traditions, which would shape future exhibitions, drew him to Mexico four times, beginning with his first visit in 1934. On his second trip, in the summer of 1939, with Chick Austin, he learned that Mexican scholars were planning an Exposition d'Art Mexicaine Ancien et Moderne (Exposition of Ancient and Modern Mexican Art) to be held at the Musée du Jeu de Paume.[153] Anticipating the onset of war in Europe in the fall, McAndrew assumed that the show would be canceled. He proceeded to inform the Museum of Modern Art about the possibility of hosting an exhibition on Mexican art in New York. Nelson Rockefeller, who had become the museum's new president in May 1939, followed up with a trip to Mexico and a successful meeting with Mexican president Lázaro Cárdenas.[154] He thanked McAndrew for "tipping us off on the Mexican show."[155] In October 1939 McAndrew was invited to Washington to participate in a conference sponsored by the State Department, Inter-American Relations in the Field of Art, which encouraged his interest in hemispheric art and politics (see Epilogue).[156]

McAndrew returned to Mexico in early 1940 in order to prepare the exhibition *Twenty Centuries of Mexican Art*. Marking the most comprehensive exhibition of Mexican art ever held in any country at that time, it was the first of several MoMA shows in the 1940s and 1950s that promoted cultural relations between Latin America and the United States and made it a key site in the formation of a "Latin American manner," as architectural historian Patricio del Real has shown.[157] The New York show, which opened in May 1940, occurred at a strategic time, when Latin America had severed its ties with Europe and gravitated instead to North America, just as the United States looked to the governments of its Latin American neighbors for political and cultural accord. *Twenty Centuries of Mexican Art* was organized with a structure and a cadre of participants similar to the earlier one projected for the Musée du Jeu de Paume.[158] Undertaken by three Mexican specialists and sponsored by the government of Mexico, the MoMA exhibition aimed to be a comprehensive demonstration of Mexican art.[159] It promoted the concept of *mexicanidad* (Mexicanness) as both a political and cultural construction of the past.[160] At a time when the oil industry had been recently nationalized under President Cárdenas and the United States had countered with extensive propaganda and diplomatic initiatives, the museum's show served as a mediating agent.[161] It must be pointed out that Nelson Rockefeller, whose personal fortune derived from the family-owned corporation Standard Oil of New Jersey, was a principal supporter of the exhibition. When Rockefeller met with President Cárdenas to discuss the exhibition of Mexican art, he also brought up the issue of the government's nationalization of the oil companies.[162] Notwithstanding Rockefeller's presumed personal agenda, *Twenty Centuries of Mexican Art* promoted *mexicanidad* as a non-governmental diplomatic and cultural initiative between Mexico and the United States—a form of Pan-Americanism.

The Museum of Modern Art devoted its building and sculpture garden to the *Twenty Centuries of Mexican Art* exhibition of pre-Spanish art, colonial art and architecture, folk and popular art, modern art, and children's art. McAndrew served as coordinating curator, with three additional roles: exhibition designer for the installation of over five thousand objects, assistant on the colonial architecture section, and designer of the restaged sculpture garden for Mexican art.[163] For the installation, he deployed once again his signature curve, this time forming a sinuous horizontal plane for a long display table (fig. 3.16). In doing so, the curve recalled those he used in the installation of the *Useful Household Objects under $5.00* show and in the Julien Levy Gallery wall, and was suggestive of organic forms emerging in both Europe and the United States around 1930 (fig. 3.14; see fig. 1.13).

McAndrew's research on colonial architecture in Mexico showed, for example, how eighteenth-century churrigueresque—what the Mexican writer and diplomat Antonio Castro Leal called the

country's "most complete and original esthetic expression"—evinced
an acculturation between European baroque and native forms.[164] It
was a poignant example of the hybrid character and open-ended-
ness of Mexican colonial architecture, which embodied McAndrew's
concept of naturalization.[165] McAndrew had originally planned for
the exhibition to feature a section on modern architecture, which
included photographs and plans obtained from Mexican architects
with whom he had worked since the summer of 1939.[166] But, on the
eve of the show, that section was canceled largely because he was
overextended. Given the theme of the show, the cancellation may
also have stemmed from the perception that modern architecture
in Mexico did not sufficiently represent the concept of *mexicanidad*,
as del Real has proposed.[167] For example, there was most likely an
awareness that the design of Juan O'Gorman's house and studios
for Diego Rivera and Frida Kahlo in Mexico City (1929–32) was too
close to Corbusian expression to convey an affiliation with vernacular
and regional traditions. McAndrew was undoubtedly disappointed
with the omission of modern architecture from the *Mexican Art* show.
Later he would envision a book on modern architecture from 1931
to 1941, but he would abandon the project in favor of further research
on colonial architecture in Mexico (see Epilogue).

McAndrew chose to bring into play the theme of *mexicanidad*
when he redesigned the sculpture garden for the display of Mexican

Figure 3.17
Chac-Mool (Resting God), Chichén Itzá, Yucatán, Mexico. Exhibited in *Three Centuries of Mexican Art*, Sculpture Garden, The Museum of Modern Art, New York, 1940 (Photographic Archive. The Museum of Modern Art Archives, New York. © The Museum of Modern Art/Licensed by SCALA / Art Resource, NY)

art from pre-Columbian to folk and popular, as if in an open-air market.[168] To do so, he replaced old pebbles with fresh ones embedded in hard clay and introduced new trees, plants, and organic ground cover as well as new structures, including seven pavilions made of plywood and lightweight canvas sunshades propped up by cedar poles.[169] He enriched the tradition of viewing sculpture in the garden by installing twenty-five pieces of pre-Spanish sculpture as well as contemporary Mexican pottery and folk art.[170] The garden now featured a monumental Aztec statue of Coatlicue (goddess of earth and death) so that it could also be seen from inside the museum through the glass walls.[171] Nearby was the stone sculpture of a resting god called *Chac-Mool* from Chichén Itzá in the Yucatán (fig. 3.17). Garden displays of pottery and objects of everyday life suggested an ongoing tradition of cultural practice and synthesis since pre-Spanish times.[172] McAndrew's ambitious and innovative installation of the *Twenty Centuries of Mexican Art* show did not go unnoticed by MoMA principals. Following its opening on May 15, 1940, Nelson Rockefeller sent McAndrew a telegram commending him for his "thrilling job of installation," which produced "the most ingenious and effective ever undertaken by the Museum."[173]

Several Museum of Modern Art exhibitions served as vehicles for advancing architectural competitions and the work of their award-winning modernist designers. At the museum this was a completely new and innovative initiative, which obliged McAndrew to draw upon his architectural training. There he promoted the contemporaneity of design ideas and the ethics of democratic process in his inaugural sponsorship (with *Architectural Forum*) of a competition for a Wheaton College Art Center in 1938.[174] The museum subsequently staged an exhibition of the winning design of Richard Bennett and Caleb Hornbostel and the projects of other award winners. If the second-prize design of Walter Gropius and Marcel Breuer had won the competition and been executed, it would have joined with McAndrew's Art Library in establishing modernism on the American campus.[175] McAndrew's department also exhibited the prize-winning designs for two other competitions, each won by modernists: Eero Saarinen, Ralph Rapson, and Frederic James's design for a theater and fine arts building at the College of William and Mary in Williamsburg (1938–39; unbuilt); and the design by Saarinen and Saarinen with Swanson for the government-sponsored Smithsonian Gallery of Art (1939; unbuilt), a competition that, according to McAndrew, "was stacked very decidedly in favor of a modern building" because Joseph Hudnut served as advisor to the jury (fig. 3.5).[176]

For his final architectural exhibition at MoMA, McAndrew advanced his concept of naturalization in an effort not only to Americanize European modernism but also to revalorize American modernism. To that end, McAndrew examined Frank Lloyd Wright's work and ideas in the architect's second exhibition at the museum, which opened in 1940. In contrast to the modest character and spontaneity of the Fallingwater show in 1938, McAndrew's *Frank Lloyd Wright, American Architect* was a grand retrospective covering a fifty-year period from his earliest association with Louis Sullivan to his most recent buildings. The planning phase of the retrospective entailed lengthy negotiations between Wright and McAndrew, who visited Taliesin in Wisconsin in the fall of 1939 and 1940.[177] Three comingled issues dominated their discussions: the installation design; a plan to construct in the sculpture garden a full-scale Usonian House, the name derived from "United States of North America" in reference to Wright's design for a simple low-cost house that could serve as a model for a reformed American society; and the exhibition catalogue.[178]As preparations moved forward, Wright's mounting expectations and demands turned excessive. He wanted a larger budget, more space, and more control over the exhibition and its catalogue, wielding the resources of the Museum of Modern Art to document his past accomplishments and publicize his new work. But, according to Kathryn Smith, other shows were on the museum's schedule, which Wright perceived as competing for funds and exhibition space.[179] A series of hurdles involving the fund-raising campaign, construction estimate, and building permit led to discord, which Wright and McAndrew sought to overcome. The size of the plot and precise location for the Usonian House also remained points of conflict.[180]

Throughout the discussions McAndrew attempted to appease the willful architect, especially over contributions to the catalogue, intended as a Festschrift in honor of Wright. McAndrew commissioned essays from leading architects and historians, including Aalto, Hitchcock, Mies, Neutra, and Mumford (who declined). He also requested a major essay from Walter Curt Behrendt, the German émigré historian, critic, and a leading authority on Wright by virtue of his book *Modern Building: Its Nature, Problems, and Forms* (1937).[181] Behrendt had been an early and steadfast voice in recognizing the significance of Wright's influence in Europe, his view informing McAndrew's notion of an Americanized modernism.[182] However, Wright told McAndrew that he was wary of a critic who "sits in judgement" and of Behrendt in particular.[183] Visiting Taliesin in mid-September 1940, McAndrew allowed Wright to read Behrendt's essay.[184] Wright alleged that Behrendt had "either ignorantly or deliberately twisted my meaning and implied untruths concerning myself and my work," and that by emphasizing his early work he had rendered him irrelevant to the new generation of architects.[185] To placate the architect, McAndrew telegraphed him: "If you will wire us what parts of article you take exception to, we will try to straighten matters out."[186] In effect, this allowed Wright to edit Behrendt's essay. The curator's efforts notwithstanding, Wright responded by announcing his withdrawal from the show.[187] Initially he did not blame McAndrew for the impasse and hoped that they would remain friends.[188]

Attempting to rescue the exhibition, McAndrew canceled the catalogue with the Behrendt essay in part because Barr had criticized it as having been censored by Wright.[189] MoMA was now prepared to give Wright the space he required for the show's installation.[190] On September 20 Wright rebounded by sending a telegram in support of the exhibition, which now included a more favorable garden site for his Usonian House as the star attraction.[191]

From the beginning McAndrew envisioned a show that would emphasize Wright's architectural thinking rather than his stylistic development. In his initial "Exhibition Outline" for the Wright retrospective (October 1, 1940), McAndrew set forth a series of overarching themes, which included the architect's concepts of "organic architecture," "reforming the house," and working "in the nature of materials."[192] Sketch plans in McAndrew's hand with Wright's annotations indicate that the ground-floor space would be divided by moveable and immoveable partitions.[193] The exhibition would contain sepia drawings, photographs, and models of the architect's iconic early work (before 1910). It also included models of more recent work, such as the Willey House in Minneapolis (1932–34); Broadacre City (1929–35); the Herbert Jacobs House in Madison, Wisconsin (1936–37); and the Johnson Administration Building (1934–39) and Herbert F. Johnson House (known as "Wingspread"; 1937–39), both in Racine, Wisconsin (fig. 3.18). But by early November, Wright would sidestep McAndrew and take control of the content, installation design, and execution of the exhibition. In place of the curator's classification by topic, Wright opted for a "bird's-eye view."[194] Barr would later fault Wright for ignoring McAndrew's original plan with its "lucid chronological exposition of Wright's development, particularly as regards his handling of space."[195] Following the opening of *Frank Lloyd Wright, American Architect* on November 12, 1940, the Usonian House would prove unfeasible.[196] Thus, in spite of McAndrew's success in raising sufficient funds to construct the house, he was forced

to abandon what he called his "pet scheme," which would have given New Yorkers the opportunity to encounter and explore a Wright house in the sculpture garden.[197]

No evidence suggests that McAndrew wrote his catalogue essay for the Wright exhibition, but his critical perspective on the architect's work informed two MoMA press releases for the show.[198] In them McAndrew opposed "the International style" to Wright's "warm humanitarian approach to architecture."[199] There too he foresaw that the "space-conception created by Wright in 1904 was destined to be the most characteristic one of modern architecture."[200] Moreover, he astutely cast Wright's compositions as a rivalry with, rather than an imitation of, organic forms and processes.

Branded by MoMA as a "Wright" installation, and publicized as such, the exhibition was criticized for lacking both clarity of organization and sufficient wall text.[201] Mumford did not publish a review of it, which signaled his waning enthusiasm for Wright.[202] Even Hitchcock admitted that while the show might convey Wright's significance as an architect, it was neither cohesive nor intelligible.[203] Their friendship notwithstanding, Wright held McAndrew responsible for the show's critical reception, its clarity all the more encumbered by the absence of a catalogue.[204] If the Fallingwater exhibition had inspired a meeting of the minds between architect and curator, the Frank Lloyd Wright retrospective led them to work at cross purposes. In spite of his difficulties with Wright, however, McAndrew would remain one of the architect's most partisan supporters. In his *Guide to Modern Architecture, Northeast States*, McAndrew called attention to Wright as a figure of historical significance and renewed vigor.[205] As emphasized in the *Guide*, and due largely to McAndrew's own efforts in reviving the architect's career, Wright's work and ideas were no longer "disguised as importations" and could now be fully appreciated as "part of our living tradition," in the sense that they were native to North American practice.[206] The 1940 show demonstrated the ongoing vitality of Wright's architecture and confirmed both Mumford's and McAndrew's analyses, which secured the architect's seminal role in the repatriation of American modernism.

For McAndrew, the year 1940 began with exhilarating prospects. He spent the first months in Mexico, having returned to prepare the *Mexican Art* exhibition. He curated the Wright exhibition and completed his *Guide to Modern Architecture, Northeast States*, the first handbook on modern architecture in America and where to find it in the northeastern region (fig. 3.19). Published in a spiral-bound format in an edition of ten thousand copies and sold at low cost (twenty-five cents), it was an indispensable resource for explorers of American modernism. The *Guide* once again laid claim to the International Style as an "importation," which also contained "American elements derived from . . . Frank Lloyd Wright and from our industrial building."[207] For McAndrew, the architecture of the present, circa 1940, still owed a debt to the International Style for its "beauty of clean lines and simple surfaces," "subtleties of free asymmetrical grouping," and "vigorous logic," which served as a "catalytic agent."[208] As Jere Abbott pointed out in his review, the *Guide* showed that even though modern buildings in the Northeast since 1930 were still sparse, representing only 1 percent of construction, they were well distributed throughout the region and thus represented a diffuse, if incipient, public acceptance of the movement.[209] The *Guide* both conceptualized and documented the presence of a regional modernism in the northeastern states. In doing so, McAndrew confirmed that modernism and regionalism were not mutually exclusive.

But the preparation of the *Guide* in addition to McAndrew's curatorial obligations, an ambitious lecture schedule to fifteen states, and his duties as visiting lecturer at Vassar only strengthened the opinion among MoMA senior staff that he was overextended.[210] McAndrew continued to remain in close touch with his Vassar colleagues, especially with Agnes Rindge, who in 1938 gave a lecture series in New York sponsored by MoMA.[211] But with two major shows weighing on McAndrew in the spring of 1940, the museum stripped him of his responsibilities as curator of industrial art. In his place, the Harvard-trained architect Eliot Noyes was appointed director of the Department of Industrial Design.[212] The *Mexican Art* exhibition was a resounding success, but the Wright exhibition was problematic

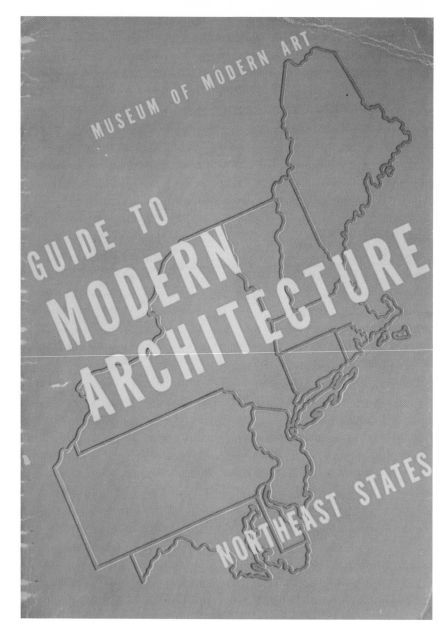

for the museum. McAndrew's dealings with Wright over revisions
to Behrendt's catalogue essay had compromised his position with
MoMA colleagues, and the show's negative reception further weakened his position.[213] There was a growing disaffection with McAndrew
on the part of the museum hierarchy. It flowed from the change in
leadership the previous year when Rockefeller assumed the pres-
idency and Clark became chairman of the board. This signaled a
new era with an emphasis on organization. The museum's executive
vice-president, John Abbott (known as "Dick"), may well have blamed
McAndrew for an overly ambitious *Mexican Art* show, but he also

faulted him for what was reported to Barr as his "lack of cooperative-ness" and "irresponsibility" during research trips to Mexico.[214] These trips diverted him from visiting Wright in Chicago and at Taliesin West, the architect's winter residence and studio in Scottsdale, Arizona. Moreover, to advance the interests of the *Mexican Art* show, McAndrew had been obliged to poach Department of Architecture staff assigned to the Wright exhibition.[215] This breach of management contributed to the delayed Wright opening.

There was additional evidence of administrative and political discord within the institution. According to Russell Lynes, relations between Clark and Barr had declined. Barr's authority was further weakened to the point that he effectively lost his curatorial position when Monroe Wheeler was named director of exhibitions (as well as publications) in March 1941.[216] This led to Barr's resignation as director in 1943.[217] McAndrew later recounted how Rockefeller "called in the professional efficiency sharks to reorganize MoMA into something self-supporting…and it failed to work, and morale was broken."[218] "Architecture shows did not make money," McAndrew claimed; how-ever, as one museum colleague told Lynes, the curator had "trouble staying within his budgets."[219] Aside from the issue of management, Clark, Goodyear, and Rockefeller had not approved of McAndrew's role on the Building Committee. Lynes also suggested that McAndrew was "not one to be over-impressed by trustees; indeed, he was not unlikely to be rather high-handed with them."[220] A MoMA colleague told Lynes candidly that McAndrew was "very elegant and just got their dander up."[221] Notwithstanding his recent praise for the cura-tor's installation of the *Mexican Art* show, Rockefeller, according to Lynes, found McAndrew generally "'incompatible' and wanted him off the staff," a decision with which Clark concurred.[222] By June 1940 McAndrew's dismissal seemed imminent. Barr, who had not been told about the decision to sack his curator, pleaded McAndrew's case with Rockefeller, museum trustees, and principals. Barr urged them to consider his "positive qualities and achievements [which] definitely outweigh whatever shortcoming he has from an adminis-trative point of view," and to take into account his "brilliant mind, an extraordinary ability to clarify the history, theory, and esthetics of modern architecture," and his "remarkable flair for anticipating trends in modern architecture."[223] Even Philip Johnson offered support to McAndrew. This was surprising because he faulted McAndrew, like Noyes, for having a "tin eye," according to Johnson's biographer Franz Schulze.[224] More to the point, Johnson feared that without a curator in place, the Department of Architecture, which he had headed during the early 1930s, might be eliminated.[225] By December, McAndrew later recalled, "I heard that the axe had fallen."[226] But due to Barr's efforts, Rockefeller agreed to delay his removal for another six months.[227] Barr wrote bluntly of the matter to Paul Sachs. McAndrew was "thrown out," he explained, because museum standards had declined since 1939, exchanging "distinction for mediocrity."[228] It was Rockefeller, Barr emphasized, who "didn't like him, believed one-sided stories against him, ignored his value to the Museum, and kicked him out."[229] In an effort to support McAndrew's future prospects for curatorial and academic work, Barr appealed to Sachs: "He is extraordinarily learned in the history of architecture, a brilliant designer, a lucid and exciting lecturer with wide knowledge and deep cultivation." Barr further described him as "a person of courage, integrity and conscience...charming and excellent company." And although he had faults, including "a certain immaturity and perhaps too much intellectual confidence," Barr conceded, "he was, I say with conviction, the most brilliant person on our staff, at once sensitive and energetic."[230] McAndrew stayed on at the museum during the spring of 1941, but by July he was gone.[231]

In spite of his forced departure, McAndrew had made significant contributions to the museum's programs and to the construction of a hybrid form of modernism. Was his tenure at the Museum of Modern Art then merely devoted to furthering the agenda of curators Johnson and Barr (and also Hitchcock) or establishing his own? McAndrew's exhibition record and his writings suggest that, on the one hand, he transformed the Department of Architecture and Industrial Art from within. His *Useful Objects* shows launched what would become MoMA's product development and marketing for mass consumption. He reframed the International Style as an evolving tradition. On the other hand, he realized that its rigid principles were inadequate to address new streams of modernism: the American organic tradition as Mumford had framed it in the Richardson-Sullivan-Wright lineage (*The Brown Decades*); the awareness of vernacular and regional traditions as both models and molders of design; and the importance of human-centered elements of design, both native and received. *Three Centuries of Mexican Art* not only examined the hemispheric political and cultural significance of the exhibited works but also promoted their diffusion in North America. In large measure, McAndrew's two Wright exhibitions restored the American architect's faltered career, while his Aalto exhibition established the Finnish architect as a leading modernist among modernists and launched his furniture as a consumer product in America.[232] McAndrew's project at MoMA had also been to adopt Barr and Cahill's pluralistic and open-ended characterization of modern art from the early 1930s and to find a way forward for architecture. Through his concept of naturalization, he forged a transatlantic synthesis of these many streams at the same time as he reconciled the empirical transformations in the International Style.

Mumford failed to appreciate all aspects of McAndrew's inclusive modernism. However, he was influenced by the curator's probing insights into the relationship between modern and vernacular, which would resonate in his own writings on regionalism. When McAndrew left the museum, Mumford had begun to solidify his polemical position against the International Style, partly because his ideology was so firmly grounded in the American organic tradition and partly because he associated internationalism with fascism.[233] In a 1947 "Sky

Line" essay in the *New Yorker*, Mumford continued to reject "sterile and abstract modernism" in favor of a "Bay Region Style," which represented humanism and regional expression.[234] With it Mumford launched a broader debate on regionalism.[235] His *New Yorker* essay led to a contentious MoMA symposium the following year, "What Is Happening to Modern Architecture?," dominated by the opposition of Barr, Hitchcock, and Johnson.[236] While McAndrew participated as a panel member, his remarks were not included in the published proceedings, nor did he record them elsewhere. However, his long-standing position on regional modernism would have mediated between the two poles. But by this time, McAndrew was no longer inclined to enter the fray; he had returned to academia and resumed his scholarship on colonial architecture in Mexico (see Epilogue).

With McAndrew's curatorial denouement in 1941, the baton shifted. His immediate successors as curator (director) of the Department of Architecture were his two former assistants: Janet Henrich (1941–42) and Elizabeth Bauer Mock (1943–46).[237] Ever since the *Trois siècles d'art aux États-Unis* exhibition of 1938, the two Vassar alumnae had carried out McAndrew's curatorial vision. On April 17, 1940, Henrich and Elizabeth Hird, a fellow McAndrew student in the class of 1937, launched their own initiative: a photographic exhibition, *Seventy-Five Years of Vassar Architecture*, shown in the members' penthouse of the museum and at other metropolitan venues.[238] The presumption was that most Vassar students interested in art were members of MoMA.[239] Although Mock had graduated from Vassar before McAndrew's arrival at the college, she was especially dedicated to the broad diffusion of his vision. Her own training and experience made her a keen observer of contemporary developments. In 1933 she had studied architecture in Wright's Fellowship at Taliesin and then at the Gewerbeschule in Basel before joining the museum in 1937.[240] Succeeding Henrich as wartime curator, Mock expanded McAndrew's search for Americanized modern architecture and regional modernism. In both her 1944 exhibition *Built in USA, 1932–44* and the influential book that carried a similar name, she examined with great acuity the currents of an evolving modernism across the American continent.[241] There she cited such regional examples as Carl Koch's cluster of eight houses on Snake Hill in Belmont, Massachusetts (1940), and government-assisted housing developments in California.[242] Thus, with the departure of John McAndrew, Elizabeth Mock championed his legacy at the same time as she drew on her own training with Wright, her transatlantic experience, and her association with Mumford (through her sister Catherine Bauer [Wurster]) to bring vernacular and regional expression to a national platform.[243]

1   MoMA announced McAndrew's appointment as curator of the Department of Architecture and Industrial Art on July 10, 1937. He officially assumed his position on September 1. When Alfred Barr informed McAndrew of his appointment in June, he understood that his new hire would be free to work for the museum during the summer. "Gets Modern Art Museum Post," *New York Times* (July 10, 1937): 3; Alfred H. Barr Jr. to John McAndrew, June 29, 1937 (John McAndrew Papers, Courtesy of Wellesley College Archives; hereafter cited as John McAndrew Papers, WCA). See also "John McAndrew Curator of Dept. of Architecture and Industrial Art," The Museum of Modern Art Press Release [unnumbered; 1937].

2   For the second term of the 1936–37 academic year, McAndrew and Agnes Rindge joined James Johnson Sweeney at the Institute of Fine Arts, New York University, to teach a graduate course titled "Aspects of Modern Art." "New York University, Graduate School, Department of Fine Arts, Announcement of Graduate Courses," *Speculum* 11 (July 1936): unpaged back matter.

3   John McAndrew, interview by Russell Lynes, Venice, October 1971 (Russell Lynes Papers, 1935–1986, Archives of American Art, Smithsonian Institution; hereafter cited as Russell Lynes Papers, 1935–1986, AAASI); Russell Lynes, *Good Old Modern: An Intimate Portrait of the Museum of Modern Art* (New York: Atheneum, 1973), 178.

4   McAndrew, interview by Lynes, October 1971 (Russell Lynes Papers, 1935–1986, AAASI).

5   Lynes, *Good Old Modern*, 177. Jere Abbott served as the first associate director of the Museum of Modern Art, beginning in 1929, but left that position in 1932 to become director of the Smith College Museum of Art in Northampton, Massachusetts.

6   In 1932 Johnson and Hitchcock curated with Barr *Modern Architecture: International Exhibition*. Johnson curated his exhibition *Early Modern Architecture: Chicago, 1870–1910* in 1933. The following year he curated *Machine Art*, while Hitchcock curated *Early Museum Architecture*. Hitchcock wrote the catalogue essay for the Le Corbusier exhibition in 1935.

7   MoMA announced the departure of Johnson (and Alan Blackburn) in December 1934. See "Two Forsake Art to Found a Party," *New York Times*, December 18, 1934, 23; "Resignation of Mr. Blackburn and Mr. Johnson," *Bulletin of the Museum of Modern Art* 2, no. 4 (January 1935): 2. On the Long episode and its aftermath as well as Johnson's efforts to cofound a conservative National Party, see Franz Schulze, *Philip Johnson: Life and Work* (New York: Alfred A. Knopf, 1994), 104–19. Concerning Johnson's directions to Fantl, see Philip Johnson to Ernestine Fantl, August 15 [1935], Department of Architecture and Design, Museum of Modern Art, New York, reproduced in Mardges Bacon, *Le Corbusier in America: Travels in the Land of the Timid* (Cambridge, MA: MIT Press, 2001), 42. Beginning in January 1935, following Johnson's

resignation, Fantl directed the department's exhibitions. "Four New Staff Appointments," The Museum of Modern Art Press Release [unnumbered; 1936]. Fantl was obliged to be guided by the Committee on Architecture and Industrial Art, whose members were Goodwin (chair), Hitchcock, Johnson, and Barr, joined by Joseph Hudnut, Catherine Bauer, John Coolidge, George Howe, and Chauncey Stillman.

8   "Architecture of H. H. Richardson," The Museum of Modern Art Press Release 1636–48, January 11–12, 1936; Henry-Russell Hitchcock Jr., *The Architecture of H. H. Richardson and His Times* (New York: Museum of Modern Art, 1936).

9   In February 1937 Fantl resigned, leaving the running of the department to the Committee on Architecture and Industrial Art.

10   On the design of the new building, see Dominic Ricciotti, "The 1939 Building of the Museum of Modern Art: The Goodwin-Stone Collaboration," *American Art Journal* 17, no. 3 (Summer 1985): 50–76.

11   Rona Roob, "1936: The Museum Selects an Architect," *Archives of American Art Journal* 23, no. 1 (1983): 25–28.

12   Roob, "Museum Selects an Architect," 28.

13   McAndrew, interview by Lynes, October 1971 (Russell Lynes Papers, 1935–1986, AAASI). See also Lynes, *Good Old Modern*, 193.

14   Barr to McAndrew, June 29, 1937 (John McAndrew Papers, WCA).

15   Lynes discusses the sessions between the architects and the Building Committee in *Good Old Modern*, 193.

16   On Stone's conversion to modernism, see Edward Durell Stone, *The Evolution of an Architect* (New York: Horizon Press, 1962), 23–24, 30.

17   McAndrew, interview by Lynes, October 1971 (Russell Lynes Papers, 1935–1986, AAASI). See also Stone, *Evolution of an Architect*, 35.

18   "The Museum of Modern Art, New York City," *Architectural Forum* 71, no. 2 (August 1939): 115–28; "New Art Museum to Open for Fair," *New York Times*, August 30, 1938, 15.

19   McAndrew, interview by Lynes, October 1971 (Russell Lynes Papers, 1935–1986, AAASI); "Museum of Modern Art, New York City," 121.

20   Margaret Scolari Barr, "Our Campaigns," *New Criterion*, Special Issue (Summer 1987): 54; Margaret Scolari Barr, "John McAndrew," unpublished manuscript [1979], 27 (Margaret Scolari Barr Papers, II.232. The Museum of Modern Art Archives, New York).

21   Lewis Mumford, "The Sky Line: Growing Pains— The New Museum," *New Yorker*, June 3, 1939, 53.

22   Mumford, "Sky Line: Growing Pains," 52.

23   There were actually two rows of perforations: eleven in the first row, which could be seen from the street, and three in a second row, which could not be seen from below. "The Museum of Modern Art," *Fortune*, December 1938, 75; Ada Louis Huxtable, "A Dubious Survival Plan for the Modern," *New York Times*, August 7, 1977, D1, quoted in Mary Anne Hunting, *Edward Durell Stone: Modernism's Populist Architect* (New York: W. W. Norton, 2013), 47–48, 155n112; Kazys Varnelis, ed., *The Philip Johnson Tapes: Interviews by Robert A. M. Stern* (New York: Monacelli Press, 2008), 67.

24   Jean-Louis Cohen, *André Lurçat, 1894–1970: Autocritique d'un moderne* (Liège, Belgium: Mardaga, 1995), 46–49.

25   Le Corbusier first designed a rooftop perforation for his Esprit Nouveau pavilion at the 1925 Exposition Internationale des Arts Décoratifs et Industriels Modernes. Le Corbusier and Pierre Jeanneret, *Oeuvre complète, 1910–1929* (1937; repr., Zurich: Girsberger, 1964), 99. Aalto employed circular skylights for his Viipuri Library in Finland (now Vyborg, Russia) (1927–35). The library figures prominently in *Architecture and Furniture: Aalto* (New York: Museum of Modern Art, 1938), plate 10. On Prouvé's use of perforations in his architecture and furniture, see Peter Sulzer, *Jean Prouvé: Highlights, 1917–1944* (Basel: Birkhäuser, 2002), 34, 78, 110, 110, 115.

26   Paul J. Sachs, "Professor Sachs' Address," *Bulletin of the Museum of Modern Art* 6, no. 5 (July 1939): 9. For a photograph and a plan of the lobby, see "Museum of Modern Art, New York City," 116.

27   McAndrew, interview by Lynes, October 1971 (Russell Lynes Papers, 1935–1986, AAASI).

28   "Museum of Modern Art, New York City," 124, 128.

29   David A. Hanks, "Spreading the Gospel of Modern Design," in *Partners in Design: Alfred H. Barr Jr. and Philip Johnson*, ed. David A. Hanks (New York: Monacelli Press, 2015), 194–95.

30   Committee member Coolidge wrote of McAndrew, with whom he shared an office at Vassar College in 1937–38 , "I believe that he was responsible for all the architectural features in the garden." John Coolidge to Mirka Beneš, August 5, 1994, quoted in Mirka Beneš, "A Modern Classic: The Abby Aldrich Rockefeller Sculpture Garden," in *Philip Johnson and the Museum of Modern Art*, ed. John Elderfield (New York: Museum of Modern Art, 1998), 146–47n65.

31   John McAndrew, ed., *Guide to Modern Architecture, Northeast States* (New York: Museum of Modern Art, 1940), 76.

32   Beneš, "A Modern Classic: The Abby Aldrich Rockefeller Sculpture Garden," 106–7. Beneš reviews the history of these gardens up to 1984 in Mirka Beneš, "Inventing a Modern Sculpture Garden in 1939 at the Museum of Modern Art, New York," *Landscape Journal* 13, no. 1 (Spring 1994): 1–20. On Johnson's gardens, see Beneš, "A Modern Classic: The Abby Aldrich Rockefeller Sculpture Garden," 104–51. On Taniguchi's garden, see Allen Freeman, "Heart Replacement: Torn Out for Construction of the Huge New Addition, MoMA's Sculpture Garden Is Back—Not Quite the Same," *Landscape Architecture* 95, no. 6 (May 2005): 106–13.

33   Beneš, "Inventing a Modern Sculpture Garden," 1.

34   McAndrew, *Guide to Modern Architecture, Northeast States*, 76.

35   Beneš, "A Modern Classic: The Abby Aldrich Rockefeller Sculpture Garden," 109.

36   "Facts on New Two-Million-Dollar Building and Sculpture Garden of the Museum of Modern Art," The Museum of Modern Art Press Release 39508–21, May 8, 1939.

37   "'Art in Our Time' Set in Cool Garden,'" *New York Times*, July 7, 1939, 19; Alice Morgan Carson, "A Garden Gallery of the Museum of Modern Art," *Bulletin of the Garden Club of America* 7 (July 4, 1939): 72–73.

38   Mumford, "Sky Line: Growing Pains," 53.

39   Lynes, *Good Old Modern*, 198.

40   Elizabeth Kassler, "The Sculpture Garden," *MoMA: A Publication for Members of The Museum of Modern Art* 4 (Summer 1975): unpaged.

41   Alfred H. Barr Jr. to Philip Goodwin, March 1942, quoted in Beneš, "Inventing a Modern Sculpture Garden," 116, 146n45.

42   Carson, "Garden Gallery of the Museum of Modern Art," 72–73; "Facts on New Two-Million-Dollar Building and Sculpture Garden of the Museum of Modern Art."

43   Mumford, "Sky Line: Growing Pains," 53.

44   Partisans of Mexican art and design, including Frances Flynn Paine, used colored pebbles in their patio designs. See Frances Flynn Paine, "In a Mexican Mirador," *House and Garden* 59 (May 1931): 73, 120. McAndrew's garden shares a similarity with, but does not appear to draw on, landscape architect Roberto Burle Marx's earliest work. As Kassler remembered, "No one at the Museum had yet heard of Burle Marx's new free-form gardens in Brazil." Kassler, "Sculpture Garden," unpaged.

45 [Alfred H. Barr Jr.] to Philip Goodwin, July 6, 1936, quoted in Roob, "Museum Selects an Architect," 27.

46 Lynes, *Good Old Modern*, 193.

47 John McAndrew, transcript of interview, Boston, February 28, 1959, Time Inc. Archives, 3, quoted in Hicks Stone, *Edward Durell Stone: A Son's Untold Story of a Legendary Architect* (New York: Rizzoli, 2011), 66, 307n24.

48 Edward Alden Jewell, "Museum of Modern Art Looks Ahead," *New York Times*, May 14, 1939, 137.

49 Beneš, "A Modern Classic: The Abby Aldrich Rockefeller Sculpture Garden," 110.

50 For an announcement of the prize winners and illustrations of their designs, see "Smithsonian Gallery of Art Competition," and "The Report of the Jury," *Architectural Forum* 71, no. 1 (July 1939): I, II, XVI. Beneš gives a vivid description of Stone's design in "A Modern Classic: The Abby Aldrich Rockefeller Sculpture Garden," 110. See also James D. Kornwolf, ed., *Modernism in America, 1937–1941: A Catalog and Exhibition of Four Architectural Competitions* (Williamsburg, VA: Muscarelle Museum of Art, 1985), 188–89, 216–17.

51 *A National Competition to Select an Architect for the Proposed Smithsonian Gallery of Art, Washington, D.C.* (Washington, DC: Smithsonian Institution, 1939), 16, quoted in Beneš, "A Modern Classic: The Abby Aldrich Rockefeller Sculpture Garden," 109–10, 145n22.

52 Beneš, "Inventing a Modern Sculpture Garden," 8.

53 Beneš, "Inventing a Modern Sculpture Garden," 11, 16.

54 John McAndrew, "Architecture in the United States," *Bulletin of the Museum of Modern Art* 6, nos. 1–2 (February 1939): 9.

55 Beneš, "Inventing a Modern Sculpture Garden," 13–15.

56 Beneš, "A Modern Classic: The Abby Aldrich Rockefeller Sculpture Garden," 121.

57 See, for example, Le Corbusier, *Oeuvre complète, 1938–1946*, ed. W. Boesiger (1946; repr., Zurich: Les Éditions d'Architecture, 1966), 82–89, 176, 178–179, 186.

58 Beneš, "Inventing a Modern Sculpture Garden," 13. On McAndrew's admiration for the El Pedregal Gardens, see John McAndrew, "Good Building by Good Neighbors," *ARTnews* 54, no. 9 (January 1956): 64. During World War II McAndrew recommended to Barragán that John Yeon work on the architectural development of the El Pedregal site. Marc Treib, *John Yeon: Modern Architecture and Conservation in the Pacific Northwest* ([Novato, CA]: ORO Editions [2016]),

260n38. See also Keith Eggener, *Luis Barragán's Gardens of El Pedregal* (New York: Princeton Architectural Press, 2001).

59 Although McAndrew claimed that "Industrial Art" was added to the Department of Architecture "to keep it mine," he had inherited the Department of Architecture and Industrial Art from the previous curatorship under Fantl. McAndrew, interview by Lynes, October 1971 (Russell Lynes Papers, 1935–1986, AAASI).

60 For a list of McAndrew's exhibitions organized for MoMA's Department of Architecture and Industrial Art from 1938 to 1940, see Lynes, *Good Old Modern*, 450–51.

61 I explore Barr's open-ended concept of modernism, his "torpedo moving through time" bound up with its cultural construction, in my essay "Modernism and the Vernacular at the Museum of Modern Art, New York," in *Vernacular Modernism: Heimat, Globalization, and the Built Environment*, ed. Maiken Umbach and Bernd Hüppauf (Stanford, CA: Stanford University Press, 2005), 32–33, 36–44.

62 The exhibition drew heavily on Abby Aldrich Rockefeller's collection of American folk art. See Holger Cahill, *American Folk Art: The Art of the Common Man in America, 1750–1900* (New York: Museum of Modern Art, 1932).

63 On Cahill's views of modernism and its origins, see Bacon, "Modernism and the Vernacular at the Museum of Modern Art," 39–41.

64 The Department of Industrial Art was formed in 1933 and the Department of Film in 1935.

65 Alfred H. Barr Jr., *Cubism and Abstract Art* (New York: Museum of Modern Art, 1936), 19.

66 Barr, *Cubism and Abstract Art*, 200.

67 Barr, *Cubism and Abstract Art*, 70.

68 Barr, *Cubism and Abstract Art*, 138, 166, 200, figs. 139, 180, 181.

69 Alfred H. Barr Jr., foreword to *Modern Architecture: International Exhibition* (New York: Museum of Modern Art, 1932), 15.

70 Bacon, *Le Corbusier in America*, 6–8.

71 Alfred H. Barr Jr., "The Necco Factory," *Arts* 13 (May 1928): 292–95, reprinted in *Defining Modern Art: Selected Writings of Alfred H. Barr, Jr.*, ed. Irving Sandler and Amy Newman (New York: Harry N. Abrams, 1986), 62–66.

72 Henry-Russell Hitchcock Jr., *The Urban Vernacular of the Thirties, Forties, and Fifties: American Cities Before the Civil War* (Middletown, CT: Wesleyan University Architectural Exhibitions, 1934). See also Janine A. Mileaf, *Constructing Modernism: Berenice Abbott and*

Henry-Russell Hitchcock (Middletown, CT: Wesleyan University, 1993).

73   Le Corbusier's shift toward organic forms in the 1930s appeared in his use of rubble masonry walls in the de Mandrot House, Le Pradet, France, near Toulon (1929–31). It was also evident in his plastic expression of concrete, as seen in the *pilotis* (supporting columns) of his Swiss Pavilion at the Cité Internationale Universitaire in Paris (1930–31) and in the Weekend House (La Petite Maison; Villa Félix) at La Celle-Saint-Cloud, France (1935), with its turf-covered reinforced-concrete vaulted roof and walls of quarry stone and glass brick. Le Corbusier's Radiant City (1930–35) project embodied the collective identity and humanist values of his "second era of the Machine Age," a theme from CIAM 4, the fourth gathering of the International Congresses of Modern Architecture. On Le Corbusier's engagement with the vernacular, see Francesco Passanti, "The Vernacular, Modernism, and Le Corbusier," *Journal of the Society of Architectural Historians* 56, no. 4 (December 1997): 438–51; Mary Caroline McLeod, "Urbanism and Utopia: Le Corbusier from Regional Syndicalism to Vichy" (PhD diss., Princeton University, 1985); Mary McLeod, "Le Rêve transi de Le Corbusier: L'Amérique 'catastrophe féerique,'" in *Américanisme et modernité*, ed. J.-L. Cohen and H. Damisch (Paris: Flammarion, in association with EHESS, 1993), 208–27. Breuer followed a similar path toward organic expression and vernacular adjustments to modern design. Marcel Breuer, "Where Do We Stand?," *Architectural Review* 77, no. 4 (April 1935): 133–36; Barry Bergdoll, "Encountering America: Marcel Breuer and the Discourses of Vernacular from Budapest to Boston," in *Marcel Breuer—Design and Architecture* (Weil am Rhein, Germany: Vitra Design Museum, 2003), 260–306.

74   McAndrew, interview by Lynes, October 1971 (Russell Lynes Papers, 1935–1986, AAASI).

75   Wright had previously exhibited in two group shows: *Modern Architecture: International Exhibition* (1932) and *Early Modern Architecture: Chicago, 1870–1920* (1933). Following the opening of Hitchcock's exhibition *Architecture of Henry Hobson Richardson* (January 14–February 16, 1936), the Architecture Committee proposed a Wright retrospective for the fall of 1936. Architecture Committee Minutes, January 21, 1936 (The Museum of Modern Art Archives, New York), quoted in Kathryn Smith, "The Show to End All Shows: Frank Lloyd Wright and The Museum of Modern Art, 1940," in *The Show to End All Shows: Frank Lloyd Wright and The Museum of Modern Art, 1940*, Studies in Modern Art 8, ed. Peter Reed and William Kaizen (New York: Museum of Modern Art, 2004), 29, 61n64.

76   John McAndrew to Donald Hoffman, December 15, 1975, quoted in Donald Hoffman, *Frank Lloyd Wright's Fallingwater: The House and Its History* (New York: Dover Publications, 1993, 2nd rev. ed.), 91. Aline Bernstein married Joseph H. Louchheim in 1935; they were divorced in 1951. Two years later she married Eero Saarinen.

77   Hoffman, *Frank Lloyd Wright's Fallingwater*, 91–92.

78   Architectural historian Franklin Toker relates that it was the Russian-émigré modernist Berthold Lubetkin who reported the exchange between Rockefeller and Hitchcock. Franklin Toker, *Fallingwater Rising: Frank Lloyd Wright, E. J. Kaufmann, and America's Most Extraordinary House* (New York: Alfred A. Knopf, 2003), 264, 445. On Johnson's fascist activity, see Schulze, *Philip Johnson*, 126–46.

79   *A New House by Frank Lloyd Wright on Bear Run, Pennsylvania* (New York: Museum of Modern Art 1938).

80   The MoMA catalogue reproduced text from *A New House by Frank Lloyd Wright on Bear Run, Pennsylvania*, Special Issue on Frank Lloyd Wright, *Architectural Forum* 68, no. 1 (January 1938): 36.

81   Neil Levine, *The Architecture of Frank Lloyd Wright* (Princeton, NJ: Princeton University Press, 1966), 472n66.

82   See, for example, Wright's discussion of "organic architecture" in his essays "In the Cause of Architecture" and "In the Cause of Architecture, Second Paper," in *Architectural Record* (March 1908 and May 1914, respectively), reprinted in *Frank Lloyd Wright Collected Writings*, vol. 1, ed. Bruce Brooks Pfeiffer (New York: Rizzoli, 1992), 84–100, 126–37.

83   "House Built Over Waterfall—Frank Lloyd Wright's Project at Bear Run," The Museum of Modern Art Press Release 38121, January 21, 1938.

84   Lewis Mumford, "The Sky Line: At Home, Indoors and Out," *New Yorker*, February 12, 1938, 58.

85   Lewis Mumford to Frank Lloyd Wright, February 6, 1932, quoted in Robert Wojtowicz, *Lewis Mumford and American Modernism* (New York: Cambridge University Press, 1996), 94, 181n91.

86   Henry-Russell Hitchcock Jr., "The Architectural Future in America," *Architectural Review* 82, no. 1 (July 1937): 2.

87   John McAndrew, foreword to *Architecture and Furniture: Aalto* (New York: Museum of Modern Art, 1938), 3.

88   McAndrew, interview by Lynes, October 1971 (Russell Lynes Papers, 1935–1986, AAASI).

89   Henry-Russell Hitchcock Jr., "Paris 1937, Finland," *Architectural Forum* 67, no. 3 (September 1937): 172B, 172C. There is no evidence to suggest that either McAndrew or Barr was in Paris in 1937 to visit Aalto's Finnish Pavilion.

90   *Architecture and Furniture: Aalto*, pls. 10, 16.

91   McAndrew, foreword to *Architecture and Furniture: Aalto*, 3–4.

92 "Two New Exhibits—Furniture and Architecture by Alvar Aalto…," The Museum of Modern Art Press Release 38316–9, March 14, 1938. See also A. Lawrence Kocher, "Furniture," in *Architecture and Furniture: Aalto*, 19.

93 McAndrew, foreword to *Architecture and Furniture: Aalto*, 4.

94 "Architects to Make Furniture," *New York Times*, July 2, 1940, 42.

95 Lewis Mumford, "The Sky Line: Chairs and Shops," *New Yorker*, April 9, 1938, 57.

96 "Architecture Section in Exhibit of American Art at Jeu de Paume," The Museum of Modern Art Press Release 38411–15, April 11, 1938.

97 John McAndrew, "Architecture," *Bulletin of the Museum of Modern Art* 5, nos. 4-5 (April–May 1938): 7.

98 Lewis Mumford, *The Brown Decades: A Study of the Arts in America, 1865–1895* (New York: Harcourt, Brace, 1931), 108–81.

99 McAndrew, "Architecture," *Bulletin*, 6–8.

100 John McAndrew, "Architecture in the United States," in *Trois siècles d'art aux États-Unis, Musée du Jeu de Paume, Paris* (Paris: Éditions des Musées Nationaux, 1938), 70.

101 McAndrew, "Architecture," 6.

102 McAndrew, "Architecture in the United States," in *Trois siècles,* 69, 75. See my discussion of McAndrew's concept of "naturalization" in "Modernism and the Vernacular at the Museum of Modern Art, New York," *Vernacular Modernism: Heimat, Globalization, and the Built Environment*, ed. Maiken Umbach and Bernd Hüppauf (Stanford, CA: Stanford University Press, 2005), 49–51; and Keith L. Eggener, "Nationalism, Internationalism and the 'Naturalisation' of Modern Architecture in the United States, 1925–1940," *National Identities* 8, no. 3 (September 2006): 243–58.

103 "Exhibition of Three Centuries of American Architecture Will Open," Museum of Modern Art Press Release 39211–4, February 11, 1939.

104 McAndrew, "Architecture in the United States," *Bulletin*, 2–12.

105 Lewis Mumford, *Sticks and Stones: A Study of American Architecture and Civilization* (New York: Horace Liveright, 1924).

106 McAndrew, "Architecture in the United States," *Bulletin*, 2–4; "Architecture in the United States," in *Trois siècles*, 70.

107 McAndrew, "Architecture in the United States," *Bulletin*, 4; "Architecture in the United States," in *Trois siècles*, 71.

108 Wolf Tegethoff, "From Obscurity to Maturity: Mies van der Rohe's Breakthrough to Modernism," in *Mies van der Rohe: Critical Essays*, ed. Franz Schultz (New York: Museum of Modern Art, 1989), 55–56. McAndrew emphasized that "Wright's work was published in Germany in 1910 and 1911, long before it was widely known here. Mies van der Rohe, Gropius, Oud, and other leaders of modern architecture have acknowledged the inspiration they found in his courageous pioneer [sic] works." McAndrew, "Architecture in the United States," in *Trois siècles*, 74. In 1928 Hitchcock published Wright's work in the Paris press. Henry-Russell Hitchcock, introduction to *Frank Lloyd Wright* (Paris: Cahiers d'art, 1928).

109 Lewis Mumford, "The Sky Line: The American Tradition," *New Yorker*, March 11, 1939, 38.

110 John McAndrew to Lewis Mumford, March 9, 1939 (Lewis Mumford Papers, folder 3642, Kislak Center for Special Collections, Rare Books and Manuscripts, University of Pennsylvania; Courtesy of the Estate of Lewis and Sophia Mumford). For an analysis of Le Corbusier's appropriation, see Bacon, *Le Corbusier in America*, 6–8.

111 McAndrew, "Architecture in the United States," in *Trois siècles*, 72; McAndrew, "Architecture in the United States," *Bulletin*, 6.

112 McAndrew, "Architecture in the United States," in *Trois siècles*, 75; McAndrew, "Architecture in the United States," *Bulletin*, 10.

113 William H. Jordy, "The International Style in the 1930s," *Journal of the Society of Architectural Historians* 24, no. 1 (March 1965): 13.

114 McAndrew, "Architecture in the United States," 10.

115 McAndrew," Architecture in the United States," in *Trois siècles*, 76; McAndrew, "Architecture in the United States," *Bulletin*, 11.

116 Lewis Mumford, "The Sky Line: Organic Architecture," *New Yorker*, February 27, 1932, 49.

117 McAndrew," Architecture in the United States," in *Trois siècles*, 75; McAndrew, "Architecture in the United States," *Bulletin*, 10.

118 McAndrew," Architecture in the United States," in *Trois siècles*, 76–77; McAndrew, "Architecture in the United States," *Bulletin*, 11–12.

119 "Architecture Section in Exhibit of American Art at Jeu de Paume," 4. See also "House of Plywood [No. 2]" in *The Town of Tomorrow: New York World's Fair 1939* (New York: New York World's Fair 1939, 1939) and "Modern Houses Top N. Y. Fair," *Architectural Forum* 69, no. 2 (August 1938): 143–58.

120 McAndrew, "Architecture in the United States," *Bulletin*, 11–12.

121 Edmond Pauty, "Trois siècles d'architecture américaine et l'évolution esthétique du building," *L'Architecture* 51 (September 15, 1938): 311–12.

122 Pauty, "Trois siècles," 320–24.

123 McAndrew, "Architecture in the United States," in *Trois siècles*, 77; McAndrew, "Architecture in the United States," *Bulletin*, 12; Pauty, "Trois siècles," 324.

124 In 1938 Gropius became chairman of Harvard's Department of Architecture.

125 "Two New Schools of Industrial Design Open" and "The New Bauhaus," *Architectural Forum* 67, no. 4 (October 1937): 22, 41, 82. László Moholy-Nagy, "Why Bauhaus Education," *Shelter* 3 (March 1938): 6–21.

126 Judith Cass, "New Bauhaus Will be Dedicated Today," *Chicago Daily Tribune*, November 9, 1937, 19. "Gropius Praises Efficiency Here," *New York Times*, May 27, 1928, 31.

127 Franz Schulze and Edward Windhorst, *Mies van der Rohe* (Chicago: University of Chicago Press, 2012), 189–90.

128 Barry Bergdoll and Leah Dickerman, *Bauhaus, 1919–1933: Workshops for Modernity* (New York: Museum of Modern Art, 2009), 12, 332.

129 Shannan Clark, "When Modernism Was Still Radical: The Design Laboratory and the Cultural Politics of Depression-Era America," *American Studies* 50, nos. 3/4 (Fall/Winter 2009): 54.

130 "Nazi-Banned Art Is Exhibited Here," *New York Times*, December 4, 1938, 40.

131 Lewis Mumford, "The Sky Line: Bauhaus—Two Restaurants and a Theatre," *New Yorker*, December 31, 1938, 40.

132 Jacques Fernand Levy, "Bauhaus and Design, 1919–1939," *Architectural Record* 85, no. 1 (January 1939): 71.

133 On "modernistic chairs," see Henry McBride, "Attractions in the Galleries," *New York Sun*, December 10, 1938, 11. On "streamlined fixtures" and "stream-lined vision," see Jerome Klein, "Modern Museum Surveys 10 Years of the Bauhaus," *New York Post*, December 10, 1938, 3.

134 On other unfavorable criticism of *Bauhaus, 1919–1928* and Barr's response to it, see Mary Anne Staniszewski, *The Power of Display: A History of Exhibition Installations at the Museum of Modern Art* (Cambridge, MA: MIT Press, 1998), 145–52.

135 John McAndrew, "'Modernistic' and 'Streamlined,'" *Bulletin of the Museum of Modern Art* 5, no. 6 (December 1938): 3. I suggest that McAndrew directed his article specifically to the criticism of McBride and Klein. See Sidney Lawrence, "Declaration

of Function: Documents from the Museum of Modern Art's Design Crusade, 1933–1950," *Design Issues* 2, no. 1 (Spring 1985): 70–71.

136 John McAndrew, foreword and introduction to *A Design Student's Guide to the New York World's Fair Compiled for P/M Magazine...by Laboratory School of Industrial Design* ([New York]: Laboratory School of Industrial Design, 1939), unpaged.

137 Sybil Gordon Kantor, *Alfred H. Barr, Jr., and the Intellectual Origins of the Museum of Modern Art* (Cambridge, MA: MIT Press, 2002), 103.

138 On the origin of Johnson's two design exhibitions, see Hanks, "Spreading the Gospel of Modern Design," 176. On the installation of the *Machine Art* exhibition, see Staniszewski, *Power of Display*, 152–60.

139 Philip Johnson, "History of Machine Art," in *Machine Art* (New York: Museum of Modern Art, 1934), unpaged.

140 "Exhibit of Useful Objects Under $5 on View," The Museum of Modern Art Press Release 381013–27, October 13, 1938.

141 Lynes, *Good Old Modern*, 180–81.

142 "Exhibit of Useful Objects Under $5 on View."

143 Staniszewski, *Power of Display*, 162, 163; see fig. 3.16.

144 Elodie Courter, "Notes on the Exhibition," in "Useful Objects Under Ten Dollars," *Bulletin of the Museum of Modern Art* 6, no. 6 (January 1940): 3–4.

145 John McAndrew, "New Standards for Industrial Design," *Bulletin of the Museum of Modern Art* 6, no. 6 (January 1940): 6; McAndrew, "Architecture in the United States," in *Trois siècles*, 72–73; McAndrew, "Architecture in the United States," *Bulletin*, 6, 8. McAndrew gives a version of Sullivan's dictum "form ever follows function." Louis H. Sullivan, "The Tall Office Building Artistically Considered," *Lippincott's Magazine* 57 (March 1896): 408–9; reprinted in *America Builds: Source Documents in American Architecture*, ed. Leland Roth (New York: Harper & Row, 1983), 345–46.

146 Hanks, "Spreading the Gospel of Modern Design," 177.

147 In 1934 MoMA held the exhibition *America Can't Have Housing?*, organized by Carol Aronovici. In 1936 its *Architecture in Government Housing* exhibition focused on the work of the PWA and the Resettlement Administration. Curated by Fantl, the show received the assistance of Bauer, who wrote the essay to its catalogue, *Architecture in Government Housing* (New York: Museum of Modern Art, 1936).

148 Frederick Gutheim and John McAndrew, "Houses and Housing," in *Art in Our Time: Tenth Anniversary Exhibition* (New York: Museum of Modern Art, 1939), 289–91.

149 Gutheim and McAndrew, "Houses and Housing," 291.

150 Gutheim and McAndrew, "Houses and Housing," 290, 305; John Yeon, "Buildings and Landscapes," Lionel H. Pries Distinguished Guest Lecture, University of Washington, May 1, 1986, unpaged. On the siting of the Watzek House and Yeon as its designer, see Treib, *John Yeon*, 51, 62–65.

151 Gutheim and McAndrew, "Houses and Housing," 311–12.

152 Gutheim and McAndrew, "Houses and Housing," 313, 314–15. W. Pope Barney served as the architect of record for the Mackley Houses.

153 Gaddis, *Magician of the Modern*, 334; Lynes, *Good Old Modern*, 222–23.

154 Rockefeller succeeded Goodyear as president of MoMA, and Clark became chairman of its board of trustees. "Modern Museum Shifts Officials," *New York Times*, May 9, 1939, 17. See also McAndrew, interview by Lynes, October 1971 (Russell Lynes Papers, 1935–1986, AAASI); Lynes, *Good Old Modern*, 222–23.

155 Nelson Rockefeller to John McAndrew, October 28, 1939 (John McAndrew Papers, WCA).

156 Cordell Hull to John McAndrew, September 30, 1939 (John McAndrew Papers, WCA).

157 Patricio del Real, "Building a Continent: The Idea of Latin American Architecture in the Early Postwar" (PhD diss., Columbia University, 2012), 5, 6, 8, 24. See especially the exhibitions *Brazil Builds* and *Latin American Architecture since 1945*. Philip Goodwin, *Brazil Builds* (New York: Museum of Modern Art, 1943); Henry-Russell Hitchcock, *Latin American Architecture since 1945* (New York: Museum of Modern Art, 1955).

158 The exhibition was initially planned for Paris as a sequel to *Trois siècles d'art aux États-Unis*. Del Real, "Building a Continent," 38–40.

159 Alfonso Caso, archaeologist and director of the National Institute of Anthropology and History, Mexico City, supervised the entire exhibition and also assembled the pre-Spanish section; Manuel Toussaint, director of the Institute of Esthetic Research of the National Autonomous University of Mexico, organized the section on colonial art, 1521–1821; the noted artist Miguel Covarrubias was responsible for the section on modern art, 1821–1940; and the painter and former museum director Roberto Montenegro assembled the section on folk art.

160 Del Real explores the concept of *mexicanidad* with its political and cultural projections in "Building a Continent," 36, 41.

161 In 1937 the Cárdenas government took control of the oil industry owned by American, British, and Dutch companies. Del Real, "Building a Continent," 42, 46–47.

162 Del Real, "Building a Continent," 44–45.

163 "Large Shipment of Art from Mexico Received," The Museum of Modern Art Press Release 40411–25, April 11, 1940; "200 Guests at Garden Party in Sculpture Garden," The Museum of Modern Art Press Release 40520–37, May 20, 1940.

164 Antonio Castro Leal, introduction to *Twenty Centuries of Mexican Art*, 15; "Twenty Centuries of Mexican Art," *Bulletin of the Museum of Modern Art* 7, nos. 2–3 (May 1940): 7.

165 On the hybrid character of Mexican culture, see Roberto Montenegro, *Twenty Centuries of Mexican Art*, 109–10. In 1935 McAndrew lectured at Vassar on the "true mexican style" as it emerged in the late seventeenth century. "McAndrew Lectures Here on Mexican Architecture," *Vassar Miscellany News*, May 18, 1935, 1, 3.

166 John McAndrew to John E. Abbott, March 4, 1940 (Curatorial Exhibition Files, Exh. #106. The Museum of Modern Art Archives, New York). See also "Twenty Centuries of Mexican Art Being Assembled for the Museum of Modern Art," The Museum of Modern Art Press Release 40220–14, February 20, 1940.

167 Del Real argues that the omission of modern architecture from *Twenty Centuries of Mexican Art*, first in Paris and then in New York, was deliberately made as part of an effort to craft a "strategic construction of Mexico's image in France, and later in the United States." See Del Real, "Building a Continent," 40–41, 70–71.

168 McAndrew, interview by Lynes, October 1971 (Russell Lynes Papers, 1935–1986, AAASI).

169 "Large Exhibition of Mexican Art in Final Preparation," The Museum of Modern Art Press Release 40507–32, May 7, 1940.

170 "Mexicans Arrive to Aid Art Show," *New York Times*, May 8, 1940, 27; Edward Alden Jewell, "The Panorama of Mexican Culture," *New York Times*, May 19, 1940, 137.

171 "Twenty Centuries of Mexican Art Opens at Museum of Modern Art," The Museum of Modern Art Press Release 40511–34, May 11, 1940.

172 "Twenty Centuries of Mexican Art," 8.

173 Nelson Rockefeller, telegram to John McAndrew, May 15, 1940 (John McAndrew Papers, WCA).

174 McAndrew was a member of the jury along with Walter Curt Behrendt, Stanley R. McCandless,

John Root, Edward Durell Stone, and Roland Wank. "Judges for Wheaton College Competition Announced," The Museum of Modern Art Press Release 38531–20, May 31, 1938. See also "An Architectural Competition," *Bulletin of the Museum of Modern Art* 5, no. 2 (February 1938): 2–3.

175 Lawrence Anderson and Herbert Beckwith subsequently employed a steel frame and curtain wall for their Alumni Swimming Pool (1939–40) on the campus of MIT.

176 "New Architectural Designs for Theatres," The Museum of Modern Art Press Release 39227–5, February 27, 1939. On Mumford's support for its modern design, see Mumford, "Sky Line: The American Tradition," 37. Hudnut served as "Professional Advisor" for the Smithsonian competition and wrote the program favoring "maximum flexibility" and "freedom of extension." "Modern Building Planned for Washington's 'Petrified Forest,'" The Museum of Modern Art Press Release 40111–3, January 11, 1940; Jill E. Pearlman, *Inventing American Modernism: Joseph Hudnut, Walter Gropius, and the Bauhaus Legacy at Harvard* (Charlottesville: University of Virginia Press, 2007), 133. See also Mina Marefat, "When Modern Was a Cause: The 1939 Smithsonian Art Gallery Competition," *Competitions* 1, no. 3 (Fall 1991): 36–49. On Hudnut's participation in the Smithsonian jury, see McAndrew, interview by Lynes, October 1971 (Russell Lynes Papers, 1935–1986, AAASI).

177 The details of Wright's exhibition, in all their complexity, are the subject of Smith, "Show to End All Shows," 12–64. See also Kathryn Smith, *Wright on Exhibit: Frank Lloyd Wright's Architectural Exhibitions* (Princeton, NJ: Princeton University Press, 2017), 126–44. McAndrew first visited Taliesin between October 20 and 26, 1939. At Wright's request, McAndrew also visited Taliesin on September 12 and 13, 1940. Frank Lloyd Wright, telegram to John McAndrew, September 9, 1940, and John McAndrew, telegram to Frank Lloyd Wright, September 10, 1940 (The Frank Lloyd Wright Foundation Archives [The Museum of Modern Art / Avery Architectural and Fine Arts Library, Columbia University, New York]; Copyright © 2017 Frank Lloyd Wright Foundation, Scottsdale, AZ; hereafter cited as FLWFA).

178 The Wright exhibition was originally scheduled to open on October 28, 1940, but was postponed. John McAndrew to Eugene Masselink, September 5, 1940; [John McAndrew] "Schedule for the Catalogue and Exhibition: The Museum of Modern Art" (FLWFA). See also [John McAndrew] "Schedule for Catalogue and Exhibition," September 5, 1940; John McAndrew, telegram to Frank Lloyd Wright, September 5, 1940 (FLWFA).

179 Initially Wright's retrospective was planned under the rubric of a joint exhibition, *Three Great Americans: Wright, Stieglitz, and Griffith*. Although the plan to exhibit Stieglitz's photographs was canceled, a large exhibition of the work of D. W. Griffith opened on November 13, 1940, the same night as the Wright

retrospective. Another show, known as *Exhibition X*, was also canceled. Smith, "Show to End All Shows," *The Show to End All Shows*, 35, 39–41.

180 Frank Lloyd Wright, telegrams to John McAndrew, September 5, and October 9, 10, and 11, 1940; John McAndrew, telegram to Frank Lloyd Wright, October 11, 1940 (FLWFA). See also Reed and Kaizen, *Show to End All Shows*, 70–102.

181 See section on Wright in Walter Curt Behrendt, *Modern Building: Its Nature, Problems, and Forms* (New York: Harcourt, Brace, 1937), 126–39.

182 See Walter Curt Behrendt, review of *Frank Lloyd Wright, Chicago* (Berlin: Ernst Wasmuth, 1911), in *Kunst und Künstler* 11, no. 9 (September 1913): 484–88; Behrendt, *Modern Building*, 139.

183 Frank Lloyd Wright to John McAndrew, May 30, 1940 (FLWFA).

184 Wright's edited version of Behrendt's essay on Wright is reproduced in Reed and Kaizen, *Show to End All Shows*, 125–33, as are other commissioned essays for the Wright exhibition catalogue.

185 Frank Lloyd Wright, telegram to John McAndrew, September 14, 1940, and letter to John McAndrew, September 16, 1940 (FLWFA).

186 John McAndrew, telegram to Frank Lloyd Wright, September 14, 1940 (FLWFA).

187 Frank Lloyd Wright to John McAndrew, September 15, 1940 (FLWFA); Frank Lloyd Wright, telegram to John McAndrew, September 16, 1940 (FLWFA).

188 Frank Lloyd Wright to John McAndrew, September 16, 1940 (FLWFA). Wright even warned of a "serious [law] suit" against the museum. Frank Lloyd Wright to John McAndrew, September 19, 1940 (FLWFA).

189 Barr offered McAndrew his views on museum policy. If the institution commissioned writers for a Wright "Festschrift," Barr held, the architect could not then "censor their remarks." On that basis the catalogue had to be abandoned. Alfred Barr, postcard to John McAndrew, undated [postmarked September 17, 1940] (Registrar Exhibition Files, Exh. #114, The Museum of Modern Art Archives, New York). Preferring not to reignite Wright's quarrel with the museum, McAndrew told him that there was no longer time to produce an "adequate catalogue" and that "the exhibition need not be incomplete" without one. McAndrew to Wright, September 18, 1940 (FLWFA).

190 Additional space for the Wright show was made possible by the cancellation of *Exhibition X*, planned by museum director and exhibition designer Leslie Cheek and Mumford as a timely vehicle to warn the nation of Hitler's objectives and to prepare it for an impending war. Smith, "Show to End All Shows," 39, 63n121.

191 Frank Lloyd Wright, telegram to John McAndrew, September 20, 1940 (FLWFA). See also McAndrew to Wright, September 18, 1940 (FLWFA).

192 The "Exhibition Outline" identified the overall premise as "reforming the house" with four themes: "the human approach," "simplification," "the open plan," and "new forms." "Exhibition Outline," October 1, 1940, reprinted in Reed and Kaizen, *Show to End All Shows*, Appendix, 210–12.

193 McAndrew's sketch plans for the installation of the first and second floors are illustrated in Reed and Kaizen, *Show to End All Shows*, 186, 187, plates 1, 2. A sketch plan identified as "Space for Wright Exhibition" (plate 1) includes annotations by McAndrew and Wright (Department of Architecture and Design Study Collection, The Museum of Modern Art, New York). A blueprint of the installation plan for the first and second floors of the exhibition (plate 2) has similar annotations. Drawing number 4000.003 (The Frank Lloyd Wright Foundation Archives [The Museum of Modern Art / Avery Architectural and Fine Arts Library, Columbia University, New York]; Copyright © 2017 Frank Lloyd Wright Foundation, Scottsdale, AZ).

194 Frank Lloyd Wright to John McAndrew, November 19, 1940 (FLWFA).

195 Alfred Barr, letter to the editor, *Parnassus* 13, no. 1 (January 1941): 3.

196 John D. Rockefeller Jr. had encumbered the lots behind the museum, on which the Usonian House would be sited, barring any large structures. Rockefeller also disapproved of Wright's solution to low-cost housing. See John D. Rockefeller Jr. to Stephen C. Clark, November 12, 1940, Rockefeller Archive Center, quoted and reproduced in Smith, "Show to End All Shows," 46–47, 63n153, 94–95. A drawing of Wright's Usonian House project (pencil on tracing paper) is reproduced in Smith, *Wright on Exhibit*, 134, fig. 4.21.

197 John McAndrew to Frank Lloyd Wright, December 2, 1940 (FLWFA). See also John McAndrew, memorandum to John E. Abbott [November 3, 1940], reproduced in Reed and Kaizen, *Show to End All Shows*, 91–93. Aside from the museum's contribution to construction costs, McAndrew had raised funds from other donors, including Goodwin and Johnson. McAndrew to Wright, September 18, 1940 (FLWFA).

198 "Greatest Living Architect Comes to Museum of Modern Art," The Museum of Modern Art Press Release 401112-67, November 8, 1920; "Museum of Modern Art Opens Large Exhibition of the Work of Frank Lloyd Wright, American Architect," The Museum of Modern Art Press Release 401112–69, November 12, 1940. McAndrew maintained that he wrote an unpublished study, "Space in the Architecture of Frank Lloyd Wright," but no manuscript survives. John McAndrew, curriculum vitae [1941] (Bio File, John McAndrew Papers, WCA).

199 "Museum of Modern Art Opens Large Exhibition of the Work of Frank Lloyd Wright, American Architect."

200 "Museum of Modern Art Opens Large Exhibition of the Work of Frank Lloyd Wright, American Architect."

201 The invitation to Wright's exhibition noted that it was "arranged by the architect himself." Frank Lloyd Wright Invitation, Museum of Modern Art, November 12, 1940 (FLWFA). See also Edward Alden Jewell, "Modern Museum Opens Two Shows," *New York Times*, November 13, 1940, 20; Geoffrey Baker, "Wright as Iconoclast," *New York Times*, November 24, 1940, X10; Milton Brown, "Frank Lloyd Wright's First Fifty Years," *Parnassus* 12, no. 8 (December 1940): 37–38. Barr confirmed that "the exhibition was planned by Mr. Wright and the installation supervised by him with the assistance of a group of very hardworking students from Taliesin." Alfred Barr, letter to the editor, *Parnassus* 13, no. 1 (January 1941): 3. For additional criticism, see Smith, "Show to End All Shows," 56–57.

202 Kathryn Smith suggests that Mumford wrote an unpublished review that expressed some criticism. She cites and quotes from an unpublished manuscript. Smith, *Wright on Exhibit*, 143–44, 258–59n169.

203 Hitchcock found a lack of cohesion between Wright's corpus prior to 1910 and the recent work produced since 1932, which he called "perhaps the finest contemporary building…in an architectural world stricken with depression." Henry-Russell Hitchcock, "Frank Lloyd Wright at the Museum of Modern Art," *Art Bulletin* 23, no. 1 (March 1941): 73.

204 Wright followed up with instructions that effectively scotched a circulating version of the exhibition. Frank Lloyd Wright to John McAndrew, December 1, 1940 (FLWFA).

205 McAndrew dovetailed his work on the *Guide* with his regular correspondence with Wright's office. John McAndrew to Eugene Masselink, April 25, 1940 (FLWFA).

206 McAndrew, *Guide to Modern Architecture, Northeast States*, 12.

207 McAndrew, *Guide to Modern Architecture, Northeast States*, 9.

208 McAndrew, *Guide to Modern Architecture, Northeast States*, 11.

209 Jere Abbott, review of McAndrew, *Guide to Modern Architecture, Northeast States*, in *Art Bulletin* 23, no. 2 (June 1941): 185–86. See also H. W. Janson, review of McAndrew, *Guide to Modern Architecture, Northeast States*, in *Parnassus* 12, no. 8 (December 1940): 24, 26.

210 Philip L. Goodwin, preface to *Built in USA, 1932–1944*, ed. Elizabeth Mock (New York: Museum of Modern Art, 1944), 6.

211 Rindge gave three lectures on modern painting and sculpture in February and March 1938 at the Dalton School. "Rindge to Lecture on Modern Painting," *Vassar Miscellany News*, February 26, 1938, 1.

212 "Director of the Department of Industrial Design, *Bulletin of the Museum of Modern Art* 7, no. 1 (April 1940): 9.

213 Although positive, a review by Frederick Gutheim was not published until January 1941. F. A. Gutheim, "'First Reckon with His Future': Frank Lloyd Wright's Exhibit at the Modern Museum," *Magazine of Art* 34 (January 1941): 32–33.

214 Alfred H. Barr to Mrs. [Abby Aldrich] Rockefeller, June 27, 1940 (Alfred H. Barr Jr. Papers, I.B.32. The Museum of Modern Art Archives, New York; hereafter cited as AHB, I.B.32. MoMA Archives, NY).

215 John Abbott, telegram to John McAndrew, February 5, 1940; and John McAndrew, memorandum to John Abbott, April 13, 1940 (Curatorial Exhibition Files, Exh. #106. The Museum of Modern Art Archives, New York).

216 "Museum of Modern Art Announces Staff Appointments and Changes," The Museum of Modern Art Press Release 41313–17, March 13, 1941.

217 Although Barr resigned as director in 1943, he assumed the position of advisory director. "Reorganization at Museum of Modern Art. Alfred H. Barr, Jr. Retires as Director," The Museum of Modern Art Press Release 431027–55, October 27, 1943.

218 Lynes, *Good Old Modern*, 220.

219 Lynes, *Good Old Modern*, 221.

220 Lynes, *Good Old Modern*, 221.

221 Lynes, *Good Old Modern*, 221.

222 Lynes, *Good Old Modern*, 221.

223 Mr. [Alfred H.] Barr, memorandum to Mr. Clark, Mrs. Sheppard, Mrs. Rockefeller, Mr. Nelson Rockefeller, Mr. Abbott, Mr. Goodwin, June 26, 1940 (AHB, I.B.32. MoMA Archives, NY).

224 Schulze, *Philip Johnson*, 180.

225 Philip Johnson to Alfred H. Barr Jr., undated [Summer 1940] (AHB, I.B.32. MoMA Archives, NY).

226 John McAndrew to Margaret Scolari Barr, undated [October 1941] (Margaret Scolari Barr Papers, II.231. The Museum of Modern Art Archives, New York).

227 Barr, "Our Campaigns," 62.

228 Alfred Barr to Paul Sachs, January 14, 1941 (Paul Sachs Correspondence HC3, folder 117. Harvard Art Museums, Harvard University, Cambridge, MA; hereafter cited as HAMHU).

229 Barr to Sachs, January 14, 1941 (Paul Sachs Correspondence HC3, folder 117. HAMHU).

230 Barr to Sachs, January 14, 1941 (Paul Sachs Correspondence HC3, folder 117. HAMHU). Russell Lynes quotes portions of the letter in *Good Old Modern*, 221–22.

231 Barr, "Our Campaigns," 63.

232 Aalto's Finnish Pavilion for the 1937 Exposition Internationale des Arts et Techniques in Paris had gained him international recognition, but not yet as a leading modernist. McAndrew informed Aalto that "a great number of architects" had visited his MoMA exhibition, notably Wright, Gropius, Breuer, Neutra, Lescaze, and Gunnar Asplund. John McAndrew to Alvar Aalto, April 16, 1938, quoted in Eeva-Liisa Pelkonen, "Aalto Goes to America," in *Aalto and America*, ed. Stanford Anderson, Gail Fenske, and David Fixler (New Haven, CT: Yale University Press, 2012), 81, 93n17. When Wright visited Aalto's Finnish Pavilion at the New York World's Fair in 1939, he was reported to have told Edgar Kaufmann Jr. that Aalto was a "genius." Juhani Pallasmaa, "Alvar Aalto: Toward a Synthetic Functionalism," in *Alvar Aalto: Between Humanism and Materialism*, ed. Peter Reed (New York: Museum of Modern Art, 1998), 34, 43n97.

233 Keith L. Eggener, "John McAndrew, the Museum of Modern Art, and the 'Naturalization' of Modern Architecture in America, ca 1940," in *Architecture and Identity*, ed. Peter Herrle and Erik Wegerhoff (Berlin: LIT Verlag, 2008), 240.

234 Lewis Mumford, "The Sky Line: Status Quo," *New Yorker*, October 11, 1947, 110.

235 Lewis Mumford, "The Architecture of the Bay Region," in *Domestic Architecture of the San Francisco Bay Region* (San Francisco: San Francisco Museum of Art, 1949), unpaged. See also Mumford's earlier publication on regionalism: Lewis Mumford, *The South in Architecture: The Drancy Lectures, Alabama College 1941* (New York: Harcourt, Brace, 1941).

236 "What Is Happening to Modern Architecture?," *Museum of Modern Art Bulletin* 15, no. 3 (Spring 1948): 1–21. On the MoMA symposium, see Liane Lefaivre and Alexander Tzonis, *Architecture of Regionalism in the Age of Globalization: Peaks and Valleys in the Flat World* (London: Routledge, 2012), 120–22.

237 Initially Henrich and Mock were each appointed as "acting curator." "Elizabeth Mock Appointed Acting Curator of the Museum's Department of Architecture," The Museum of Modern Art Press Release 43908–48, September 8, 1943.

238 The photographic exhibition of Vassar architecture was prepared for the New York Vassar Club and also shown at the University Women's Center at the New York World's Fair in early 1940. Agnes Rindge, "II The Art Department," in "Open House: The College at Work," *Vassar Alumnae Magazine* 25 (June 15, 1940): 22; "Photos Depict Vassar: Exhibition Will Cover 75 Years of College Architecture," *New York Times*, April 15, 1940, 22.

239 In 1939 an out-of-town MoMA membership cost ten dollars, the member receiving free admission to lectures and films, free copies of five publications per annum, and a subscription to the *Bulletin*. "Art Notes," *Vassar Miscellany News*, February 11, 1939, 5.

240 McAndrew, interview by Lynes, October 1971 (Russell Lynes Papers, 1935–1986, AAASI); Lynes, *Good Old Modern*, 223.

241 Elizabeth Mock, "Built in the USA—Since 1932," in *Built in USA, 1932–1944*, ed. Mock, 9–25. The show comprised the Architecture section of MoMA's fifteenth anniversary exhibition *Art in Progress*. During its planning, McAndrew was a member of the Architecture Committee, chaired by Goodwin.

242 Mock included such government-sponsored public housing as Baldwin Hills in Los Angeles, designed by Reginald D. Johnson and Wilson, Merrill & Alexander with Clarence Stein as consulting architect, a Federal Housing Administration (FHA) "limited-dividend rental development" (1942), and the Farm Security Administration–sponsored farm community at Chandler, Arizona, designed by Burton D. Cairns and Vernon DeMars (1936–38). See *Built in USA, 1932–1944*, ed. Mock 54–57, 62–63.

243 On Mock's important role in advancing regionalism at MoMA, see Liane Lefaivre, "Critical Regionalism: A Facet of Modern Architecture since 1945," in *Critical Regionalism: Architecture and Identity in a Globalized World*, ed. Liane Lefaivre and Alexander Tzonis (Munich: Prestel, 2003), 24; Lefaivre and Tzonis, *Architecture of Regionalism in the Age of Globalization*, 116–19. Before she married William Wurster, Bauer had had "a love affair" with Mumford, which he described briefly in Lewis Mumford, *Sketches from Life: The Autobiography of Lewis Mumford, the Early Years* (New York: Dial Press, 1982), 459.

IV. EPILOGUE

In June 1941 John McAndrew left his curatorial post at the Museum of Modern Art but still maintained ties to it. In spite of his difficulties with Nelson Rockefeller and senior staff, he would serve on the museum's Architecture Committee from 1941 to 1947. During his final six months at MoMA (January–June 1941), McAndrew pursued several projects. With Elizabeth Mock he wrote the popular book *What Is Modern Architecture?* (1942), based on two circulating exhibitions.[1] As lead author, McAndrew examined recent developments in American and European modernism through the Vitruvian prism of "utility," "strength," and "beauty," thereby invoking his formative academic training.[2] Moreover, he imposed his perspective on modernism, finding accord among International Style principles, regional modernism, and a Mumfordian position endorsing both "free forms of nature" and a harmonious relationship between a building and its natural setting.[3] Once again John Yeon's Watzek House in Portland, Oregon (1936–38), which had figured in MoMA's *Art in Our Time* exhibition (1939), served as a major example. In the summer of 1940 McAndrew had finally visited the house along with Edgar Kaufmann Jr. and Eliot Noyes (see fig. 3.15).[4]

During the spring of 1941 McAndrew also wrote the article "Design in Modern Architecture," in which he continued to frame modernism through a Vitruvian reformulation: construction, function, and design. Now design (Vitruvian beauty) was understood to mean a "deliberate aesthetic intention" in order for a building to be "a work of art."[5] Joining utility with beauty, McAndrew held that the "consistent expression of function" served as a "powerful aesthetic device."[6] There he went beyond the formalist analysis underlying Henry-Russell Hitchcock and Philip Johnson's International Style to explain how one aesthetic treatment might be contingent upon a structural element (e.g., steel reinforcing rods within concrete to produce the "thin and elegant curving ramps" of Berthold Lubetkin and Tecton's Penguin Pool, Regent's Park Zoo, London [1933–34]), while another aesthetic treatment might be embodied in a new spatial configuration, such as an "open plan" or an "abstract composition."[7] There, too, McAndrew's article addressed the relationship between architecture and modern painting by pointing out the congruence of formal elements in Le Corbusier's Villa Savoye (1929–31) and his 1920 *Still Life with a Stack of Plates*, which had informed the color palette of the Vassar Art Library (see Chapter Two) (see figs. 2.41 and 2.42). And finally, the article called upon architects to learn from vernacular building traditions: structural systems of modern factories on the one hand and folk architecture on the other.

McAndrew had not finished his master of architecture degree and was, therefore, without a key credential were he to return to academia. So his best option was to address the remaining task of the thesis requirement, and he finally received his degree from Harvard's Graduate School of Design in June 1941. With Alfred Barr's help, McAndrew was named Sachs Research Fellow at Harvard University in 1941. But the ongoing war in Europe obliged him to relinquish the research and travel fellowship.[8] Thus, with an architecture degree but no museum, university, or research appointment in hand, he turned in an unlikely direction.

In August 1941 McAndrew went to Mexico, where, it seems, his pursuits could do double duty. It was his fourth trip. This time he shared an apartment with John Yeon, on the corner of Liverpool and Havre Streets in what was then the select and cosmopolitan Zona Rosa neighborhood of Mexico City. Earlier, during the spring of 1940, McAndrew had joined Yeon in Mexico while he prepared MoMA's *Twenty Centuries of Mexican Art* show. In an effort to advance Yeon's career, McAndrew had suggested Yeon's name to organizers of the New York World's Fair, who were in the throes of commissioning demonstration rooms for its "America at Home" display, according to architectural historian Marc Treib.[9] Although they spent several months together, the two men would separate by late 1941. Yeon would enter the armed forces and be deployed overseas. Upon Yeon's departure McAndrew confided to Margaret Barr that he felt "pretty numb."[10]

McAndrew's first task upon his arrival in Mexico was to explore the country, often with the renowned art historian Manuel Toussaint, visiting colonial churches, monasteries, and convents. McAndrew's study of Mexican colonial architecture was funded by two new sources, both awarded in the summer of 1941: a Fogg Museum Fellowship in Modern Art and a grant from the US government, discussed below.[11] McAndrew planned to write a book together with Toussaint, who had organized the section on colonial art for *Twenty Centuries of Mexican Art*. Although the book they envisioned, *Mexican Architecture, 1521–1821*, was never completed, McAndrew did publish with Toussaint a scholarly article based on their research, titled "Tecali, Zacatlán, and the Renacimiento Purista in Mexico," in 1942.[12]

But all along, McAndrew hoped to return to academia, as he told Toussaint and also Margaret Barr, with whom he maintained an extensive correspondence.[13] During the fall of 1941 he also attempted to secure an academic appointment for the following year at either the University of California, Berkeley, or Brooklyn College, though unsuccessfully.[14] What's more, he was eager to return to Vassar College, were it not for the likelihood that the idea would be thwarted by Agnes Rindge. Since his departure from Poughkeepsie, he had perceived her attitude toward him to be one of "ambivalence"—and understandably so.[15]

McAndrew's activities in Mexico took him on another mission that mixed scholarship with what would become wartime intelligence. In addition to the Fogg fellowship, he received a grant from the Office of the Coordinator of Inter-American Affairs (OCIAA) for his research project with Toussaint.[16] A product of Franklin D. Roosevelt's administration, the OCIAA was officially founded and sponsored by the US Department of State, which had appointed Nelson Rockefeller as coordinator in August 1940.[17] (In March 1945 the OCIAA was renamed the OIAA—the Office of Inter-American Affairs.) Rockefeller's position facilitated a close watch over his business interests in Latin America. It obliged him to resign his post as president of MoMA even as he remained on its board of trustees, where he continued to be apprised of the museum's programs and objectives.[18] Earlier, in October 1939, McAndrew had a brief association with the Department of State when he participated in a conference it sponsored, Inter-American Relations in the Field of Art, in Washington, DC, under the leadership of Secretary of State Cordell Hull.[19] Now McAndrew joined the OCIAA's field of operations in Mexico. On the one hand, Rockefeller had faulted the MoMA curator's administrative competence. On the other hand, he respected McAndrew's intellect, fluent Spanish, knowledge of Mexican art and culture, and social skills, all of which were useful to Rockefeller's project in the Americas. In assembling his new agency of Inter-American Affairs, Rockefeller looked expressly within the Museum of Modern Art network by enlisting most notably the Harvard modernist Lincoln Kirstein, trustee (later president) John Hay Whitney, and guest curator (later director) René d'Harnoncourt.[20] Rockefeller also recruited two MoMA administrators, John Abbott and Monroe Wheeler, as chairmen of art and publications, respectively, in addition to Wallace K. Harrison, who succeeded Rockefeller as coordinator in December 1944.[21]

The OCIAA's ostensible purpose was to strengthen the economies of Latin America and forge hemispheric solidarity. But there was another more strategic objective. Its principal goal was to bolster American authority and thereby counter what the US government judged to be the Axis intent on destabilizing the region.[22] It sought to prevent Axis influence in Latin America through the blacklisting and elimination of companies owned by Axis nationals.[23] In addition to economic cooperation and direct attempts to check Axis sway, the OCIAA mission focused on a range of activities, including transportation, health, food supply, propaganda, and education. The office vigorously promoted unity within the Americas in the form of propaganda cloaked as cultural programs, especially print media, radio, and motion pictures.[24] Toward that objective, the OCIAA also offered grants for research in Latin American studies, among them McAndrew's project with Toussaint, in addition to sponsored exhibitions, including those held at the Museum of Modern Art in New York.[25]

During the war years McAndrew served the OCIAA as intelligence collector and goodwill ambassador, aided by his "genius for socializing," the fact that he was "highly cultivated in many fields," and what Margaret Barr called his "unsuppressible [*sic*] joie de vivre."[26] In Mexico City he carried on an energetic social schedule with Latin American and foreign elite, including government officials. He also traveled throughout Latin America. But any OCIAA assignments, aside from his project with Toussaint, remain unknown. If McAndrew were involved in significant covert activity, he received little remuneration for it. He was unremittingly pressed for money. By the spring of 1942 he had run out of OCIAA funds and planned to rely on monies given to him by his friend Edgar Kaufmann. He was loath to ask OCIAA principals for more.[27] Although McAndrew had received the first installment of his Fogg grant, he had not yet used it because he intended to shift course in favor of a new project: a book on modern architecture covering the period from 1931 to 1941.[28] His ambitious plan, however, was still unformed, and he would later abandon the project.

From 1942 to 1944 McAndrew traveled throughout Mexico pursuing research on its colonial architecture. He also gave lectures both inside and outside the academy. In 1942 he held the post of lecturer at the National Autonomous University of Mexico. Two years later he joined Toussaint as professor at the National Institute of Anthropology and History.[29] He also organized exhibitions of the works of Pablo Picasso (1943) and José Clemente Orozco (1944) and installed nearly a dozen other shows in museums, libraries, and galleries in Mexico.[30] His friends worried about his finances. In July 1944 Barr wrote to d'Harnoncourt, expressing his concern over McAndrew's lack of compensation for "very valuable services rendered both to Mexican institutions of various sorts and to our own work in the Embassy or other channels."[31] After McAndrew's death, his wife, Betty, told Margaret Barr that during the war years in Mexico, "John had worked for the CIA."[32] Although the Central Intelligence Agency was not formed until 1947, its forerunners were both the OCIAA and the Office of Strategic Services (OSS), founded in 1942. Having reached the age of thirty-seven in 1941, McAndrew was exempt from the Selective Service. Yet his work with the OCIAA and its affiliation with the Department of State drew him not only to the center of hemispheric politics at the intersection of culture but also to national service.

Like McAndrew, Agnes Rindge maintained close ties with MoMA's inner circle and the former habitués of the Askew salon during the war years. From 1941 to 1942 Rindge also worked for the OCIAA, but she was based in New York. There she served as executive secretary and consultant in the Division of Art, arranging for traveling exhibitions of Latin American art works within the United States.[33] While she continued her faculty appointment at Vassar College, she obtained leave during the academic year 1943–44 to hold the position of assistant executive vice president at the Museum of Modern Art under John Abbott. During that time, she wrote and narrated the ten-minute color film, *Alexander Calder: Sculpture and*

Constructions (1944), based on a retrospective at the museum in 1943. The film was first shown at Vassar in 1945.[34]

Toward the end of 1944, with World War II drawing to a close, McAndrew was ready to return to the United States. Barr, who had taught at Wellesley College from 1926 to 1929, intervened on McAndrew's behalf in communications with Wellesley art professor Bernard Heyl and art professor emerita Myrtilla Avery.[35] In early 1946 McAndrew resumed his academic life, taking a position as lecturer at Wellesley College.[36] The following fall he was named associate professor.[37] Unlike most teaching faculty, McAndrew taught a wide range of courses in both the modern and pre-modern fields. While he specialized in modern art and architecture as well as Spanish art, as he had at Vassar College, he also taught the introductory course (with colleagues) as well as courses in painting of Northern Europe, medieval architecture, and Renaissance and baroque architecture. For twenty-three years he was a member of the Wellesley faculty, until his retirement in 1968. He was considered by colleagues to be the Department of Art's "most brilliant and influential teacher" as well as its most "popular."[38]

During the 1940s McAndrew returned briefly to the practice of architecture with designs for two houses: one in Mexico City (1947–48) and another in Manchester, Connecticut (1948–49). The first was the result of his association with the German-born Mexican architect Max Cetto. In collaboration with McAndrew, Cetto designed a house for the US diplomat Robert C. Hill in the San Angel neighborhood of Mexico City; it was located on a street leading to what would become the El Pedregal gardens, at a time when Luis Barragán was first engaged in the development of the Pedregal lava fields (fig. 4.1).[39] For a house that Barragán intended to build in San Angel, McAndrew had suggested "the idea of an invisible one, with lava walls and glass walls."[40] That thought must have stuck with McAndrew during his design collaboration with Cetto.

The place-centered Hill House was both modern and Mexican. Its flat roofs and blocks of limestone and pink cantera—a quarried volcanic rock native to Mexico—joined with large glass windows to form the main volumes of the house just as garden walls and terraces defined its courtyards.[41] The tensional relationship of its walls and chimney recalled not only the work of Frank Lloyd Wright but also that of De Stijl architects and Ludwig Mies van der Rohe. The house embodied McAndrew's vision of modernism infused with vernacular architectural elements, in effect a "naturalized" Latin American modernism. However, McAndrew departed Mexico before construction had begun. Presumably he visited the house on his return to Mexico City in the fall of 1953 as a visiting lecturer on an extensive tour to seven Latin American countries for the US Information Service.[42]

For a decade McAndrew served concurrently as a professor and as director of the Wellesley College Museum, known as the Farnsworth Museum (1948–58). In that capacity he represented the college as client for the new art museum, the Mary Cooper Jewett Arts

Center. In the fall of 1955 Paul Rudolph received the commission as a result of a closed competition among a short list of candidates drawn up by McAndrew, which included Eero Saarinen, Edward Durell Stone, Marcel Breuer, Hugh Stubbins, and Paul Rudolph. Most were experienced and highly respected architects with whom McAndrew had previously worked during his curatorship at MoMA. That was not the case with the young Rudolph. McAndrew knew Rudolph and his early work with Ralph Twitchell in Sarasota, Florida, at least since the spring of 1950, when Chick Austin, at that time the director of the Ringling Museum in Sarasota, had hosted Agnes Rindge and him, among others, for a two-week "History of Art" seminar in conjunction with Florida State University, at which McAndrew gave a talk on baroque architecture and Rindge gave one on baroque art.[43] Impressed with Rudolph's Sarasota buildings, McAndrew expressed the Department of Art's preference in a letter to Wellesley president Margaret Clapp, inferring that Rudolph would be "likely to produce the most distinguished design…one of *quality*."[44]

McAndrew seems to have had a personal stake in shaping Rudolph's final design. During the two-year phase of the project's design development, the museum director worked with Department of Art chair Agnes Abbot to supply Rudolph with continual critiques, especially on the articulation of the building's exterior.[45] Rudolph's early scheme called for a patterned block supported by a ground floor arcade, which evoked the Doge's Palace in Venice.[46] The use of a Venetian model not only resonated with postmodernism but also

Figure 4.2
Paul Rudolph. Jewett
Arts Center, Wellesley
College, Wellesley,
Massachusetts, 1955–
58 (© Wayne Andrews
/ Esto)

anticipated McAndrew's associations with Venice and its architecture, discussed below. The final design of the Jewett Arts Center (1955–58) shared a "new formalism" with Mies van der Rohe's Seagram Building in New York (1954–58), Edward Durell Stone's US Embassy in Delhi (1956–59), and Minoru Yamasaki's McGregor Memorial Conference Center for Wayne State University in Detroit (1958), according to the architectural historian and critic William Jordy (fig. 4.2).[47] In his article "The Formal Image: USA" (1960), Jordy attributed to these and other recent buildings a turn toward neoclassical massing and ornament, largely abandoned by the modern movement of the 1920s and 1930s. The Jewett Arts Center, which incorporated the Farnsworth Museum in 1958, also served an urban function as both a "gateway" and an edge to Severance Green and to the adjacent Collegiate Gothic buildings of Green and Pendleton Halls.[48] It comprised a neutral glass box clad in what architectural historian Timothy Rohan has called "delicate screens" of anodized aluminum drawn from Le Corbusier's brise-soleils.[49] Combined with the formal language of modernism, Rudolph's historicism was an attempt both to contextualize the building within Wellesley's Gothic campus and to shape public space.[50] But the arts center's return to ornament was not without its critics. In

1960 Jordy cautioned that the Jewett Arts Center and other buildings "augur an increasing abstractness and historicism in much of modern architecture, such that it may quite literally cease to be modern in the sense that its imagery grows from the urgency of modern life."[51]

To accompany a 1960 editorial by McAndrew, the editors of *Museum News* included a text that not only cited his contribution to the design of the Museum of Modern Art building but also affirmed his advisory role in planning the Jewett Arts Center.[52] Find an architect "sympathetic to your needs," McAndrew counseled readers in his editorial: "If the building is fine, part of the credit is yours; if not, yours may be half the fault."[53] Clearly, McAndrew felt that he was responsible for selecting the right architect and helping to craft the building's design such that he could also share its success.

During the Wellesley years McAndrew transformed his personal life, as Agnes Rindge had done in 1945 when she married Philip W. Claflin, a US Army captain. In 1953 McAndrew married Betty Amory Bartlett (1906–86), following in the path of Chick Austin and other friends within his circle of gay men who were married. The McAndrews bought pictures together and formed a collection of largely modern works. To friends Betty spoke in jest about their collecting collaboration: "It was my money and his eye!"[54] These years also marked a definitive rift in his friendship with Philip Johnson, McAndrew still holding him accountable for his earlier fascist activities.[55]

During his tenure as director of the Wellesley Art Museum, McAndrew "built up that collection as a study collection," which, as with the Vassar Art Gallery, formed "a direct connection between the classes and the study of objects," according to Eleanor Garvey, who served as Wellesley curator.[56] McAndrew pursued a spirited acquisition program, enlisting such friends and MoMA colleagues as Edgar Kaufmann Jr., Jere Abbott, and Dorothy Miller to make donations to Wellesley. Moreover, both John and Betty made generous gifts to the museum. In recognition of the director's many contributions, the Jewett Arts Center would present the *Exhibition in Honor of John McAndrew* (1969).[57]

McAndrew also produced critical essays on modern art and architecture largely in the art press. Once again, he drew upon his singular blend of formal, technical, and cultural analysis, but now his writing was largely directed to postwar building. In his 1953 article "Our Architecture Is Our Portrait," McAndrew selected examples from the recent MoMA exhibition *Built in USA: Post-war Architecture* to make the point that "a good modern building can look natural almost anywhere in America."[58] At last, he felt, modern architecture had been fully naturalized, Americanized. Houses, he insisted, were either "formal ones," both "classic and intellectual"—Mies's Farnsworth House in Plano, Illinois (1945–51) and Johnson's Glass House in New Canaan, Connecticut (1949–50)—instinctively "romantic" (those of Frank Lloyd Wright), or somewhere in between (Marcel Breuer in Connecticut, Walter Gropius in Massachusetts, Paul Rudolph in Florida, Richard Neutra in California).[59]

Even the postwar house had to take a back seat to the excitement of American commercial and industrial architecture whose refined construction and glazed surfaces suggested both technical achievement and drama—hallmarks of the early 1950s in such works as Saarinen & Associates' General Motors Technical Center in Detroit (1948–51) and Skidmore, Owings & Merrill's Lever House in New York (1950–52). These buildings reflected the aspirations of an expanding postwar corporate culture. The General Motors Technical Center held a special interest for McAndrew because his former Vassar student Aline Bernstein Louchheim had married its lead designer, Eero Saarinen, in 1953. McAndrew's 1956 article "First Look at the General Motors Technical Center," for *Art in America*, combined technical acumen with visual acuity, unmistakable when he discussed, for example, the way in which the "doors and windows and striking black steel verticals (at once mullions *and* structural support) all agree to a five-foot measure, or module."[60] With the help of Ezra Stoller photographs, McAndrew was able to convey the character of the different parts of the building complex disposed around a lake. There, too, he parsed their play of forces between large scale and human scale, man and machine (especially evident in the Dynamometer Building), a static curtain wall with mullions (Skylight Building) opposing the "technical daring" of the dome adjacent to it, and a prismatic building giving way to a dramatic interior whose "Constructivist" stairway of "creamy travertine" formed "a circle pulled up into a helix…by stainless steel suspension rods" (Research Building).[61] Holding fast to the traditions of the Bauhaus and the Cranbrook Academy of Art of enriching architecture through art—and following the example of such American postwar buildings as Harkness Commons and Graduate Center at Harvard University (1948–52), designed by Gropius and TAC (The Architects Collaborative)—the GM Technical Center integrated sculpture by Antoine Pevsner, Alexander Calder, and Harry Bertoia.[62] In short, McAndrew understood the surging corporate climate and optimism of postwar America as well as GM's ethos of increasing product interchangeability with a stratagem of planned obsolescence embodied in the complex, which introduced another chapter in an Americanized modernism.[63] More broadly, he grasped the tempo of corporate architecture and, in the work of its best practitioners, the power of buildings to convey their culture and to excite.

McAndrew knew as much about the history of American commercial building as he did about the corporate architecture of his own time. Thus, he was well equipped to respond insightfully to Edgar Kaufmann's 1956 Louis Sullivan centennial exhibition at the Art Institute of Chicago. In his article "Who Was Louis Sullivan?" for the journal *Arts*, McAndrew framed Sullivan's architecture in relation to the modern movement of the 1920s. According to McAndrew, when Gropius visited Chicago [with him, in 1937], "he said that had the *avant-garde* in Europe known the Carson-Pirie-Scott Building [1899–1904], the evolution of modern architecture there might have been accelerated by fifteen years" (see Chapter 3, note 126 and fig. 3.13).[64] McAndrew was able to make meaningful connections between the first generation of modernists and such early Chicago pioneers as Sullivan, much as Hitchcock had also done for architecture and Barr had done for painting (see Chapter Three). But Gropius's statement is especially significant because in it he recognizes the radical precedent set by an American building in the evolution of international modernism and Sullivan's importance as a proto-modernist.

With the opening of the Jewett Arts Center in 1958, the year after McAndrew ended his directorship of the Wellesley College Museum, he returned to Mexico, this time to resume his wartime investigation of the way in which European forms had been naturalized by local Mexican practice. His scholarship resulted in the insightful and prodigious study *The Open-Air Churches of Sixteenth-Century Mexico*, for which he received the 1965 Alice Davis Hitchcock Award from the Society of Architectural Historians.[65] The walled outdoor courtyards of churches in New Spain, with their oratories and chapel, were a survival from the sixteenth-century conversion of indigenous Mexicans by mendicant friars. Rather than deriving from a European precedent, McAndrew determined, "the forecourt with its auxiliary architecture...was a new element, synthesized locally from older [Mexican] models in order to satisfy new demands."[66] In his review of the book, George Kubler, the eminent historian of pre-Columbian and Spanish colonial art, understood McAndrew's underlying concept of a naturalized, in this case Latin Americanized, architecture, endorsing his "method of argument" as "rigorous."[67]

Following his retirement, events in Italy drew McAndrew to the study of its Renaissance and baroque architecture and, more specifically, to its Venetian architecture. In 1971, responding to the devastating floods of November 1966 and their destruction of Italian cities, chief among them Venice and Florence, McAndrew officially founded the Boston-based organization Save Venice Inc. to assist in restoration work.[68] He was joined in this effort by his wife, Betty, and Sydney J. Freedberg, the renowned art historian at Harvard University who had been his former Wellesley colleague. During the 1970s McAndrew served as president of Save Venice and then chairman of its board. Joining members of the organization, they raised one million dollars to preserve and restore buildings, sculpture, and frescoes in Venice. Notable architectural restoration projects included the facades of the Ca' d'Oro and the Scola Grande di San Marco, the Doge's Palace, the church of Santa Maria dei Miracoli, and the Cathedrals of Murano and Torcello. In 1974 McAndrew published the *Catalogue of the Drawings Collection of the Royal Institute of British Architects: Antonio Visentini*.[69] He was completing his book on *Venetian Architecture of the Early Renaissance* at the time of his death in Venice in 1978.[70] For his efforts on behalf of Venice, McAndrew was made Grande Ufficiale of the Order of Merit of the Republic of Italy in 1974, a recipient of the Torta Prize in 1976, and an honorary fellow of the Venetian Institute of Sciences, Arts and

Letters.[71] From modernist to preservationist, McAndrew had come full circle.

John McAndrew's varied careers as architect, professor, historian, museum curator, museum director, and preservationist were intertwined. His commitment to an integrated form of modernism suffused his scholarship and academic life, as it did his extensive museum and design work. Notwithstanding McAndrew's close associations with Barr and Johnson (in the early years) and other Harvard modernists, as well as his firsthand knowledge of the new architecture in both Europe and the United States, he was reluctant to promote his Vassar College Art Library interior, as previously seen (see Preface, page 34; fig. 2.8). Most likely, this was because he considered its design, as well as that of the Vassar Cooperative Bookstore and the Taylor Art Gallery, to be "remodeling commissions," executed before he had received his architecture degree (see figs. 2.9, 2.12, and 2.31).[72] McAndrew was also sensitive to the weight of Rindge's position as champion of Vassar's new Art Department headquarters, following his departure for the Museum of Modern Art in 1937. We might speculate on another reason. Deep within the formation of modernism is a set of values giving artistic expression to modern times. The notion that art and architecture reflected a culture of the "present" meant that as the "present" inevitably changed, so would aesthetic expression.[73] McAndrew may have thought of an art library interior as a provisional typology open to continual renovation, as he did his first sculpture garden at MoMA. Moreover, he may have considered the polychromed surfaces of the Art Library to be experimental and, like all experimental design, subject to revision. As it turned out, McAndrew's intention to design a modern interior shaped by the vernacular tendencies of his time and his "functional thinking," as Rindge recognized, would be enduring values. Of course, McAndrew's functionalism did not rest on Bauhaus thinking alone but was shaped by Corbusian ideals with the aim of transforming the utilitarian into art by means of a purist palette and the architectonic or constructive use of colors with their physiological and psychological effects. The judicious restoration of the Art Library, completed in 2009 by Platt Byard Dovell White Architects, has revitalized the interior by preserving original fabric, whenever possible, combined with interventions to increase technical and managerial efficiency for the digital age. In doing so, the restoration has preserved not just a landmark interior but the essential character of McAndrew's design.

McAndrew's vision of modernism, evinced in his Art Library and Art Gallery interiors as well as his curatorship at the Museum of Modern Art, reframed the modern movement in America from different perspectives. The Art Library challenged the traditional view of American modernism as a Harvard-MoMA axis by positioning Vassar College as a new focal point. Along with Frederick Kiesler's Film Arts Guild Cinema and Chick Austin's Morgan Memorial office, the Art Library validated the role of applied color and its capacity to layer space within the theory and practice of American modernism, thus contesting International Style orthodoxy. As curator, McAndrew crafted MoMA exhibitions that lent further provocation. American modernism could no longer be mainly judged as a mere importer of European avant-garde design. His exhibitions and slim, but no less significant, body of writing defined the modernist project as cross-cultural, hybrid, and open-ended. On the one hand, modernism in America embodied homegrown achievements—the architecture of Frank Lloyd Wright, industrial buildings, and skyscrapers. McAndrew revalorized them as American contributions to international modernism. On the other hand, American modernism was also constructed of European importations given to "naturalizations" by virtue of local conditions, technology, and culture. Moreover, regional modernisms engaged vernacular practices, organic materials, climate, topography, and locale—all constituents of architecture in the Americas. McAndrew's ambition had been to synthesize both native and received traditions. In the end, he lent his critical voice to the formation of an American position on prewar modernism, which confronted established assumptions while advancing a more pluralistic vision. McAndrew went on to champion the postwar shift toward formal abstraction whose integration with art captured the spirit of his earlier Vassar Art Library interior.

1   The circulating exhibitions were *What Is Modernism? I (1938–41)* and *What Is Modernism? II (1939–42)*. A third exhibition, *What Is Modernism? III (1943–45)*, circulated after the publication of the book *What Is Modern Architecture?* (New York: Museum of Modern Art, 1942).

2   *What Is Modern Architecture?*, 7–12. Although McAndrew was the book's lead author, he considered it a departmental collaboration. John McAndrew to Alfred H. Barr Jr., April 9, 1942 (Alfred H Barr Jr. Papers, I.B.32. The Museum of Modern Art Archives, New York; hereafter cited as AHB, I.B.32. MoMA Archives, NY).

3   *What Is Modern Architecture?*, 18.

4   John McAndrew to Henry-Russell Hitchcock Jr., July 29, 1940 (Henry-Russell Hitchcock Papers, 1919–1987, Archives of American Art, Smithsonian Institution).

5   John McAndrew, "Design in Modern Architecture," *Art Education Today* (New York: Teachers College, Columbia University, 1941), 29.

6   McAndrew, "Design in Modern Architecture," 31.

7   McAndrew, "Design in Modern Architecture," 30, 36.

8   John McAndrew, curriculum vitae [ca. 1949] (Bio File, John McAndrew Papers, Courtesy of Wellesley College Archives; hereafter cited as John McAndrew Papers, WCA).

9   On Yeon's demonstration room design for the "America at Home" display, see Marc Treib, *John Yeon: Modern Architecture and Conservation in the Pacific Northwest* ([Novato, CA]: ORO Editions [2016]), 83–85. See also John McAndrew, ed., *Guide to Modern Architecture, Northeast States* (New York: Museum of Modern Art, 1940), 61.

10   John McAndrew to Margaret Scolari Barr, undated [late 1941] (Margaret Scolari Barr Papers, II.231. The Museum of Modern Art Archives, New York; hereafter cited as MSB, II. 231. MoMA Archives, NY).

11   In June 1941 McAndrew accepted the Fogg Museum Fellowship, although it was not announced until 1942. "John McAndrew Gets Fogg Grant," *New York Times*, January 25, 1942, 37; "McAndrew Awarded Fogg Fellowship," *Harvard Crimson*, January 26, 1942, accessed December 18, 2012, https://www.thecrimson.com/article/1942/1/26/mcandrew-awarded-fogg-fellowship-pjohn-mcandrew/.

12   John McAndrew with Manuel Toussaint, "Tecali, Zacatlán, and the Renacimiento Purista in Mexico," *Art Bulletin* 24, no. 4 (December 1942): 311–25.

13   John McAndrew to Margaret Scolari Barr, August 1, 1941 (MSB, II.231. MoMA Archives, NY).

14   John McAndrew to Margaret Scolari Barr, undated [Fall 1941] and [late 1941]; John McAndrew to Alfred Barr, October 4, 1941, and November 28 [1941] (MSB, II.231. MoMA Archives, NY).

15   McAndrew to Margaret Scolari Barr, undated [late 1941] (MSB, II.231. MoMA Archives, NY). See also Chapter Two, note 157.

16   McAndrew's curriculum vitae [ca. 1949] (Bio File, John McAndrew Papers, WCA) lists this as "grant from Co-ordinator for Latin-American Affairs, 1941." When McAndrew's study with Toussaint was published in the *Art Bulletin*, he identified the funding agency as the Committee for Inter-American Artistic and Intellectual Relations. McAndrew with Toussaint, "Tecali, Zacatlán, and the Renacimiento Purista in Mexico," 311n1.

17   Cary Reich, *The Life of Nelson A. Rockefeller: Worlds to Conquer, 1908–1958* (New York: Doubleday, 1996), 182–87; "Defense Post Goes to N. Rockefeller," *New York Times*, August 17, 1940, 6. See also Claude Curtis Erb, "Nelson Rockefeller and United States–Latin American Relations, 1940–1945 (PhD diss., Clark University, 1982).

18   On January 9, 1941, Rockefeller resigned and John Hay Whitney was elected museum president. "John Hay Whitney Succeeds Nelson A. Rockefeller as President of Museum of Modern Art," The Museum of Modern Art Press Release 41108–2, January 8, 1941.

19   Cordell Hull to John McAndrew, September 20, 1939 (John McAndrew Papers, WCA).

20   Toby Miller and George Yúdice, *Cultural Policy* (London: Sage Publications, 2002), 41.

21   *History of the Office of the Coordinator of Inter-American Affairs: Historical Reports on War Administration* (Washington, DC: Government Printing Office, 1947), opp. pp. 150, 152.

22   Founded as the Office for Coordination of Commercial and Cultural Relations between the American Republics, it was renamed the Office of the Coordinator of Inter-American Affairs (OCIAA) in July 1941. Gisela Cramer and Ursula Prutsch, "Nelson A. Rockefeller's Office of Inter-American Affairs (1940–1946) and Record Group 229," *Hispanic American Historical Review* 86 (November 2006): 785–86. See also Gisela Cramer and Ursula Prutsch, "Nelson A. Rockefeller's Office of Inter-American Affairs and the Quest for Pan-American Unity: An Introductory Essay," in *¡Américas unidas! Nelson A. Rockefeller's Office of Inter-American Affairs (1940–46)*, ed. Gisela Cramer and Ursula Prutsch (Madrid: Iberoamericana, 2012), 15–51.

23   See Cramer and Prutsch, "Nelson A. Rockefeller's Office of Inter-American Affairs," 786, 791.

24   Monica Ann Rankin, "¡México, La Patria! Modernity, National Unity, and Propaganda during World War II" (PhD diss., University of Arizona, 2004), 116, 213–43.

25   Cramer and Prutsch, "Nelson A. Rockefeller's Office of Inter-American Affairs," 797; Catha Paquette, "Soft Power: The Art of Diplomacy in US-Mexican Relations, 1940–1946," in Cramer and Prutsch, ¡Américas unidas!, 143–80; Cathleen M. Paquette, "Public Duties, Private Interests: Mexican Art at New York's Museum of Modern Art, 1929–1954" (PhD diss., University of California, Santa Barbara, 2002), 208–35.

26   PJF [Peter J. Fergusson], "John McAndrew," Wellesley College Friends of Art Newsletter 14 (1977–78); Margaret Scolari Barr, "John McAndrew," unpublished manuscript [1979], 25 (Margaret Scolari Barr Papers, II.232. The Museum of Modern Art Archives, New York; hereafter cited as MSB, II.232. MoMA Archives, NY).

27   In February 1942 McAndrew sent a report to the OCIAA that documented his extensive research in Mexico. John McAndrew to David H. Stevens, February 28, 1942 (AHB, I.B.32. MoMA Archives, NY). In a subsequent letter to Barr, McAndrew revealed: "the [OCIAA] grant had been so difficult to extract, had seemed to be a little grudgingly given, and had involved humbly accepting favors from NR [Nelson Rockefeller] and JEA [John E. Abbott]—all of which were so distasteful that I had not considered asking for additional funds." McAndrew to Barr, April 9, 1942 (AHB, I.B.32. MoMA Archives, NY).

28   John McAndrew to Alfred H. Barr Jr., March 7 [1942] and April 9, 1942 (AHB, I.B.32. MoMA Archives, NY). In 1941 McAndrew planned to write an article for the Journal of the Warburg Institute titled "Modern Architecture: The Last Ten Years." John McAndrew, curriculum vitae [ca. 1941] (Bio File, John McAndrew Papers, WCA).

29   McAndrew, curriculum vitae [ca. 1949] (Bio File, John McAndrew Papers, WCA).

30   John McAndrew, "Mexico, 1941–44" [list of activities] (AHB, I.B.32. MoMA Archives, NY); McAndrew, curriculum vitae [ca. 1949] (Bio File, John McAndrew Papers, WCA).

31   Alfred H. Barr Jr. to René d'Harnoncourt, July 18, 1944 (Alfred H. Barr Jr. Papers [AAA: 2170]. The Museum of Modern Art Archives, New York).

32   Margaret Scolari Barr, "John McAndrew," 28 (MSB, II.232. MoMA Archives, NY).

33   "Professor Rindge Works for Defense," Vassar Miscellany News, September 27, 1941, 2.

34   Alexander Calder: Sculpture and Constructions, with cinematography by Herbert Matter, was produced by the Museum of Modern Art. Notice, Vassar Miscellany News, January 10, 1945, 1.

35   Alfred Barr to John McAndrew, December 1, 1944 (John McAndrew Papers, WCA).

36   Wellesley College, "Wellesley College Bulletin Catalogue Number 1945–1946" (1945), 38, The Wellesley College Catalogs, Book 41, http://repository.wellesley.edu/catalogs/41.

37   Wellesley College, "Wellesley College Bulletin Catalogue Number 1946–1947" (1946), 41, The Wellesley College Catalogs, Book 40, http://repository.wellesley.edu/catalogs/40.

38   Sydney J. Freedberg, Fogg Art Museum Newsletter 15 (April 1978): 6; PJF [Peter J. Fergusson], "John McAndrew" (John McAndrew Papers, WCA).

39   During the mid-1940s McAndrew suggested to Barragán that he might consider Yeon as designer for his El Pedregal development. Treib, John Yeon, 260n38.

40   John McAndrew to John Yeon, November 6, 1945 (John Yeon Archives, Portland, OR). I wish to thank Keith Eggener and Marc Treib for generously providing me with a copy of the letter.

41   Susanne Dussel Peters, Max Cetto, 1903–1980: Arquitecto Mexicano-Alemán (Azcapotzalco, Mexico: Universidad Autonoma Metropolitana, 1995), 167; "Tres casas del arquitecto Max Cetto," Arquitectura 26 (January 1949): 20–27. For an extended analysis of the Hill House and its garden, see Juan Manuel Heredia, "The Work of Max Cetto: Restorations of Topography and Disciplinarity in Twentieth Century Modern Architecture" (PhD diss., University of Pennsylvania, 2008), 169–80, figs. 89–106.

42   McAndrew gave lectures in Mexico, Cuba, Colombia, Guatemala, Panama, Venezuela, and Ecuador. See clippings and Betty McAndrew, "Notes on John's clippings from Latin-American lecture trip 1953 Fall" (John McAndrew Papers, WCA).

43   John Rhodes, "The Jewett Arts Center," in The Landscape & Architecture of Wellesley College, ed. Peter Fergusson, James F. O'Gorman, and John Rhodes (Wellesley, MA: Wellesley College, 2000), 208. By 1950 Rudolph and Twitchell, his partner, had built more than a dozen houses in the Sarasota area. See Christopher Domin and Joseph King, Paul Rudolph: The Florida Houses (New York: Princeton Architectural Press, 2002); "Third Annual History of Art Seminar, Sarasota Florida April 3–15, 1950," The Florida State University and John and Mable Ringling Museum of Art (John McAndrew Papers, WCA).

44   Rhodes, "Jewett Arts Center," 207.

45   Rhodes, "Jewett Arts Center," 218–19; Timothy Rohan, "The Dangers of Eclecticism: Paul Rudolph's Jewett Arts Center at Wellesley," in Anxious Modernisms: Experimentation in Postwar Architectural Culture, ed. Sarah Williams Goldhagen and Réjean Legault (Montreal and Cambridge, MA: Canadian Centre for Architecture and MIT Press, 2000), 196.

46   Rhodes, "Jewett Arts Center," 213–15.

47   William H. Jordy, "The Formal Image: USA," *Architectural Review* 127 (March 1960): 158.

48   Rohan, "Dangers of Eclecticism," 197.

49   Rohan, "Dangers of Eclecticism," 191–92.

50   On Rudolph's call for modern buildings to be more contextual and to reflect their urban character, see Rhodes, "Jewett Arts Center," 210.

51   Jordy, "Formal Image," 163.

52   John McAndrew, "Points of View," *Museum News* 39, no. 3 (November 1960): 13.

53   McAndrew, "Points of View," 13.

54   Peter J. Fergusson, interview by the author, Wellesley, Massachusetts, April 25, 2013.

55   Fergusson, interview by the author, April 25, 2013. See also Rhodes, "Jewett Arts Center," 203.

56   Oral History Interview with Eleanor M. Garvey, February 28–June 13, 1997 (Archives of American Art, Smithsonian Institution).

57   *Exhibition in Honor of John McAndrew: Wellesley College Museum, Jewett Arts Center, March 4–April 13, 1969* (Wellesley, MA: The College, 1969).

58   John McAndrew, "Our Architecture Is Our Portrait," *New York Times*, January 18, 1953, SM12. While Johnson served as director of the Department of Architecture and Design, he was assisted in the book and exhibition by Hitchcock and curator Arthur Drexler. Henry-Russell Hitchcock and Arthur Drexler, eds., *Built in USA: Post-war Architecture* (New York: Simon & Schuster [1952]).

59   McAndrew, "Our Architecture Is Our Portrait," SM12.

60   John McAndrew, "First Look at the General Motors Technical Center," *Art in America* 44, no. 2 (Spring 1956): 27.

61   McAndrew, "First Look at the General Motors Technical Center," 28–29, 31.

62   McAndrew, "First Look at the General Motors Technical Center," 30–31.

63   Reinhold Martin, *The Organizational Complex: Architecture, Media, and Corporate Space* (Cambridge, MA: MIT Press, 2003), 140–41.

64   John McAndrew, "Who Was Louis Sullivan?," *Arts* 31 (November 1956): 23.

65   John McAndrew, *The Open-Air Churches of Sixteenth-Century Mexico: Atrios, Posas, Open Chapels, and Other Studies* (Cambridge, MA: Harvard University Press, 1965).

66   McAndrew, *Open-Air Churches of Sixteenth-Century Mexico*, 202.

67   George Kubler, review of McAndrew, *Open-Air Churches of Sixteenth-Century Mexico*, in *Art Bulletin* 47, no. 4 (December 1965): 525.

68   From 1967 to 1971 the organization was originally part of the Venice Committee of the International Fund for Monuments, but in 1971 it formed the tax-exempt organization Save Venice Inc. "Save Venice Inc.," accessed April 2, 2015, www.savevenice.org/about-save-venice/boston-chapter/.

69   John McAndrew, *Catalogue of the Drawings Collection of the Royal Institute of British Architects: Antonio Visentini* (Farnborough, Hants, UK: Gregg, 1974). For a list of McAndrew's publications compiled by Professor Lilian Armstrong, see "John McAndrew, former Professor Emeritus, Wellesley College, Publications" (John McAndrew Papers, WCA).

70   John McAndrew, *Venetian Architecture of the Early Renaissance* (Cambridge, MA: MIT Press, 1980).

71   John McAndrew, curriculum vitae [undated] (Bio File, John McAndrew Papers, WCA); obituary [written by Fello Atkinson], "Professor John McAndrew," *London Times*, February 21, 1978 (John McAndrew Papers, WCA).

72   John McAndrew, curriculum vitae [1941] (Bio File, John McAndrew Papers, WCA).

73   For analyses of the culture of the "present" and its importance in the formation of modernism, see Preface, note 2.

A COMPLETE LIST OF EXHIBITIONS HELD AT THE VASSAR COLLEGE ART GALLERY, 1923-1940

COMPILED BY ELIZABETH NOGRADY

Paintings by Samuel Halpert, Guy Pène du Bois, George Luks, Augustus Vincent Tack, John Sloan and Gifford Beal, courtesy of Kraushaar Galleries, New York
January 8–February 1, 1923

Oriental Rugs, from the collection of James F. Ballard
February 9–March 1, 1923

Paintings by Modern Masters of Spain, Germany, France, Russia, Italy, Belgium and America, loaned by Société Anonyme, Inc., New York
April 4–May 12, 1923

Paintings by Helen L. Sorensen
April 18–30, 1923

Paintings by Thomas Gainsborough, Mme Vigée Le Brun, Sir William Beechey, Francesco Mazzola, George Romney, Jacob Ochtervelt, Sir Joshua Reynolds, Lorenzo Lotto, Gaspard de Crayer, and Giuliano Bugiardini, courtesy of Ehrich Galleries, New York
May 14–June 12, 1923

Sketches by James Scott
May 22–June 4, 1923

Paintings of the Maine Coast by C. K. Chatterton
September 26–October 31, 1923

Paintings by Wassily Kandinsky, organized by Société Anonyme, Inc., New York
November 1923

Medici Prints of Italian and Flemish Masters
Opened November 4, 1923

Italian Water Colors by Irene Weir
Opened November 12, 1923

Paintings by Felicie Waldo Howell, A.N.A.; Water Colors by Modern Artists Including George Luks, courtesy of Kraushaar Galleries, New York
November 26–December 19, 1923

The Photographic Work of Edward Crosby Doughty
December 10–19, 1923

Graphic Art of Czechoslovakia, from the collection of Henry J. John
January 8–February 1, 1924

Chinese Draperies, from the Seaman Collection
Opened January 15, 1924

Robert Henri Paintings, courtesy of Macbeth Gallery, New York
January 30–February 28, 1924

Portrait of John Burroughs by Walter Beck
Opened February 11, 1924

French Art of the 17th and 18th Centuries, from various private collections
February 29–March 10, 1924

Paintings and Lithographs by New Society Artists
March 1–28, 1924

Modern Paintings, courtesy of New Gallery, New York; *Works by Modern English Illustrators*
April 9–30, 1924

Paintings by Jane Peterson of Gloucester and Venice
May 1–June 10, 1924

Paintings, courtesy of Grand Central Art Galleries, New York
September 1924

Paintings of Land and Sea Scapes, loaned by the Painters' and Sculptors' Galleries Association, New York
October 1924

Jewelry Designs for the Cartier Scholarship Prize, loaned by the Art Center, New York
October 15–November 20, 1924

Paintings by Rockwell Kent, courtesy of Wildenstein &
Co., New York
October 22–November 20, 1924

New England Sketches by Agnes Rockwell Jones
November 1924

Paintings of C. K. Chatterton
November 25–December 19, 1924

Pastel Paintings by Walter Beck
December 6–19, 1924

Paintings by Arthur B. Davies, from the collection
of Mrs. W. T. Bush
1925

Modern Painting, courtesy of Montross Gallery,
New York
January 7–30, 1925

*Medieval Art, Tapestries, Stained Glass, Carved Wood
and Stone, Leather and Iron Work*, courtesy of the House
of P. W. French, New York, and Demotte, Paris
January 8–30, 1925

Costume Dolls, loaned by Bonwit, Teller and Company
Closed February 16, 1925

French Paintings, courtesy of Durand-Ruel, New York
Closed February 28, 1925

Etchings by William Meyrowitz
Opened March 1, 1925

Matisse, courtesy of the Fearon Galleries, New York;
Modern American Paintings, courtesy of the Kraushaar
Galleries, New York
March 3–27, 1925

*Works by Members of the Faculty of the Grand Central
School of Art, New York City: Wayman Adams, George
Elmer Browne, George Pearse Ennis, Edmund Graecen
and Sigurd Skou*
April 1–25, 1925

American Painting, courtesy of Macbeth Art Gallery,
New York
May 7–June 16, 1925

Water Colors by Contemporary American Artists, courtesy
of Montross Gallery, New York
October 1–31, 1925

Drawings and Lithographs by Modern French Masters,
courtesy of Weyhe Gallery, New York
November 1–30, 1925

*Oil Paintings by C. K. Chatterton and Katharine Liddell
of Vassar College*
December 1, 1925–January 6, 1926

Paintings by French Impressionists, courtesy of Scott and
Fowles, New York, and Durand-Ruel, New York
January 1926

American Paintings, courtesy of Ferargil Galleries,
New York
February 1926

*Modern Painting, French Post-Impressionists and
Contemporary American Painters*, courtesy of the Ferargil
Galleries, New York
September 28–October 20, 1926

Wood-cuts, Etchings and Lithographs, courtesy of Keppel
Gallery, New York; M. Knoedler & Co., New York;
J. B. Neumann, New York; Weyhe Gallery, New York;
and the Print Club of Philadelphia
October 25–November 15, 1926

Paintings by Maurice Fromkes, courtesy of Milch Gallery,
New York
November 22–December 10, 1926

Paintings by C. K. Chatterton
December 13, 1926–January 18, 1927

An Architect's Sketchbook by Charles Collens
January 8–22, 1927

Jugoslavian Peasant Art, from the collection of
K. Kostich
January 18–February 7, 1927

Fifty Prints of the Year: Second Annual Exhibition,
organized by the American Institute of Graphic Arts
January 22–29, 1927

*Ingres: Fifty-Nine Drawings by the Great French Draftsman
of the Nineteenth Century*, courtesy of de Hauke & Co.,
New York
January 29–February 7, 1927

Watercolors by Merton Clivette, courtesy of George
Hellman, the New Gallery, New York
February 9–24, 1927

American Decorative Arts, loaned by the New York
Society of Craftsmen and Individual Artists;
Finnish Textiles, loaned by the Art Center, New York
March 8–24, 1927

Modern European Art since 1900, courtesy of F. Valentine
Dudensing Gallery, New York; de Hauke & Co.,
New York; Kraushaar Galleries, New York; J. B.
Neumann, New York; Société Anonyme, New York;
Marie Sterner Gallery, New York; Wildenstein & Co.,
New York; and Weyhe Gallery, New York
April 8–27, 1927

*American Water Colors from the Annual Exhibition,
1927,* organized by the American Federation of Arts,
New York
May 4–June 8, 1927

Paintings by C. K. Chatterton
October 1–31, 1927

Paintings by Gifford Beal
November 1–30, 1927

Lithographs by George Bellows and Etchings by Whistler, Millet, Eby, Roth, Woodbury, Hassam, Bracquemond, Appian and Lalanne
December 1–17, 1927

Paintings by Edward Hopper and Allen Tucker
January 1–31, 1928

Paintings and Drawings by Bernard Karfiol
February 1–29, 1928

Oil Paintings, Water Colors and Pastels by Mrs. Edith Varian Cockcroft
March 1–23, 1928

Modern Oil Paintings
May 12–June 12, 1928

Paintings by C. K. Chatterton
October 1–31, 1928

Paintings by Modern American Artists, courtesy of Downtown Gallery, New York
November 19–December 21, 1928

Paintings, courtesy of Kraushaar Galleries, New York
January 13–February 9, 1929

Second Annual American Print Makers
February 11–March 11, 1929

Oils and Water Colors by Carolyn C. Mase and Alice Judson
March 11–22, 1929

Works by Jacques Callot illustrating Commedia dell'Arte, on loan from the Theatre Arts Monthly Collection of Seventeenth-Century Prints
April 2–27, 1929

Paintings by Modern American Artists, courtesy of Macbeth Gallery, New York
April 29–May 18, 1929

Paintings by Impressionists and Post Impressionists
May 22–June 11, 1929

Paintings by James Scott
October 15–November 15, 1929

Representative Collection of Prints by Daumier, loaned by William M. Ivins Jr., curator of prints, the Metropolitan Museum of Art, New York
December 2–20, 1929

Paintings by C. K. Chatterton
February 3–21, 1930

The Geneva Drawings by Violet Oakley, N.A.; Paintings and Etchings by Margery A. Ryerson '09
March 1–21, 1930

Lithographs, Etchings, and Drawings, courtesy of the Print Makers Association
April 1930

Paintings by Ruth Lambert Palliser
April 7–30, 1930

Color Prints, organized by the Metropolitan Museum of Art, New York
Opened May 1, 1930

Paintings by Modernists, courtesy of Daniel Gallery, New York
May 12–June 16, 1930

Recent Paintings of New England by C. K. Chatterton
October 1–31, 1930

Paintings by Contemporary American Artists, courtesy of Downtown Gallery, New York
November 1–30, 1930

Modern Sculpture and Prints, courtesy of Weyhe Gallery, New York
December 1–19, 1930

Paintings, Water Colors, Drawings, Lithographs and Etchings by Gifford Beal, courtesy of Kraushaar Galleries, New York; *Oil Sketches and Drawings by Maurice Sterne*, courtesy of Kraushaar Galleries, New York
January 7–31, 1931

American Paintings, organized by the College Art Association, New York
February 1931

Prints by Old Master Engravers, courtesy of M. Knoedler & Co., New York
March 1–27, 1931

American Print Makers Fourth Annual Exhibition, courtesy of Downtown Gallery, New York
Closed April 30, 1931

Modern French Painting, organized by the College Art Association, New York
May 4–June 1931

Modern Austrian Painting, organized by the College Art Association, New York
October 6–31, 1931

Wood Blocks by Lilian Miller '17
November 1–14, 1931

Water Colors and Paintings by Members of the Vassar Faculty
November 12–30, 1931

Photographs by Women Practitioners and Drawings by Students in the Cambridge School of Architecture
November 15–30, 1931

Paintings by Zubiaurre, loaned by the International Art Center of the Roerich Museum, New York
December 1–18, 1931

Seascapes and Water-Fronts, organized by the College Art Association, New York
January 4–31, 1932

Modern Sculpture, courtesy of Weyhe Gallery, New York
February 1–29, 1932

Old Master Prints, courtesy of M. Knoedler & Co., New York
March 1–25, 1932

Etchings and Lithographs, courtesy of Downtown Gallery, New York
Opened March 23, 1932

Watercolors Made by Americans, organized by the College Art Association, New York
May 9–June 13, 1932

Photographs of Persian-Islamic Architecture, loaned by the American Institute for Persian Art and Archaeology, New York
October 10–November 5, 1932

Nineteenth-Century French Art and Modern Lithographs, from the collection of Walter Squire
Opened October 29, 1932

Paintings and Drawings by Eugene Berman and Pavel Tchelitchew, courtesy of Julien Levy Gallery, New York; loaned by the Wadsworth Atheneum, Hartford, Connecticut; and from various private collectors
November 6–December 4, 1932

Paintings and Water Colors by Philena Lang, Marjorie D. MacCracken, Gertrude Smith, Bernice E. Tonks, Margaret F. Washburn and Lois Whitney; *Facsimiles of Flemish 16th-Century Drawings*, courtesy of Prestel-Gesellschaft, Frankfurt am Main
December 5–16, 1932

Drawings by Sculptors, organized by the College Art Association, New York
January 4–29, 1933

German Sixteenth-Century Facsimile Drawings, courtesy of Prestel-Gesellschaft, Frankfurt am Main
January 5–31 January 1933

Italian Baroque Painting and Drawing: Sixteenth, Seventeenth and Eighteenth Centuries, organized by the College Art Association, New York
January 23–February, 11, 1933

Sculpture by Americans, organized by the College Art Association, New York
February 27–March 18, 1933

Seventeenth-Century Dutch Facsimile Drawings, courtesy of Prestel-Gesellschaft, Frankfurt am Main
March 11–April 15, 1933

Designs for Modern Stained Glass, loaned by D'Ascenzo Studios, Philadelphia
March 18–24, 1933

Wood-blocks by Julius John Lankes
April 4–15, 1933

Chatterton Paintings
April 17–May 11, 1933

Photographs of Modern Architecture, loaned by the Museum of Modern Art, New York
May 11–29, 1933

Paintings by Anton Otto Fischer
May 22–June 12, 1933

Exhibition of Student Work
June 1–12, 1933

Paintings and Water Colors by Philena Lang, Marjorie D. MacCracken, Gertrude Smith, Bernice E. Tonks, Margaret F. Washburn and Lois Whitney
October 7–22, 1933

Chinese Paintings through the Ages, organized by C. Edward Wells for the College Art Association, New York
October 23–November 12, 1933

French Houses of the Early Eighteenth Century, organized by Wesleyan University Architectural Exhibitions
November 11–December 1, 1933

Water Colors by John Goss
November 14–30, 1933

Photographs of Roman Baroque Church Facades, organized by Wesleyan University Architectural Exhibitions
December 4–15, 1933

Russian Art, from the collection of Alfred H. Barr Jr., courtesy of Marie Sterner Gallery, New York, and loaned by the Nicholas Roerich Museum, New York
January 10–31, 1934

Photographs of Civic Works designed by Gilmore D. Clarke for the Westchester County Parks Commission, loaned by the Westchester County Parks Commission
January 14–February 15, 1934

Architectural Fantasies by Emilio Terry
February 5–March 5, 1934

Baroque Drawings
February 16–March 23, 1934

Flemish and Dutch Old Masters, courtesy of Walter L. Ehrich, Ehrich Galleries, New York
March 1–23, 1934

Polish Art
April 1–30, 1934

Eighteenth-Century French Drawings
April 23–May 6, 1934

Post-War European Paintings, loaned by the Wadsworth
Atheneum, Hartford, Connecticut and Smith College,
Northampton, Massachusetts; from various private
collections; courtesy of various galleries; *Contemporary
American Sculpture*, courtesy of Downtown Gallery,
New York
May 7–June 11, 1934

National Collegiate Photography
June 1934

East Indian Art, courtesy of Heeramaneck Galleries,
New York
October 4–November 1, 1934

*Tiepolo Drawings of the Eighteenth Century and Venetian
Prints*, courtesy of Weyhe Gallery, New York, and from
the collection of John McAndrew; *Portrait Photographs
by George Platt Lynes*, courtesy of Julien Levy Gallery,
New York
October 15–November 1, 1934

*Color Reproductions of First-Century Frescoes from the Villa
of Mysteries, Pompeii*
November 1–22, 1934

Piranesi Prints of Roman Architecture, courtesy of
Weyhe Gallery, New York, and from the collection
of John McAndrew
November 1–25, 1934

Self Portraits in Prints from the Collection of Elmer Adler,
organized by the College Art Association, New York
November 5–24, 1934

Sculpture by Emma Lou Davis '27
November 5–December 1, 1934

Gauguin's Tahitian Idyll, loaned by the Museum of
Modern Art, New York
December 1–17, 1934

Eight Modes of Modern Painting, organized by the
College Art Association, New York
December 3–22, 1934

Drawings from the Astoria, Queens, Housing Project
January 9–14, 1935

Photographs by Clarence Ward of French Gothic Churches
January 9–February 9, 1935

Portrait of Madame Cézanne *by Paul Cézanne*, from the
collection of Adolph Lewisohn
January 18–28, 1935

Drawings by Henry Hill Pierce, Jr.
January 18–31, 1935

Photographs of Romanesque Churches of Apulia, from the
collection of Kingsley Porter
January 28–February 20, 1935

Modern Sculpture and Drawings by Sculptors, organized
by the College Art Association, New York
February 1–28, 1935

Model and Drawings of the Middlesex Village Project,
loaned by the Cambridge School of Architecture and
Landscape Architecture, Cambridge, Massachusetts
March 4–12, 1935

Works by the Pictorial Photographers of America, courtesy
of Margaret de M. Brown; *Photographs by Man Ray*
Opened April 22, 1935

Romantic Paintings, Seventeenth to Twentieth Centuries
organized in conjunction with the conference *Some
Correlations in Romantic Art, Literature & Music*, Vassar
College
May 1–June 10, 1935

*Cambodian and Siamese Stone and Wood Sculpture,
Javanese Puppets and Masks*, courtesy of Yamanaka
and Co., New York, and organized by the College Art
Association, New York
October 7–27, 1935

Reproductions *of Engravings and Drawings by
William Blake*
Closed October 25, 1935

Architecture by Le Corbusier
October 30–November 6, 1935

Piranesi: Roma Antica
October 30–November 7, 1935

Reproductions of Mexican Frescoes by Diego Rivera,
organized by the Museum of Modern Art, New York
December 2–20, 1935

*Ninety-Seven Etchings, Engravings and Drypoints by
Albrecht Dürer*, from the collection of Lessing J.
Rosenwald, organized by the College Art Association
January 6–25, 1936

Three Picture Exhibition: Henri Matisse, Interior with a
Violin Case; *André Derain*, Still Life; *Georges Rouault*,
The Spectacled Man, organized by the Museum of
Modern Art, New York
January 8–18, 1936

Pencil Drawings by Beatrice Field
January 25–February 10, 1936

*Paintings by Old Masters of Sixteenth and Seventeenth
Centuries*, courtesy of Jacques Seligmann & Co.,
New York; Arnold Seligmann, Rey & Co., New York;
and Ehrich-Newhouse Galleries, New York
February 1–29, 1936

Posters by Cassandre, organized by the Museum of
Modern Art, New York
March 2–20, 1936

Paintings and Lithographs by Eugene Kingman
March 9–20, 1936

Paintings by Courbet and Corot, loaned by Smith College, Northampton, Massachusetts; courtesy of Wildenstein & Co., New York; and from the collection of Mr. and Mrs. Lloyd B. Westcott, New York
March 9–April 30, 1936

Plates of Chinese Painting in the Boston Museum
March 9–April 30, 1936

Sculptures by Calder and Flanagan
March 9–June 8, 1936

German and Italian Prints, courtesy of M. Knoedler & Co., New York
November 2–22, 1936

Two Italian Seventeenth-Century Paintings: Annunciation by G. B. Caracciolo, loaned by the Wadsworth Atheneum, Hartford; and *St. Sebastian*, School of Caravaggio, loaned by the Fogg Art Museum, Harvard University, Cambridge, Massachusetts
November 2–December 12, 1936

Photographs by Clarence Kennedy of Sculptures by Desiderio da Settignano
November 2–December 18, 1936

Italian Baroque Paintings, loaned by the Metropolitan Museum of Art, New York and the Wadsworth Atheneum, Hartford, Connecticut, and courtesy of Durlacher Brothers, New York
January 7–31, 1937

Fishmarket in Rome *by Hubert Robert and Eighteenth-Century French Facsimiles; Two Bronzes and a Drawing by Gaston Lachaise*, loaned by the Whitney Museum of American Art, New York
January 9–May 15, 1937

Photographs, Drawings, etc. of the Great Abbey of Cluny, from the collection of Professor Kenneth John Conant, Harvard University, with drawings by Kenneth John Conant; *Photographs Illustrating the Development of French Gothic Architecture*
January 9–February 8, 1937

Facsimiles of Paintings and Prints by Pieter Bruegel the Elder, courtesy of Raymond & Raymond, Inc., New York
March 1–26, 1937

Vital Statistics, courtesy of American Folk Art Gallery, New York
April 6–18, 1937

Drawings of Old Modern Masters, courtesy of Durlacher Brothers, New York; Julien Levy Gallery, New York; and Weyhe Gallery, New York
May 1937

Processes of Paintings, loaned by the Fogg Art Museum, Harvard University, Cambridge, Massachusetts
May 4–23, 1937

Photographs of Modern Architecture, loaned by the Museum of Modern Art, New York, and from the collections of John McAndrew and Liam Lescaze; *Abstract Paintings and Constructions*, loaned by the Wadsworth Atheneum, Hartford, Connecticut, and the Museum of Modern Art, New York
May 20–June 9, 1937

Facsimiles of Prints of Master E. S., from the collection of Dr. Richard Krautheimer
November 15–1 December 1, 1937

Paintings by Pavel Tchelitchew, courtesy of Julien Levy Gallery, New York
January 1–23, 1938

Ballet Caravan Collaborators, courtesy of Julien Levy Gallery, New York
January 5–23, 1938

Photographic Enlargements of the Medieval Minor Arts, loaned by the Walters Art Gallery, Baltimore, Maryland
February 1–15, 1938

Paintings, Water Colors and Drawings by C. K. Chatterton and Sculpture by Elizabeth Geiger
February 1–26, 1938

Photographs of Roman Baroque Church Facades, organized by Wesleyan University Architectural Exhibitions, Middletown, Connecticut
February 1–28, 1938

Facsimiles of Paintings and Prints by Pieter Bruegel the Elder
Closed February 8, 1938

Romances Capitonnées *by Alice Halicka*, courtesy of Julien Levy Gallery, New York
March 1–25, 1938

Six Young American Painters, courtesy of East River Gallery, New York
March 1–25, 1938

Seventeenth- and Eighteenth-Century Old Masters
April 1–May 1, 1938

Spanish Government Posters, under the auspices of the American Student Union, organized by the Museum of Modern Art
April 5–15, 1938

Abstract and Absolute Art, loaned by the Museum of Modern Art, New York, and courtesy of the Valentine Gallery, New York and Naum Gabo
May 1–31, 1938
Drawings Under $100, courtesy of Durlacher Brothers, New York
Opened May 5, 1938

Paintings of the High Tatras, Poland, by Clarence A. Brodeur; Oil Paintings by Representative Painters of the Hudson River School
October 13–31, 1938

Original Water Colors On Celluloid from Walt Disney's
Snow White and the Seven Dwarves, courtesy of Julien
Levy Gallery, New York
October 13–31, 1938

The Four Ages of Man *by Valentin de Boulogne*, courtesy
of Julius H. Weitzner, Inc., New York; The Card
Players *by Caravaggio*, loaned by the Fogg Art Museum,
Harvard University, Cambridge, Massachusetts;
Facsimiles of Engravings by the Master E. S.
November 1938

Collection of Seventeenth- and Eighteenth-Century
Prints Given to the Art Department by
Mrs. William Reed Thompson
November 1–30, 1938

Drawings and Watercolors by Mary Drake Coles
November 1–30, 1938

Landscape Architecture, organized by the New York
Chapter of the American Society of Landscape
Architects
November 1–December 31, 1938

Abstract Paintings by Benjamin G. Benno, courtesy of
Nierendorf Galleries, New York; *The Prints of Georges*
Rouault, organized by the Museum of Modern Art,
New York
January 3–25, 1939

Murals by Jared French, courtesy of Julien Levy Gallery,
New York
January 24–February 7, 1939

Paintings by C. K. Chatterton and Sculpture by Elizabeth
Geiger
February 1–26, 1939

Painting and Sculpture by Dutchess County Artists
March 2–22, 1939

Art Exhibitions in Paris, 1937–1938, under the auspices
of the Department of French
March 3–23, 1939

Sculpture of India (Eliza Buffington Memorial Exhibition)
April 12–May 12, 1939

Fifteenth- and Sixteenth-Century Engravings, Woodcuts, and
Etchings, loaned by Wesleyan University, Middletown,
Connecticut
April 15–May 15, 1939

Photographs of Germany and Reproductions of German Art,
under the auspices of the Department of German
Closed April 29, 1939

Three Centuries of American Architecture, organized by the
Museum of Modern Art, New York
May 1939

Nineteenth-Century Paintings, from the collection of
Dexter Mason Ferry
May 1–June 1, 1939

The World of Today Pictured in Oils, Watercolors, Gouaches,
Drawings, and Prints by New York Artists, organized by the
National Art Society
May 1–October 31, 1939

Sculpture by Robert Laurent, courtesy of Downtown
Gallery, New York
May 15–June 15, 1939

Sculptures in Wood by Genevieve Karr Hamlin
October 31–November 27, 1939

One Picture by Picasso [La Toilette], loaned by the
Museum of Modern Art, New York; *Prints and*
Illustrations, courtesy of Wittenborn and Company,
New York
October 31–December 23, 1939

Sculpture in Limited Editions, courtesy of Robinson
Galleries, New York
December 1– 23, 1939

Photographs by George Platt Lynes
Closed December 23 1939

Original Paintings for the Cover of the New Yorker, loaned
by the Junior League of Boston
January 1940

Engravings and Woodcuts by Albrecht Dürer, loaned by
Wesleyan University, Middletown, Connecticut
January 1940

Medieval Art, courtesy of various galleries and on loan
from various private collectors
January 23–February 15, 1940

Original Drawings by James Thurber, courtesy of Marie
Harriman Gallery, New York
February 1–February 28, 1940

Drawings by Contemporary American Sculptors, from the
collection of Hans van Weeren-Griek
February 14–March 7, 1940

Drawings and Watercolors by Eugene Berman, courtesy of
Julien Levy Gallery, New York
March 1–30, 1940

Work by Mr. Lewis Rubenstein
April 1940

Chinese Paintings, on loan from various private
collectors
May 1–30, 1940

Drawings by Old Masters, courtesy of Durlacher Brothers,
New York
May–June 1, 1940

Watercolors by Jean-Marie Guislain
October 1940

The Ballet: History Art and Practice, organized by the
Museum of Modern Art, New York; *Original Designs for
Ballet from the Lifar Collection*, loaned by the Wadsworth
Atheneum, Hartford, Connecticut
October 17–November 4, 1940

*Reproductions of Drawings and Watercolors by
William Blake*
October 17–November 4, 1940

Fifty Paintings by Paul Klee, organized by the Museum
of Modern Art, New York
October 17–November 25, 1940

Tennessee Negro Homes by Maurice Crosser, courtesy of
Julien Levy Gallery, New York
October 17–November 25, 1940

Recent Work by C. A. Brodeur, from the collection of
Mrs. Ocker
November 29–December 18, 1940

Italian Baroque Paintings, courtesy of Jacob Heimann
Gallery, New York
Closed December 18, 1940

ACKNOWLEDGMENTS

The ongoing collaboration among the Vassar Art Department, the Vassar College Libraries, and the Frances Lehman Loeb Art Center has been vital to the research and realization of this book—in many ways it speaks to the way the Art Department was set up to work in the 1930s. We at Vassar are immensely grateful to Mardges Bacon for showing us the real accomplishments of our predecessors.

The idea for a book on John McAndrew's modernist vision and his design of the Vassar Art Library emerged from a lecture Bacon presented in the fall of 2009 in connection with its rededication, following a judicious restoration by the firm of Platt Byard Dovell White Architects. Nicholas Adams initiated the idea for a scholarly piece with Vassar's sponsorship, but its precise nature was yet to be determined. To mark the sesquicentennial of Vassar College in 2011, Professor Adams invited Professor Bacon to give a second lecture, focusing on the Art Library and incorporating her new research. At that lecture, Molly Nesbit, then chair of the Department of Art, suggested that the new research could form the core of a book, and she set out to make that happen. Princeton Architectural Press shared Vassar's enthusiasm for the book and agreed to publish it.

The project turns out to be a welcome collaboration between Bacon and Art Department faculty. The book includes vivid color photographs by Professor Andrew Tallon with captions by Professor Tobias Armborst. Professors Susan Donahue Kuretsky and Molly Nesbit, together with Art Librarian Thomas E. Hill, offer readers a spirited Introduction. In recognition of their abiding support for the book, the authors thank Kevin C. Lippert and Rob Shaeffer, publisher and senior acquisitions editor, respectively, at Princeton Architectural Press. We also express our gratitude to the editor Nina Pick. This book could not have been published without the enduring support of Professors Molly Nesbit and Peter Charlap, each of whom have served as chair of the Art Department, as well as Stephen Dahnert, acting vice president for finance and administration at Vassar College.

Mardges Bacon expresses her appreciation to Barry Bergdoll and Francesco Passanti, both of whom read an early draft of her text and offered their critical comments. She extends her gratitude to Charles A. Platt and Serena Losonczy, of Platt Byard Dovell White Architects, as well as to Joan C. Berkowitz, of the engineering firm SuperStructures + Architects, each of whom were especially helpful in responding to questions about the restoration of the Art Library. Chelsea Weathers, picture editor for this book, was exceptionally resourceful and creative. For sharing her knowledge of Museum of Modern Art documents and history, Bacon thanks Wendy Jeffers.

Bacon also benefitted greatly from insightful discussions with and assistance from Nicholas Adams, Mirka Beneš, Lilian Armstrong, Peter Fergusson, Thomas Fisher, Janice Hunt, Susan Donahue Kuretsky, Molly Nesbit, Miles David Samson, Robert Smith, Nancy Stieber, Hicks Stone, Paul Turner, Christopher Wilk, and Robert Wojtowicz. She also thanks her family, especially her husband, Charles Wood, and son-in-law, Ian Sue Wing.

Bacon is indebted to the staff members of the museums, archives, and libraries who generously assisted her research. Most especially, she wishes to thank Thomas E. Hill, art librarian at Vassar College, and Dean Rogers, special collections assistant, Archives & Special Collections Library, Vassar College Libraries, for their tireless efforts over many years on behalf of this project. Eugene R. Gaddis, former William G. DeLana Archivist, Wadsworth Atheneum, Hartford, Connecticut, offered invaluable information on A. Everett Austin and John McAndrew. Bacon also received the generous assistance of Ian Graham and Mary Yearl (Wellesley College Archives, Wellesley, Massachusetts); Michelle Elligott, Michelle Harvey, and the late Rona Roob (Museum Archives, The Museum of Modern Art, New York); Wendy Hurlock Baker, Margaret Zoller, and Marisa Bourgoin (Archives of American Art, Smithsonian Institution, Washington, DC); Janet Parks, Margaret Smithglass, and Carolyn Yerkes (Avery Architectural & Fine Arts Library, Columbia University Libraries, New York); Roxanne Palmatier and Brian Green (Snell Library, Northeastern University, Boston); Tracey Schuster (Getty Research Institute, Los Angeles); Megan Schwenke (Harvard Art Museums, Cambridge, Massachusetts); Juliana Kuipers and Tim Driscoll (Harvard University Archives, Cambridge, Massachusetts); Marie Difilippantonio (Jean & Julien Levy Foundation for the Arts, Newtown, Connecticut); Mattias Herold (Department of Painting and Sculpture, The Museum of Modern Art, New York); Susan K. Anderson (Library, Philadelphia Museum of Art); Michele Hiltzik Beckerman (Rockefeller Archive Center, Sleepy Hollow, New York); Arnaud Dercelles (Fondation Le Corbusier, Paris); Moira Fitzgerald (Beinecke Rare Books & Manuscript Library, Yale University, New Haven, Connecticut); Stacey Stachow (Wadsworth Atheneum, Hartford, Connecticut); and Margo Stipe (Frank Lloyd Wright Foundation, Scottsdale, Arizona). She also thanks Joshua Lynes.

Elizabeth Nogrady, the Andrew W. Mellon Curator of Academic Programs at the Frances Lehman Loeb Art Center, would like to thank Samantha Kohl for her assistance in the preparation of the list of exhibitions held in the Vassar College Art Gallery.

ABOUT THE CONTRIBUTORS

Tobias Armborst is associate professor of art and director of urban studies at Vassar, where he has been teaching since 2008. He is also a practicing architect and urban designer currently planning urban landscape projects in Detroit; St. Louis; Cambridge, Massachusettts; and Antwerp, Belgium. The co-author of *The Arsenal of Exclusion and Inclusion* (2017), he received a master of architecture in urban design from the Harvard Graduate School of Design and a Diplom-Ingenieur from the Rheinisch-Westfälische Technische Hochschule Aachen in Germany.

Mardges Bacon is Matthews Distinguished University Professor of Architecture Emerita at Northeastern University. The recipient of a Guggenheim Fellowship, her publications include *Le Corbusier in America: Travels in the Land of the Timid* (MIT Press, 2001), *Ernest Flagg: Beaux-Arts Architect and Urban Reformer* (Architectural History Foundation and MIT Press, 1986), and numerous contributions to books and scholarly journals, including the *Journal of the Society of Architectural Historians*. She also served as editor and wrote a critical introduction to a volume of essays, *"Symbolic Essence" and Other Writings on Modern Architecture and American Culture by William H. Jordy*, published in conjunction with the Temple Hoyne Buell Center for the Study of American Architecture at Columbia University (Yale University Press, 2005).

Thomas Hill has been the librarian of the Vassar College Art Library since 1986. He holds a PhD in English from Columbia University with a specialization in medieval literature, and his scholarship concerns the reading of courtly romance in the context of scholastic philosophy and psychology. His book, *"She, this in blak": Vision, Truth, and Will in Geoffrey Chaucer's* Troilus and Criseyde, was published in 2006. He also produces and hosts *The Library Café*, a weekly radio interview program aired on WVKR about scholarship, libraries, and the formation and circulation of knowledge.

Susan Donahue Kuretsky, Sarah Gibson Blanding Professor of Art at Vassar College, received her AB degree from Vassar and her PhD from Harvard University. A specialist in Dutch art of the seventeeth century, she has published a monograph on the Dutch genre painter Jacob Ochtervelt and diverse articles on Rembrandt as a printmaker. She is the co-author of the catalogue of Dutch paintings at the Detroit Institute of Arts and produced the traveling exhibition *Time and Transformation in Seventeenth Century Dutch Art.*

Molly Nesbit is professor of art history in the Department of Art at Vassar College and a contributing editor of *Artforum*. Her books include *Atget's Seven Albums* (Yale University Press, 1992) and *Their Common Sense* (Black Dog, 2000). Since 2002, together with Hans Ulrich Obrist and Rirkrit Tiravanija, she has been curating the succession of *Utopia Stations*, an ongoing collective book, exhibition, seminar, web, and street project. *The Pragmatism in the History of Art* (Periscope, 2013), is the first volume of *Pre-Occupations*, a series collecting her essays; the second, *Midnight: The Tempest Essays*, was published in 2017 by Inventory Press.

Elizabeth Nogrady graduated from Vassar College in 1999 with a degree in art history, and went on to receive her PhD from the Institute of Fine Arts, New York University. A specialist in seventeenth-century Dutch and Flemish art, she has held curatorial positions in the Department of Drawings and Prints at the Morgan Library & Museum, European Paintings at the Metropolitan Museum of Art, and Old Master Paintings at Christie's, New York. Currently she is the Andrew W. Mellon Curator of Academic Programs at the Frances Lehman Loeb Art Center.

Andrew Tallon is associate professor of art at Vassar College, where he teaches medieval art, architecture, and pre-modern acoustics. He received a PhD from Columbia University, an MA from the University of Paris-Sorbonne, and a BA from Princeton University. He is the co-author of *Notre-Dame de Paris*, published in French; an English edition is forthcoming from the University of Pennsylvania Press. His second book (in progress) is entitled *The Structure of Gothic*. The recipient of grants from the Samuel Kress Foundation and the Andrew Mellon Foundation, he is a former director of the International Center of Medieval Art and of AVISTA, and is co-founder and a director of the US-based charitable association the Friends of Notre-Dame.